Revitalising

Economies in a
Post-COVID-19 World

Socioeconomic Issues in the New Normal

Highly Recommended Titles

Impact of COVID-19 on Asian Economies and Policy Responses
edited by Sumit Agarwal, Zhiguo He and Bernard Yeung
ISBN: 978-981-122-937-4

*Combating a Crisis: The Psychology of Singapore's Response
to COVID-19*
by David Chan
ISBN: 978-981-122-055-5

Prevention and Control of COVID-19
editor-in-chief Wenhong Zhang
ISBN: 978-981-122-049-4 (pbk)

Revitalising

Economies in a
Post-COVID-19 World

Socioeconomic Issues in the New Normal

Editor

Hooi Hooi Lean

Universiti Sains Malaysia, Malaysia

 **World Scientific**

NEW JERSEY · LONDON · SINGAPORE · BEIJING · SHANGHAI · HONG KONG · TAIPEI · CHENNAI · TOKYO

Published by

World Scientific Publishing Co. Pte. Ltd.

5 Toh Tuck Link, Singapore 596224

USA office: 27 Warren Street, Suite 401-402, Hackensack, NJ 07601

UK office: 57 Shelton Street, Covent Garden, London WC2H 9HE

Library of Congress Cataloging-in-Publication Data
Names: Lean, Hooi Hooi, editor.
Title: Revitalising ASEAN economies in a post-COVID-19 world :
    socioeconomic issues in the new normal / editor, Hooi Hooi Lean.
Description: Hackensack, NJ : World Scientific Publishing Co. Pte. Ltd., [2022] |
    Includes bibliographical references and index.
Identifiers: LCCN 2021049421 | ISBN 9789811228469 (hardcover) |
    ISBN 9789811228476 (ebook) | ISBN 9789811228483 (ebook other)
Subjects: LCSH: COVID-19 Pandemic, 2020---Economic aspects--Southeast Asia. |
    COVID-19 Pandemic, 2020---Social aspects--Southeast Asia. | COVID-19 (Disease)--
    Economic aspects--Southeast Asia. | COVID-19 (Disease)--Social aspects--Southeast Asia. |
    Economics--Southeast Asia--Sociological aspects.
Classification: LCC HC441 .R475 2022 | DDC 362.1962/41400959--dc23/eng/20211208
LC record available at https://lccn.loc.gov/2021049421

British Library Cataloguing-in-Publication Data
A catalogue record for this book is available from the British Library.

For any available supplementary material, please visit
https://www.worldscientific.com/worldscibooks/10.1142/12046#t=suppl

Desk Editor: Jiang Yulin

Typeset by Stallion Press
Email: enquiries@stallionpress.com

Printed in Singapore

About the Editor

Hooi Hooi Lean is a professor of Economics at the School of Social Sciences, Universiti Sains Malaysia. She obtained her honors bachelor degree of Economics majoring in Statistics from the University of Malaya, Master of Science (Statistics) from the Universiti Sains Malaysia, and Ph.D. (Economics) from the National University of Singapore. She served as a post-doctoral visiting scholar to the Department of Economics at Monash University, Australia. Dr. Lean has been a visiting scholar at a number of prestigious international universities, including Sungkyunkwan University (Korea), Tamkang University (Taiwan), CEREFIGE Universitè Nancy 2 (France), Auckland University of Technology (New Zealand), Georg-Simon-Ohm University of Applied Sciences (Germany), and University of Rennes 2 (France).

Prof. Lean has authored more than 170 scholarly articles and academic book chapters. Her works have been published in many reputed international journals and publications. Her H-index is 46 and there are more than 9,000 citations to her works on Google Scholar. She has also presented on various topics at many major international conferences held worldwide. In addition to these talks in the academic circuit, she has been invited to give talks at some private corporations, organisations, and educational institutions. She has also provided consultancy works to the private sector, government agencies, and non-governmental organisations.

Prof. Lean has been recognised as among the Top Research Scientists Malaysia by Academy of Sciences Malaysia in 2018. She received

Malaysia's Research Star Award in 2017 from the Ministry of Higher Education Malaysia and Clarivate Analytics, and the National Academic Award in 2015 from the Ministry of Higher Education Malaysia. She was listed as top 2% scientists in the world by Stanford University. She has been listed in the Who's Who in the World since 2009 and granted the prestigious title of "Researcher of the Week" in GDNet East Asia in 2012 for her excellent contributions. She has been awarded the ASEAN-ROK Academic Exchange Fellowship Programme in 2007, the Democratic Pacific Union (DPU) Visiting Fellowship in 2008, the International HERMES Fellowship Programme in 2009, and Faculty Exchange Fellowship from Georg-Simon-Ohm University in 2012. Dr. Lean has also won the "Sanggar Sanjung" Excellent Award for Publication continuously since 2009, the "Hadiah Sanjungan" Best Award for Publication 2006–2011, and the Excellent Service Award 2010 & 2014 from the Universiti Sains Malaysia. Dr. Lean has received Newton Research Grant from Research Councils United Kingdom; the Fundamental Research Grant Scheme and Research University Grant from the Ministry of Higher Education Malaysia.

Prof. Lean is a fellow of the East Asian Economic Association. She serves as an associate editor for the *Singapore Economic Review, Frontiers in Energy Research, Malaysian Journal of Economics,* and the *International Journal of Economics and Management.* She is also an editorial board member of *Asian Journal of Economics and Finance, Energy Research Letters, Journal of Asian Finance, Economics and Business,* and *Journal of Risk and Financial Management.* She is also on the editorial board as an advisory member of the *Indonesian Capital Market Review* and the *Labuan Bulletin of International Business & Finance.* She has reviewed more than 200 papers for various academic journals and received Peer Review Award from Publons in 2018. She has supervised many undergraduate and postgraduate students and has organised several international conferences/seminars/workshops. Besides her work in the academic sphere, she also contributes towards the various multi-cultural communities in Malaysia and religious development. She holds several private or community-based positions such as Deputy President of Malaysia Silk Road Society, Consultative Panel of Young Buddhist Association of Malaysia Penang State Liaison Committee, Board of Governor of the Penang Buddhist Association Dharma Sunday School, a committee member of the Penang Buddhist Association.

Contents

Preface

The World Health Organisation (WHO) proclaimed the COVID-19 outbreak as a global pandemic on 11 March 2020. The first infection case in ASEAN was reported on 13 January 2020 in Thailand. As of late March 2020, the pandemic had spread to all 10 ASEAN member states (United Nations, 2020). The numbers have since been rising in ASEAN, with more than 15,532 confirmed cases and more than 529 deaths as reported on 9 April 2020 (ASEAN, 2020c). According to the Risk Assessment for International Dissemination of COVID-19 to the ASEAN Region strengthened by the ASEAN Biodiaspora Virtual Centre (ABVC), the ASEAN region had over 1,422,400 reported cases and at least 32,300 deaths as of 23 December 2020 (ASEAN, 2020c).

The joint response of the ASEAN Health Sector to COVID-19 was harmonised to maintain and further improve regional health cooperation and efforts in responding to the effects and spread of COVID-19 infections (ASEAN, 2020c). As each ASEAN member state announced its first case, individual national prevention and control measures were implemented to combat the outbreak. Regional health mechanisms were quickly enabled to help national measures, adapt to gaps in necessity, and facilitate timely awareness and information sharing. The grave threat posed by the pandemic had strengthened regional cooperation and collaboration among the member states and partners (ASEAN, 2020a).

The coronavirus outbreak has undoubtedly and seriously affected ASEAN's economy. At the beginning of the COVID-19 pandemic, the primary concern was the potential effects on supply chains due to the immediate shutdown of factories in Hubei province. As many countries followed suit by instituting nationwide lockdowns, community quarantine measures, stay-at-home directives, temporary company closures, contract tracing, sanitary practices, and travel bans to combat the outbreak, the pandemic had caused immediate disturbances and massive disruptions in economic activities throughout the region in tandem with the rest of the world, as shown by a decrease in tourist flows, instability in air, land, and sea travels, and a significant deterioration in consumer, producer, and business confidence (ASEAN, 2020b).

ASEAN member countries were observed to bear economic losses inequitably due to variable prevailing conditions and factors. Supply chain disturbances caused by lockdowns and quarantine steps, for example, affected countries that were more dependent on merchandise trade, such as Malaysia, Singapore, Cambodia, Vietnam, and Thailand. Countries that were more reliant on inward foreign remittances, such as the Philippines, are being hit hard as the quantum of remittances decline, reducing consumption, demand, and investment. So too for countries with a high dependency on tourism. The member countries announced various fiscal aid packages to assist their affected households and businesses. The fiscal positions of these countries are likely to deteriorate due to the forced increased expenditures and resultant weakening economic conditions. According to the International Monetary Fund (IMF), the downturn in Southeast Asian countries could hit 15% of GDP. The national debt is also predicted to double (United Nations, 2020).

However, beyond the efforts of preventing and containing the spread of the virus, ASEAN's most significant challenges are the social and economic crisis of historic proportions that are beginning to unfold. The COVID-19 pandemic has brought massive, unseen-before interruptions in all sectors of the ASEAN economies. It is therefore imperative to assess the extent to which the pandemic has impacted the social and economic aspects of the region. This book intends to highlight the social and economic impacts of the COVID-19 pandemic in ASEAN and suggest ways on how to mitigate them. The book has nine chapters which specifically cover the details of seven of the ASEAN member states. The chapters are arranged alphabetically beginning with Brunei, then Cambodia, Indonesia, Malaysia, Singapore, Thailand, and Vietnam, in sequential order.

The first chapter, titled "Impact of COVID-19 on Brunei Darussalam Economy", is co-written by Gamini Premaratne, Aishath Shahudha Abdulla, and Farah Amer Hishamuddin. This chapter provides a comprehensive analysis of the impact of the COVID-19 viral outbreak on the Brunei Darussalam economy and its key economic sectors. This analysis identifies the sultanate's social and economic policy responses to the COVID-19 infections and summarises the lessons learnt for the benefit of the business community and the economy. The outbreak underscored the opportunity for businesses and government to prioritise dynamic policies to facilitate and operationalise new growth prospects.

The second chapter, titled "Cambodia's Response to COVID-19 and its Socioeconomic Dimensions", is authored by Júlia Garcia-Puig. This chapter discusses how the country's rebound is subject to the performance of its major international trade partners and business allies. Likewise, the chapter delves into the microeconomic effects, emphasising the subsequent social ramifications, especially among the most vulnerable of their population demographics. It is argued that the current Cambodian government measures are insufficient to mitigate the growing poverty levels and needs of the population which are compounded by the pandemic.

Aris Ananta, Windhiarso Ponco Adi Putranto, and Ahmad Irsan A. Moeis collectively contributed the third chapter titled "COVID-19 and the Economy: How Indonesia Responded". This chapter shows how Indonesia responded to the economic issues which emerged during the pandemic; and how the Indonesian government responded to relieve the economic suffering of their people, how individuals coped with the crisis, how the business community adapted their behaviour to survive, and how resilient the Indonesian macro-economy was. Six months after the start of the pandemic, the economy was already improving while the number of daily infections unfortunately kept rising. Some people and some businesses enjoyed economic opportunities despite the pandemic, particularly those who were able to use online activities, adapt and practise tight health protocols.

Chapter 4, aptly titled "The Impact of the COVID-19 Pandemic on Malaysia's Economy", is written by Dzul Hadzwan Husaini and I. The chapter describes and discusses the impacts of the devastating COVID-19 pandemic based on the use of selected key macroeconomic indicators. The authors also review the existing economic policy on combating and mitigating the effects of the pandemic. It is concluded that the severe adverse impact of the pandemic on the macroeconomy is very significant and extremely "game-changing". However, it shows some improvement with the implementation of the various Malaysian government stimulus packages which were implemented throughout that unforgettably eventful year that was 2020.

The fifth chapter, titled "COVID-19 Pandemic and the Malaysian Tourism", is by Tze-Haw Chan and Jin Hooi Chan. This chapter analyses the impacts of the coronavirus pandemic specifically on the Malaysian tourism industry. With the supporting data of updated statistics, this chapter further presents the disastrous strikes caused by the pandemic and resultant countermeasures on the domestic tourism value chain, the hotel and accommodation lines, and the aviation industry. The relevant policy responses and potential post-pandemic tourism recovery are also discussed. The chapter concludes that the recovery will likely be progressive along the UNWTO's Scenario 1 (before or by the year 2023) but will still be subjected to domestic policy efficacy and global responses.

Sook-Rei Tan, Wei-Siang Wang, and Wai-Mun Chia co-contributed the sixth chapter appropriately titled "Financial Stress of Singapore in the Time of COVID-19". This study extends the existing literature on the use of the Financial Stress Index (FSI) to assess the financial conditions of Singapore during the COVID-19 crisis. The findings suggest that (1) excessive stresses were detected during 9 March–21 April 2020, a period which corresponded to the evolution of the COVID-19 health threat into a global pandemic as well as the beginning of the initial Singapore's Circuit Breaker period; and (2) the dynamics of Singapore's FSI is more significantly due to the prevailing global financial factors than it is to the severity of the domestic COVID-19 condition.

"Impacts of COVID-19 Pandemic on Thai Fruit: A Case Study of Longan Supply Chain" is jointly written by Roengchai Tansuchat, Tanachai Pankasemsuk, and Chanita Panmanee. This chapter investigates and analyses the effects of COVID-19 and the Thai government measures towards the fruit supply chain in Thailand, together with reviewing on-season longan fruits as a case study. The labour markets were significantly affected, particularly seasonal foreign harvest workers. These effects are in accordance with the agricultural overproduction scenario, farm prices and export price decreases, and other variable factors that influence export volumes. In the case of the on-season longan production, the shortage of fruit harvesting workers caused by disease preventive measures implemented, including the prohibition of cross-border travel, were highlighted as significant problems. Additionally, the required 14-day quarantine measures which were imposed greatly lessened the number of brokers, traders, and agricultural workers available. The noteworthy results derived from their research study leads to their policy recommendations for the emerging "new normal" practices of the marketplace.

The eighth chapter, very suitably titled "COVID-19 in Vietnam: Perception of Urban Workers and Compliance with the National Social Distancing Policies", is jointly authored by Thanh-Long Giang, Tham Hong-Thi Pham, Thi-Thu Do, and Manh-Phong Phi. This chapter explores how people in Vietnam perceived various measures in containing COVID-19 and how they complied and evaluated different government policies in controlling the pandemic. The study found that people showed quite good compliance to the national social distancing policies. They recommended that appropriate measures stabilising social and economic activities within the country should be continuously implemented. Sufficient goods and services for people to meet their basic needs during social distancing should be continuously maintained.

The last chapter is authored by Thanh-Long Giang with the title "Successful Social Distancing to Contain COVID-19: Mapping the Readiness of the Vietnamese Households". This study examines how well the households were prepared to contain COVID-19 in Vietnam under the implementation of the first national social distancing initiative by mapping their related indicators when presenting their distinctive living conditions. The results showed that Vietnam's social distancing measures which were carried out in late April 2020 were successful because they were applicable and implementable along with the readiness of all households which were stocked with sufficient resources and necessities. Early governmental interventions and timely social assistance measures combined with the Vietnamese households' readiness to comply with safety and health measures had strongly determined Vietnam's success in combating the pandemic and economic survival.

Three other countries, namely, the Philippines, Laos, and Myanmar, have not been covered in detail with an individual chapter of their own due to various reasons beyond my control. It was not my specific intention to exclude these countries in this book. I would have gladly welcomed any academic contributions on these countries and their countermeasures. It is hoped that perhaps later editions of this book, if I am fortunate enough to undertake, will and may be updated and contain more detailed analysis and individual chapters on these three countries as well.

Neither the editor nor the publisher can guarantee the exact accuracy of statistical data and facts, nor the time sequence occurrences of the events described within the chapters in this book. We shall not attempt to do so, as it is solely the responsibility and prerogative of the individual contributors who are independently responsible for their own works. Their scholarly contributions are accepted in good faith and trust without prejudice and gratefully acknowledged to form this book as a work of academic contribution.

I hope this book will be useful to academics, researchers, students, stakeholders, professionals, and policymakers in the region. It will also be a reference resource and supplementary advisory companion to other economies that might face similar situations either now or in the future. I would like to make an observation that the book, while recording aspects of the historical unfolding of the deadly COVID-19 pandemic and high-lighting the economic countermeasures and factors in different countries within ASEAN, can serve its readers by offering hope, confidence, and optimistic insights for a suffering ASEAN specifically and the rest of the world in general.

Despite the continuing gloom and doom, there is an undying blazing hope and optimism for us during these trying times and also once again during the eventual post-pandemic recovery period which one and all will be able to recount to our children and grand children. I am of the firm belief as with all our contributing writers that humanity will prevail and eventually overcome this deadly plague and economically disastrous period to achieve general health, prosperity, and happiness once more sometime in the not-too-distant future!

We do not claim the book to be a fully comprehensive work, nor an exhaustive study on the complicated and far-reaching issues and situations caused by the worldwide pandemic. We will hope that the book stimulates future research studies and interest in the topics covered and will welcome constructive feedback and encourage other future writers to begin their own exploration and research in order to increase the aggregate literature and collective knowledge about this unprecedented worldwide pandemic and economic phenomena which has come upon mankind like no other event has since The Great Biblical Flood of Ancient times!

Acknowledgements

I sincerely thank all the contributors and reviewers of this book for their excellent commitment and fine contributions. Some authors also served as the referees towards the improvement efforts in upgrading and improving the quality of the chapters. I thank Yulin and staff from World Scientific Publishing for their suggestions and continuing support throughout this publication process. In addition, Busayo Victor Osuntuyi is acknowledged for his excellent research assistance. Last but not least, I thank Professor Wing-Keung Wong for his continuous guidance and invaluable encouragement and insights.

References

ASEAN. (2020a). ASEAN health sector efforts in the prevention, detection and response to Coronavirus disease 2019 (COVID-19). https://asean.org/?static_post=updates-asean-health-sector-efforts-combat-novel-coronavirus-covid-19.

ASEAN. (2020b). Economic impact of Covid-19 outbreak on ASEAN. 1 (Issue April). https://asean.org/storage/2020/04/ASEAN-Policy-Brief-April-2020_FINAL.pdf.

ASEAN. (2020c). Stronger health systems: Our lifeline in a pandemic (Issue December). https://asean.org/storage/ASEAN-Rapid-Assessment_Final-23112020.pdf.

United Nations. (2020). Policy brief: The impact of COVID-19 on South-East Asia. https://www.un.org/ldcportal/policy-brief-the-impact-of-covid-19-on-south-east-asia.

Chapter 1

Impact of COVID-19 on Brunei Darussalam Economy

Gamini Premaratne[*,‡], Aishath Shahudha Abdulla[*,§],
and Farah Amer Hishamuddin [†,¶]

Universiti Brunei Darussalam, Brunei
†BIBD Asset Management, Brunei
‡gamini.premaratne@ubd.edu.bn
§17h0348@ubd.edu.bn
¶farah.hishamuddin@bibd.com.bn

Abstract

COVID-19 highlighted the fragility of the sectors and the economies, tested by lockdowns and quarantines. This chapter aims to provide a comprehensive analysis of the impact of the COVID-19 outbreak on the Brunei Darussalam economy and its key sectors. Further, it explores the policy responses undertaken and their impact to control the COVID-19 transmission within Brunei. This analysis identifies the social and economic policy responses to COVID-19 and summarises the invaluable lessons learnt in the context of businesses, sectors, and the economy. It

---

[*] Corresponding author.

is observed that Brunei economy had a positive growth during the pandemic due to its effort to enhance economic diversification to overcome the challenges faced by high dependence on the oil and gas sector. It facilitated the growth of agriculture, forestry, and fisheries sectors, wholesale and retail sectors, communication sector, and non-oil and gas sector despite the restrictions of the pandemic. The outbreak underscored the opportunity for businesses, sectors, and government to prioritise dynamic policies to facilitate and operationalise new growth prospects, which were among the reasons for the growth of Brunei amidst the COVID-19.

Keywords: Brunei Darussalam; COVID-19; economic impact; sectoral impact; economic diversification.

1. Introduction

COVID-19, the novel coronavirus, has threatened the entire globe without any boundaries and is still causing many countries to limit their social and economic activities. Tedros Adhanom Ghebreyesus, Director-General of the World Health Organisation (WHO), stated, "Over the years we have had many reports, reviews and recommendations all saying the same thing: the world is not prepared for a pandemic. COVID-19 has laid bare the truth: when the time came, the world was still not ready" (WHO, 2020b). On 31 December 2019, a cluster of pneumonia cases was identified by the Wuhan Health Commission in Wuhan, Hubei Province in China, which was later recognised as a novel coronavirus, now known as COVID-19. The virus quickly spread across and beyond the country in a short period to most of the world, with the first official positive case of the novel coronavirus outside of China reported in Thailand on 13 January 2020. By 30 January 2020, there were a total of 7,818 positive cases worldwide, with 82 cases detected in 18 countries outside of China, according to the WHO statistics (WHO, 2020a). One year later, there were 85,603,742 positive cases and 1,853,068 deaths, which shows that the world was not prepared for a pandemic (WHO, 2020c). The world is still searching for ways to control the transmission of COVID-19, while new variants of the virus have started to rise in many countries.

The United Nations' (UN's) framework for the Immediate Socio-Economic Response to the COVID-19 crisis emphasises that the

Table 1: COVID-19 confirmed positive cases, deaths, recovery (John Hopkins Coronavirus Resource Centre, 2021), population size, and population density (World Bank, 2019) in ASEAN; author's contribution based on data.

Country	Confirmed	Deaths	Recovered	Population	Population Density
1 Indonesia	1,482,559	40,081	1,317,199	270,625,568	142.56
2 Philippines	693,048	13,095	580,062	108,116,615	357.69
3 Malaysia	338,168	1,248	322,416	31,949,777	95.96
4 Myanmar	142,315	3,204	131,774	54,045,420	82.28
5 Singapore	60,253	30	60,086	5,703,569	7,953.00
6 Thailand	28,443	92	26,873	69,625,582	135.90
7 Vietnam	2,579	35	2,265	96,462,106	308.13
8 Cambodia	1,872	5	1,056	16,486,542	92.06
9 Brunei	206	3	188	459,500	81.40
10 Laos	49	0	45	7,169,455	30.60

COVID-19 outbreak is much more than a health crisis as the infected cases surge worldwide. It impacts communities and economies at their cores, while the pandemic's effect differs from nation to nation. In Southeast Asia, the most populous nation, Indonesia, has the most infected cases (1,482,559) and deaths (40,081) as of March 2021, followed by the second most populous nation, the Philippines, with 693,048 infected cases and 13,095 deaths. Laos, the third least-populous country, with the lowest population density of 30.60, had 49 infected cases and zero deaths (Table 1).

With the smallest population and the second-lowest population density in ASEAN, Brunei Darussalam had 216 cases by 8 April 2021. Brunei had its first positive COVID-19 case on 9 March 2020. Exactly 1 year after the pandemic's advent, by 9 March 2021, Brunei had suffered 192 confirmed positive cases and only 3 deaths. This figure is considerably lower than other countries worldwide.

Brunei Darussalam's Government of His Majesty, The Sultan and Yang Di-Pertuan, gave precedence to public health, safeguarding employment, and aiding businesses from the onset of the pandemic. This ASEAN member state's government has been able to contain the virus transmission speedily through a range of measures such as the "test, trace, and isolate" plan, transparent communications, and social distancing measures starting from 16 March 2020 (CSPS, 2021). These interventions radically changed Brunei residents' socio-economic lifestyle. The outbreak was successfully controlled within a month as there was no community transmission since early May 2020, resulting in the slowing down of virus transmission. The initial 100 detected cases were triumphantly controlled, resulting in the containment of the pandemic (Wong, Koh, *et al.*, 2020).

Thus, this chapter examines the economic impact of COVID-19 on Brunei and will address four major questions: (1) What are the steps taken by the government to control the outbreak? (2) What are the impacts of the COVID-19 crisis on Brunei economy? (3) What sectors are affected by COVID-19, and if so, to what extent? and (4) What are the steps taken by the government to achieve economic recovery?

The chapter will be structured as follows: firstly, the background of COVID-19 worldwide and in Brunei; secondly, breakdown of Brunei's macroeconomy, sectoral development, and supporting policies for economic recovery, and lastly, the lessons learnt and opportunities from COVID-19 to Brunei.

2. Background of Brunei

Brunei Darussalam, officially known as Negara Brunei, translated as Abode of Peace, is one of the oldest kingdoms and smallest nations in ASEAN and globally. It is one of the few absolute monarchies left globally. Located on the northwest coast of Borneo's island in Southeast Asia, Brunei spans over 5,765 square kilometres. The country has two disconnected segments of unequal size, bounded to the north by the South China Sea, and has a common border with Sarawak, the East Malaysian state.

Brunei is recognised for its large crude oil and natural gas reserves, which has fuelled the nation's economy for the past 90 years since its discovery in 1929. It accounts for approximately 65% of GDP and makes the country the third-largest oil producer in Southeast Asia, with the second-highest GDP per capita in ASEAN. Thus, proceeds from the crude oil and natural gas sector enable the Brunei government to support a generous welfare state where citizens pay no personal income taxes, and enjoy almost free medical services and education, attaining 97.2% adult literacy rate in 2018. The Brunei government is highly centralised, and the investment in the medical sector has risen; from 1.2% of GDP (BND 269 million) in 2014 to 1.8% of GDP (BND 300 million) by 2020. It also has a budget allotted for outbreaks and public health emergencies of BND 15 million (USD 10.5 million) (Wong, Koh, *et al.*, 2020). This made Brunei comparatively well-prepared for the pandemic despite the inexperience and limited capacity to handle large-scale pandemic outbreaks.

Brunei typically consists of multigenerational households, and a social structure centred on strong family bonds and religious interactions (Ahmad, 2018; Ullah and Kumpoh, 2019). These characteristics of multiple borders, lack of experience handling large-scale outbreaks, and household characteristics make Brunei considerably fragile to outbreaks and swift domestic transmission of the virus. Nonetheless, Brunei's export-oriented, energy-dense economy, low population, and population density leave the country prosperous than its ASEAN neighbours, which has greatly aided in slowing down the viral transmission.

3. COVID-19 Transmission in Brunei

WHO announced a global pandemic following the transmission of the novel coronavirus, COVID-19's epidemic to most countries, and ASEAN economies were among the first to be hit with the virus due to close geographical proximity to China. The first positive case in Brunei was reported on 9 March 2020. It was related to the most significant international cluster of cases from the annual 4-day religious congregation (Tablighi) in Kuala Lumpur, Malaysia, attended by 16,000 people worldwide, including 75 people from Brunei (Ministry of Health, 2020). The participants took part in prayers, meals, and speeches and slept at the mosque, while some took part in cooking and cleaning. Seventy-one cases (52.6%) out of the 135 positive cases reported from March till April had an epidemiological link to this cluster (Wong, Chaw, *et al.*, 2020).

It led to the outbreak rising to 100 infected cases within the first 2 weeks (Figure 1), and by 31 March 2020, the number of cases surged to 127 with 1 death. It was one of the biggest and the sole COVID-19 cluster of cases in Brunei for 2020. Henceforth, the positive cases' progression gradually slowed with the timely stringent measures implemented. Within

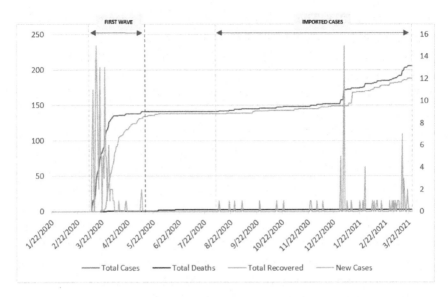

Figure 1:   COVID-19 confirmed positive cases, deaths, and recovery cases in Brunei. (Author's contribution based on data from John Hopkins Coronavirus Resource Centre, 2021).

the first 2 months, Brunei had effectively controlled the virus propagation, as the virus spread hit a plateau at 141 cases since 6 May. The increase of infected cases beginning from the 142nd case (7 May) is primarily due to imported cases, with a total of 206 cases, out of which 64 cases are imported as of 25 March 2021. However, immediate 14-day quarantine in the special quarantine facilities allowed the nation to prevent the virus from spreading domestically, allowing the residents of Brunei to live an almost normal, everyday life.

4.   COVID-19 Outbreak in Brunei and ASEAN

Brunei, the Islamic Sultanate, has a population of 459,500 (2019), including foreigners (DEPS, 2020) with a population density of 81.40 persons per square kilometre (2019), which is the second-lowest in ASEAN. Brunei and Laos have the two lowest population densities in ASEAN. The strikingly low population density of 30.60 persons per square kilometre (2019) and third-lowest population of 7,169,455 (2019) can be the reasons for Laos's success in containing the virus from spreading. It is likely that a low population and low population density are a great advantage as that makes it easier to track and trace the spread of the virus and to quickly test and quarantine those who may have been exposed, to control the spread of the pandemic.

5. COVID-19 Policies and Restrictions

The early success of Brunei is primarily due to its steadfast control measures through rigorous contact tracing, ring-fencing, domestic lockdowns, and compulsory quarantining of the detected cases and their links (Wong, Koh, *et al.*, 2020). Over 10 days from the first detection of a COVID-19 case on 9 March, a succession of interventions (Appendix) were executed: such as school closures, the prohibition of mass gatherings including weddings, sports events, mosque closures, and strict inbound and outbound international travel restrictions and domestic travel restrictions. These interventions succeeded as Brunei had only 141 positive cases by 20 May 2020.

Despite Brunei having various legislations for crisis management, it was inexperienced in curbing the pandemic outbreak due to the rare implementation of the current crisis management measures. Nonetheless, Brunei used its small population to effectively enforce pandemic containment, trace, test, and public risk communication strategies (Wong, Koh, *et al.*, 2020).

The government identified that daily transparent and updated communication could circumvent mass panic and achieve community cooperation, especially effectively implement the social distancing measures. The public communications strategies utilised were daily press conferences headed by the Minister of Health and other ministers, which were broadcasted live on national television and social media channels. Likewise, a 24-hour health advice line, a government Telegram channel, and a mobile application (BruHealth) were created, which were used as case-tracing systems combined with artificial intelligence and advanced data analytics that links all health care facilities in Brunei (Wong, Koh, *et al.*, 2020). BruHealth is used by more than 90% of the adult population, which is a key factor for the success in curbing the outbreak. These communication strategies provided accessibility to key information such as the virus transmission status, the government's policies, and restrictions which enabled the public to be up to date and combat misinformation to effectively mitigate the virus outbreak. All these strategies allowed to build the public trust in the Brunei government's crisis management strategies, which was a crucial factor that allowed the Brunei pandemic situation, economy, sectors, and businesses to recover swiftly.

As the number of infected cases vastly declined due to the stringent public health measures imposed at an early stage of the pandemic, Brunei government launched its economic recovery plans to reinforce the development of businesses and the growth of the economy. In the next section, the impact of the pandemic on Brunei economy and its sectors will be discussed.

6. Brunei Macroeconomy

The economy of Brunei has been negatively impacted by COVID-19 restrictions due to its impact on the movement of people in the community, shutdown of businesses, and the global economic downturn such as from the slowdown of external demand and slump in oil and gas prices. Nonetheless, service sectors largely recovered following the ease of COVID-19 restrictions.

The country's economy has been comparatively resilient, with an annual positive growth of 1.2% (2020), although it is a drop from 3.9% (2019) due to a 9% increase in the non-oil and gas sector despite the 4.9% fall in the oil and gas sector (Ministry of Finance and Economy, 2020a). This is the steepest in comparison to the global financial crisis of 2007–2008 and the plunge in global oil prices from 2014–2016. The reason why Brunei managed to have an annual positive economic growth of 1.2%, despite the low global demand and low global oil prices, is the country's focus on economic diversification.

Based on Brunei's quarterly data, the growth plummeted from 7.1% (BND 4.8 billion) in Q4 2019 to a negative growth of 1.4% (BND 4.1 billion) in Q4 2020 due to the drop in oil and gas sector's growth from –4.0% in Q1 2020 to –8.6% in Q4 2020 (Figure 2). This steep fall in growth is primarily due to the drop in oil and gas mining in Brunei from 6.9% in Q4 2019 to –8.8% in Q4 2020 (Figure 3). Oil and gas proceeds

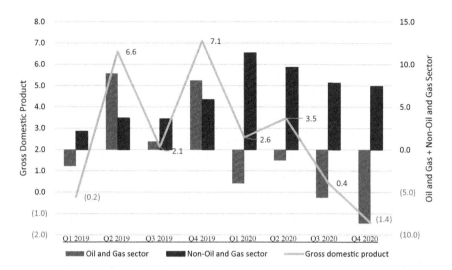

Figure 2: Percentage growth of gross domestic product (GDP), oil and gas and non-oil and gas sector. (Author's contribution based on data from Ministry of Finance and Economy, Department of Economic Planning and Statistics, 2021).

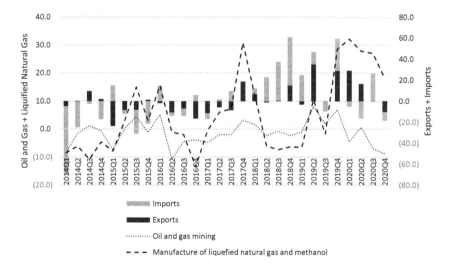

Figure 3: Percentage growth of oil and gas mining, manufacture of liquefied natural gas and methanol, exports and imports. (Author's contribution based on data from Ministry of Finance and Economy, Department of Economic Planning and Statistics, 2021).

sunk by nearly 60% in comparison to 2019, as oil prices plunged to USD 42 per barrel in 2020 from USD 69 per barrel in 2019. The oil production dropped to 111,000 barrels per day in 2020 from 121,000 barrels per day in 2019 (CSPS, 2021). This resulted in the oil revenue dropping from BND 4,873.370 million in 2019 to BND 3,645.608 million in 2020 (CEIC Data, n.d.). The fall in oil and gas sector growth is due to low external demand, lockdowns, and quarantines, causing limited transportation, resulting in the oil-producing countries to be the most affected. These restrictions led to the drop in domestic activities and slowdown of the economy in Brunei.

Manufacturing of liquefied natural gas (LNG) and methanol experienced a surge in growth before COVID-19 (Figure 3). In Q4 2019, the sector grew by 28.5%, which was witnessed in the preceding Q4 2017 with 30.9% growth, which is the highest over the preceding 6 years from 2014–2020. Once the outbreak emerged, manufacturing of LNG and methanol sector's growth persisted at 32.2% during Q1 2020 before declining by 13.7% (falling to 833,570 million British thermal units per day) in the subsequent quarters (CSPS, 2021). The decline in the manufacturing of LNG and methanol, aside from the cause being the outbreak, was also due to supply chain issues in securing a steady source of natural gas needed to produce LNG.

Economic diversification has been one of the central national development goals since the second National Development Plan 1962–1966. The Ninth National Development Plan (2007–2012)'s long-term development plan, called Vision 2035 (Wawasan 2035), is to transform Brunei into a "dynamic and sustainable economy". This is to overcome the challenges faced by the high dependence on oil and gas sector, which results in the high unemployment and low economic growth (Ministry of Finance and Economy, 2020b). Thus, the country envisions developing the non-Oil and Gas Sector as well as strengthening the five priority sectors: (1) downstream oil and gas; (2) agri-food; (3) technology and ICT; (4) tourism and hospitality; and (5) business and financial services.

During COVID-19, Brunei showcased its resilience due to the non-oil and gas sector, which comprises agriculture and industry (e.g. manufacture of food and beverages, construction, petroleum, and chemical products) and services (communication, transport, finance, wholesale and

Table 2: Contribution % of domestic exports of oil and gas and non-oil and gas sectors. (Ministry of Finance and Economy, Department of Economic Planning and Statistics, 2021).

Contribution % of Domestic Exports of Oil and Gas and Non-Oil and Gas Sectors		
Year	Oil and Gas Sector	Non-Oil and Gas Sector
2017	91.9%	8.1%
2018	94.6%	5.4%
2019	85.2 %	14.8%
2020	51.4 %	48.6 %

retail trade, health services). These sectors advanced rapidly through the pandemic, keeping Brunei's economy strong despite the faltering oil sector. The non-oil and gas sector accounted for 55.2% of GDP in Q4 2020, while the oil and gas sector accounted for 44.8% of GDP (Ministry of Finance and Economy, 2020a). The non-oil and gas sector's export contribution (Table 2) surged by 33.8%, from 14.8% (2019) to 48.6% (2020), which is unlike the preceding years from 2017–2020. This resulted in the economic dependence of the oil and gas sector dropping by 40.5%, from 91.9% (2017) to 51.4% (2020) over 4 years.

2020 began with the agriculture, forestry, and fishery sector at –1.5% in Q1 2020, booming at striking 27.5% growth in Q4 2020, more than any other sector had for the past 6 years, while all the other sectors declined during the pandemic (Figure 4). Industry sector owing to the drop in oil and gas sector had a major decline from 11.4% in Q4 2019 to –0.8% in Q4 2020, while services sector was faring at a 0.7% in Q4 2019 and declined to –3.0% in Q4 2020.

COVID-19 has stressed the significance of food security and the fragility of global supply chains, which was tested by lockdowns and quarantines worldwide. For a small country like Brunei that relies on 80% of its food requirements on imported goods, out of which 75% of the food requirements comes from ASEAN countries, the impact was hard felt (Kwek, 2016). Scarcity of meat products and fresh vegetables, pharmaceutical products such as face masks and hand sanitisers,

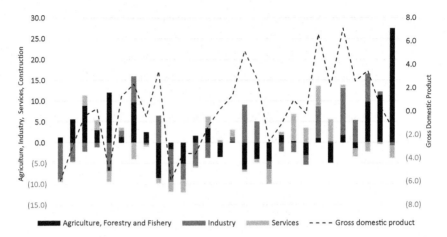

Figure 4:   Quarterly GDP growth contribution by economic sector for the year 2014–2020. (Author's contribution based on data from Ministry of Finance and Economy, Department of Economic Planning and Statistics, 2021).

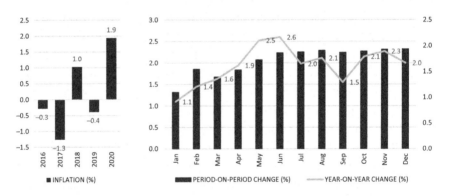

Figure 5:   Inflation rate from 2016–2020 (left) and inflation percentage change yearly and periodically for 2020. (Author's contribution based on data from Ministry of Finance and Economy, Department of Economic Planning and Statistics, 2021).

resulted in the consumer prices experiencing a steep rise from 1.1% in January to 2.6% in June 2020 (Figure 5). In June 2020, inflation rate stabilised at 1.9%, yet it is the highest Brunei economy has experienced since 2000–2019, with an average inflation rate of 0.3% (CSPS, 2021).

The COVID-19 outbreak resulted in a steep rise in prices of insurance premium (18% rise), air travel (13% rise), imported fresh vegetables (30%

rise), meat products, such as beef, lamb, mutton, mineral water and soft drinks (6% rise), and jewellery (27% rise) in comparison to 2019. Air travel prices rose to accommodate the costs from the drop in operations due to the pandemic safety restrictions. Jewellery prices rose due to a rise in prices of precious metals. Fresh vegetables and meat products' prices rose owing to the lockdowns resulting in scarce supply in exporting countries (CSPS, 2021). On the contrary, prices fell for lodging services, package vacations, and financial services, resulting in the boost in local tourism and the gradual recovery of the hotel subsector by the end of 2020.

The rise in food prices followed by a fall in quantity encouraged the country to search for food alternatives. The fisheries industry and the live-stock and poultry industry emerged as a strong substitute, catering to the rise in demand with a rapidly growing sector. The fisheries industry grew from 9.8% in Q1 2020 to a striking 47.4% in Q4 2020, while livestock and poultry (beef, chicken, and egg) grew from 7.9% in Q1 2020 to 24.0% in Q4 2020 (Figure 6). In total, the agriculture, forestry, and fishery sectors grew by 27.5%, aided by a rise in production of livestock and poultry, paddy, and aquaculture (shrimp and fish). This highlighted Brunei's resil-ience and the nations adaptability to the changes of demand and supply.

7. Sectoral Impact of COVID-19

COVID-19 pandemic, despite being a medical shock, had adversely impacted Brunei economy, far greatly in the service sector than industrial sector in comparison to preceding recessions such as the Global Financial Crisis 2007–2009. This was a direct result of the pandemic safety guide-lines that restricted the mobility and face-to-face interactions of its resi-dents, altering the demand structure and consumer behaviour. It has extensively altered the structure and operations of major sectors due to lockdowns and border closure, accrued to a decline in mobility, shortage in food supply altering the consumer demand and prices of goods and services domestically. Thus, subsectors such as hotels, restaurants, whole-sale and retail, reliant on mobility and face-to-face interactions, saw a significant decline. Adapting to the new safety guidelines by enhancing digitalisation, innovation, and employing remote working allowed certain

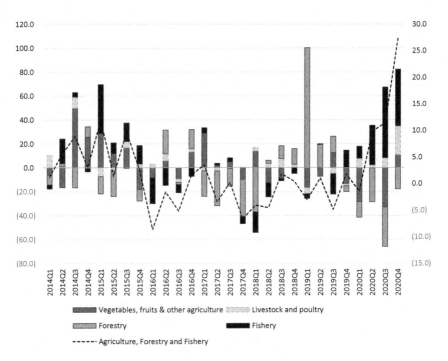

Figure 6:   Quarterly contribution to GDP growth by agriculture, forestry, and fishery sector from 2014–2020. (Author's contribution based on data from Ministry of Finance and Economy, Department of Economic Planning and Statistics, 2021).

sectors such as the communication sector to flourish at the peak of the pandemic.

Adhering to the new normal social distancing guidelines at the peak of the pandemic, accrued to a contraction in household income, consumption, and local demand, which was further exacerbated by the weak global demand. It led to the fall in recreational and cultural activities, eating-out, and travel activities domestically. Businesses revenue plunged during Q1 and Q2, amidst the peak of the pandemic when the COVID-19 restrictions were stringent. It stemmed in bankruptcies and temporary shutting down of businesses and dismissal of employees.

These changes had negatively affected the growth of specific sectors (Figure 7) such as air transport (fell from 3.8% in Q4 2019 to –83.6% in Q4 2020), land transport (fell from 9.3% in Q4 2019 to –51.0% in Q4

	2018Q1	2018Q2	2018Q3	2018Q4	2019Q1	2019Q2	2019Q3	2019Q4	2020Q1	2020Q2	2020Q3	2020Q4
Agriculture, forestry and fishery	−4.0	−4.5	1.9	0.4	−3.0	1.0	−4.8	1.8	−1.5	9.8	11.4	27.5
Livestock and poultry	2.9	3.6	7.6	2.3	−5.1	0.3	−5.2	−1.4	7.9	2.5	8.2	24.0
Forestry	−37.0	2.6	10.7	13.2	100.3	19.0	13.7	−4.8	−12.9	−28.3	−33.1	−17.9
Fishery	−17.1	−11.8	−1.8	−4.9	−3.8	0.5	−16.9	14.6	9.8	32.8	59.1	47.4
Industry	5.0	−2.0	−2.2	−2.3	−2.3	7.7	0.5	11.4	5.3	6.7	0.8	−0.8
Oil and gas mining	1.7	−2.3	−0.7	−2.3	−1.0	8.0	1.8	6.9	−4.4	0.7	−6.9	−8.8
Manufacture of liquefied natural gas and methanol	12.2	−6.0	−7.4	−6.3	−6.5	10.5	−1.7	28.5	32.2	27.8	27.0	18.1
Manufacture of food and beverage products	−4.9	−5.3	−6.3	−0.9	−5.3	−4.9	−6.2	3.9	12.8	8.7	34.6	30.8
Other manufacturing	29.5	45.5	7.4	20.7	1.5	−11.9	−9.7	−19.8	1.1	−10.7	−18.5	5.7
Electricity and water	0.0	16.0	6.4	22.9	9.9	12.9	3.4	−7.7	1.6	−7.7	−0.5	−0.2
Construction	24.4	6.5	−2.5	6.0	−3.3	−4.3	−5.1	13.8	8.5	−0.7	2.1	4.4
Services	−0.7	−3.5	0.7	6.4	3.5	4.9	5.1	0.7	−1.9	−2.2	−0.4	−3.0
Wholesale and retail trade	1.9	3.2	−1.2	5.2	11.2	5.5	9.5	2.1	1.3	−0.4	4.2	7.5
Land transport	−8.9	7.3	−5.0	−4.8	−14.0	−6.7	−10.5	9.3	−35.9	−56.4	−45.5	−51.0
Air transport	8.5	5.2	1.3	5.6	11.4	10.9	10.8	3.8	−20.6	−93.1	−92.1	−83.6
Communication	−0.7	0.8	−2.9	−1.0	0.2	3.2	−1.4	−1.1	17.3	19.7	23.8	−0.9
Hotels	19.3	−9.9	2.9	3.3	22.6	6.3	3.6	6.1	−4.0	−55.5	−12.3	−4.8
Restaurants	3.3	6.3	1.6	3.5	9.3	6.6	5.2	4.6	1.7	−16.2	−7.4	2.5
Health services	−3.8	13.8	2.3	0.8	3.5	10.5	10.1	5.8	6.3	−14.1	5.3	9.8
Education services	−2.6	0.4	1.9	0.2	2.3	10.2	−2.8	4.1	−1.1	−18.7	−0.6	−9.1
Business services	−1.8	5.2	2.4	3.3	−14.4	0.1	4.4	−3.1	12.1	13.2	1.1	−6.5
Government services	−1.1	4.3	4.6	5.5	2.7	−1.6	2.1	1.7	−5.1	−4.6	−4.0	−2.4

Figure 7: Quarterly economic growth of economic sectors for year 2018–2020. (Author's contribution based on data from Ministry of Finance and Economy, Department of Economic Planning and Statistics, 2021).

2020), industry (fell from 11.4% in Q4 2019 to −0.8% in Q4 2020), oil and gas mining (fell from 6.9% in Q4 2019 to −8.8% in Q4 2020), services (fell from 0.7% in Q4 2019 to −3.0% in Q4 2020), hotels (fell from 6.1% in Q4 2019 to −4.8% in Q4 2020), and restaurants (fell from 4.6% Q4 2019 to 2.5% Q4 2020).

On the contrary, COVID-19 has aided some sectors to flourish and overcome the challenges such as lack of supply and high demand faced during the outbreak. At Q3 2020, with the ease of restrictions laid by Brunei government allowing restaurant dine-ins, opening of gyms, schools, hotels, the service sector gradually began to recover. The sectors that flourished included agriculture, forestry, and fishery (1.8% Q4 2019 to 27.5% Q4 2020), livestock and poultry (−1.4% Q4 2019 to 24.0% Q4 2020), fishery (14.6% Q4 2019 to 47.4% Q4 2020), manufacture of food and beverages (3.9% Q4 2019 to 30.8% Q4 2020), and wholesale and retail trade (2.1% Q4 2019 to 7.5% Q4 2020). The following sections will discuss the majorly affected economic sectors due to the COVID-19 outbreak.

7.1 *Air transport and tourism sector*

The COVID-19 outbreak has radically impacted travel and tourism globally. Control measures, such as travel restrictions, community lockdowns, and compulsory quarantines, have caused the air transport sector to contract from –20.6% in Q1 2020 (BND 13.32 million) to –92.1% in Q3 2020 (BND 1.75 million). Brunei government approximated the loss of revenue to the civil aviation industry to be USD 114 million, which is the lowest among the ASEAN member countries with a projected loss of 8,500 jobs in 2020 (Othman, 2020b).

Due to the travel restrictions and border closure, tourist arrivals decreased from 79,199 in Q2 2019 to a mere 202 in Q2 2020; meanwhile, air freight activity (cargo based on aircraft) dropped by 75.1% (Figure 8). The tourist arrivals fell even further by 70% in March 2020 with lower than 10% of flights in operation by December 2020 in Brunei

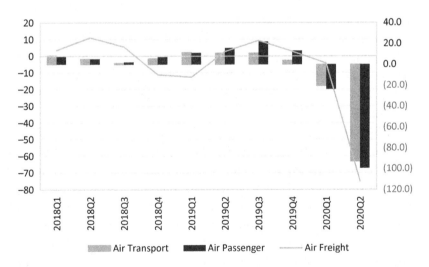

Figure 8:   Air passenger activity and air freight activity. (Author's contribution based on data from Ministry of Finance and Economy, Department of Economic Planning and Statistics, 2021).

International Airport. To accommodate safe travel between Brunei and Singapore for short-term business and official trips, the two governments established a green lane reciprocal arrangement in September 2020 (Wong, Chaw, *et al.*, 2020).

Despite the air transport and tourism sectors being the hardest hit in Brunei, the pandemic restrictions brought unexpected benefits to the local economy. Prior to COVID-19, residents of Brunei extensively travelled overseas, which significantly increased the outflow of monies to other countries. Official figures show that Brunei residents spent over BND 1.16 billion only in Malaysia in 2019, BND 1.12 billion in 2018 and BND 1.25 billion in 2017, which is approximately each Brunei resident spending an average of BND 2,755 in 2019 in Malaysia (The Scoop, 2020). Furthermore, solely in the East Malaysian state Sarawak, 1.29 million visitors from Brunei were documented in 2019 (Chung, 2020).

With lockdown in place and ban on non-essential travels for all residents of Brunei, the trend and appeal to travel abroad for vacations shifted to other sectors; namely, domestic hotels, restaurants, communication, and wholesale and retail industry. The monies spent overseas before COVID-19 now circulating domestically within Brunei ever since the pandemic has helped the economy to gradually recover and sustain the impacted sectors.

7.2 *Hotel and retail industry*

The hotel industry, the restaurant industry, and the retail industry in Brunei experienced significant obstacles in the early months of COVID-19. The apprehension of getting contracted with the virus, social distancing regulations, and lockdowns severely affected the income of households and revenue of businesses such as restaurants, hotels, and wholesale and retail industry.

Before the pandemic in Q4 2019, the hotel industry had a 6.1% increase in growth (BND 1.14 million), which dropped to −55.5% (BND 2.60 million) in Q2 2020 during the pandemic (from BND 10.86 million in Q1 2020). The restaurant industry was up by 4.6% in Q4 2019 (BND 41.54 million) and experienced a drop of −16.2% (BND 36.87 million) in Q2 2020 during the pandemic (from BND 46.95 million in Q1 2020).

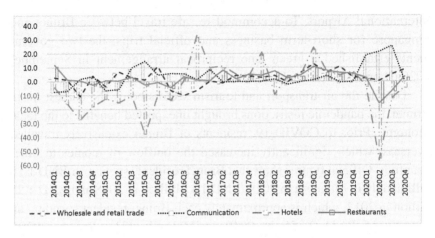

Figure 9:   Quarterly contribution to GDP growth by service sector from 2014–2020; wholesale and retail, communication, hotels and restaurants. (Author's contribution based on data from Ministry of Finance and Economy, Department of Economic Planning and Statistics, 2021).

The wholesale and retail industry had a 2.1% growth in Q4 2019 (BND 20.03 million) and experienced a drop of –0.4% (BND 257.47 million) in Q2 2020 during the pandemic (from BND 307.41 million in Q1 2020) (Figure 9).

Business activities gradually recovered with the ease of restrictions in Q3. The recovery can be seen in particular in the food and beverage industry with the restrictions of dining-in eased and in the hotel industries with the promotion of staycations for residents of Brunei. The hotel industry gradually started to recover from negative growth of 55.5% (BND 2.60 million) in Q2 2020 to 12.3% (BND 5.49 million) in Q3 2020. Hotel occupancy rates plunged to 18.3% in June but recuperated by the end of the year to some extent (CSPS, 2021). Similarly, restaurant and wholesale and retail industries had an improvement of –7.4% (BND 41.58 million) in Q2 2020 and 4.2% (BND 227.94 million) in Q3 2020. Despite showing negative growth in these industries, the revenue generated in these sectors after the ease of restrictions is larger than the revenue before the onset of COVID-19. This can be explained by the unanticipated benefits of the border closure for the entire 2020, which stemmed in a hike in demand for hotels (as a form of staycation), restaurant, and retail services domestically.

The residents of Brunei are well-known for their love for food and eating out within the country and out. During Q4 2019, the restaurant industry grew by 4.6% (BND 41.54 million), but the banning of dining-in in restaurants on 18 March 2020 had a consequence of the industry being severely affected in Q2 2020 with a drop of 16.2% (BND 36.87 million). This highlighted the importance of improving online food ordering and delivery system within the country. New businesses gradually began to emerge to cater to the rise in the demand in the sector. However, as the nation slowly eased its restriction, eating out became a form of recreational activity. Despite the restaurants initially functioning at 30% room capacity until middle of June 2020, the lack of mobility beyond Brunei borders allowed the industry to recover as the demand for food rose slowly. By the end of Q4 2020, the restaurant industry's growth rose to 2.4% (BND 42.56 million).

As Brunei imposed a lockdown on 12 March 2020, closing schools and higher education institutions and work from home hiked the demand for communication services for work, education, and entertainment purposes. The communication sector in Brunei grew from –1.1% (BND 62.60 million) in Q4 2019 to +23.8% (BND 108.48 million) in Q3 2020 (Figure 9) and also ensued in the growth in computer and telecommunication equipment –4% (Q42019) to +24% (Q42020) (Figure 10). Demand for books, newspapers, and stationeries had a significant decline as physical schools were closed for the major part of 2020. The plunge of books, newspapers, and stationeries was mainly seen at Q2 2020, which dropped to –45%. However, it recovered steadfastly by Q4 2020 with a +87% growth in sales as schools and offices re-opened by the end of the year, regaining the demand for books and stationaries.

Locked within the borders of Brunei for the major part of 2020, residents began searching for avenues for entertainment. Sales of recreational goods increased to 17% (Figure 10) during Q2 2020 and continued to stay relatively high for 2020. On the other hand, the sales of petrol and cars rose with the ease of restrictions within Brunei. The sale of petrol rose in Q3 2020 by 23% and the motor vehicle sale of cars rose in 2020 by 5%

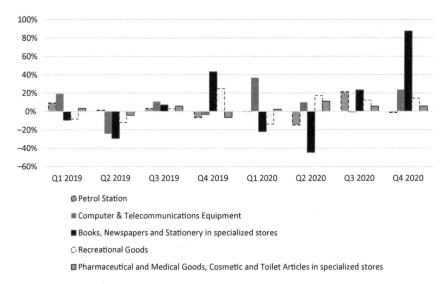

Figure 10:   Quarterly retail sales index of petrol state, computer items, books and stationeries, recreational goods, and pharmaceutical and medical goods from 2019–2020. (Author's contribution based on data from Ministry of Finance and Economy, Department of Economic Planning and Statistics, 2021).

(from 11,909 in 2019 to 12,505 in 2020) with the ease of restrictions, out of which 98% is for passenger vehicles (Table 3). Brunei is the only ASEAN country that had a growth in motor vehicle sales, while the rest of the ASEAN nations had a dramatic plunge in sales.

COVID-19 also brought about significant changes to buying patterns of Brunei residents as they move away from supermarkets to the neighbourhood mini-marts and department stores during the peak of the pandemic. At Q1 2020, the sales in supermarkets rose to 25% from 2% in Q4 2019, due to panic buying of face masks, disinfectants, and hand sanitisers and hoarding behaviour from fear of food and other items running out (Borneo Bulletin, 2020) after COVID-19 was announced as a global pandemic (Figure 11). The sale of food and beverages in specialised stores dropped to –5% in Q2 2020, as people stopped purchasing non-essential items due to heightened safety restrictions causing such stores to be temporarily closed down.

Table 3: Motor vehicle sales volume and percentage change from 2019–2020. (ASEAN Automotive Federation, 2021).

Country	Passenger Vehicles	Passenger Vehicle Contribution %	Commercial Vehicles	Commercial Vehicles Contribution %	2020	2019	% Change
1 Brunei	12239	98%	266	2%	12505	11909	+5%
2 Indonesia	388886	70%	143141	26%	552027	1030126	–48%
3 Philippines	69638	31%	154155	69%	223793	369941	–40%
4 Singapore	46986	83%	9437	17%	56423	90429	–38%
5 Thailand	343494	43%	448652	57%	792146	1007552	–21%
6 Myanmar	12867	73%	4840	27%	17707	21916	–19%
7 Malaysia	474104	91%	48469	9%	522573	604281	–14%
8 Vietnam	221274	75%	75360	25%	296634	322322	–8%

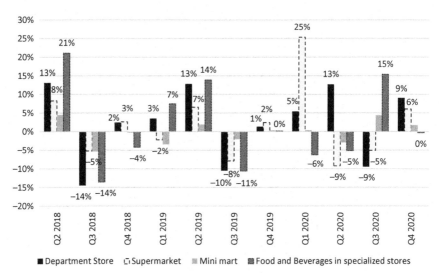

Figure 11:   Quarterly retail sales index of department stores, supermarkets, mini marts and food and beverages in specialised stores from 2018–2020. (Author's contribution based on data from Ministry of Finance and Economy, Department of Economic Planning and Statistics, 2021).

The sale in department stores rose to 13% in Q2 2020 from 5% in Q4 2019, which was due to shift in spending behaviour from supermarkets (which dropped to –9% in Q2 2020) to department stores. The shift in sales was due to the avoidance of places that may be crowded, accessibility of more variety of items in one place reducing the chances of crowds and search time needed to purchase the required items.

At Q3 2020, as the restrictions were eased and life within Brunei gradually started to shift towards an almost normalcy, the sales of department stores dropped to –9% and supermarkets to –5%, while increasing the sales of neighbourhood mini-mart by 4% and food and beverages in specialised stores to 15%. This was concomitant with the restriction of dining-in being eased, recovering the social life within Brunei. Nevertheless, sales of department stores and supermarkets recovered by 9% and 6% in Q4 2020, respectively.

These alterations in spending habits and lifestyle occasioned the sustenance of industries and stakeholders within Brunei despite the pandemic. It allowed the sectors and the economy to flourish against the drawbacks of COVID-19 and eased the economy to recover faster than expected.

8. Supporting Policies for Economic Recovery

Using a "Whole of Nation Approach", policy and measures were imposed supporting industries and individuals most affected by the COVID-19 crisis with three main aims:

(1) to maintain the wellbeing of the public: (i) building of a National Isolation Centre, National Virology Laboratory, and (ii) COVID-19 relief fund,
(2) to protect jobs: (i) full Supplemental Contributory Pension (SCP) contributions for self-employed individuals, (ii) free online training and contract extension aimed to equip jobseekers with relevant work experience and training in relevant fields, and
(3) to support and assist businesses: (i) 30% government buildings rental discount in selected industries, (ii) 50% corporate income tax discount, (iii) 15% discount on water and electricity bills, and (iv) temporary exemption of customs and excise duties on personal hygiene products (Ministry of Health, 2020).

These policies will assist in boosting Brunei's industries, sectors, and economy to recover faster and bounce back to normal.

9. Lessons Learnt and Opportunities

Brunei Darussalam has been exceptionally successful in controlling the COVID-19 outbreak and the economy, despite the lack of experience in handling large-scale outbreaks, by giving precedence to public health, daily risk communication, safeguarding employment, and aiding businesses from the onset of the pandemic. All these strategies allowed Brunei government to build the public's trust in their crisis management strategies, which allowed the small ASEAN state's pandemic situation, economy, and sectors to recover swiftly and have a long-term economic footprint.

The emergence of the COVID-19 pandemic highlighted several lessons learnt as a result and opportunities identified. The pandemic highlighted the benefits of economic diversification, which propelled the progression of Vision 2035 (Wawasan 2035) to transform Brunei into a "dynamic and sustainable economy". The pandemic allowed Brunei to move further away from the dependence on the oil and gas sector and develop the non-oil and gas sector, which was significantly seen in the agri-food sector, technology and ICT sector, and downstream oil and gas sector.

Consequently, despite bottlenecks in the supply chain logistics, hindering the availability of certain products, the food, agriculture, forestry, and fishery sectors grew at an unprecedented level to overcome the food shortage and hiking food price issues. The communication sector grew significantly to cater to the rise in demand due to remote working lifestyle amidst the pandemic.

COVID-19 caused drastic changes in consumer behaviour and lifestyle in terms of entertainment, recreational, and social activities, where most of these activities before the outbreak were primarily engaged in (over BND 1 billion) outside of Brunei, typically in Malaysia. The pandemic came as a blessing for Brunei as the border closure and lockdown allowed the diversion of these funds to circulate within Brunei.

Following the lockdown and the stringent travel restrictions throughout 2020, residents began searching for entertainment, recreation, and shopping avenues, with limited options, within the borders of Brunei. This allowed the initially pandemic-affected industries, such as hotels, restaurants, wholesale and retail industries, and the motor vehicle industry, to recover quickly due to changes in demand structure and lifestyle. This also showed the need for Brunei to develop local tourism, resorts, and attractions even further within the nation to increase the potential of boosting tourism catered not only for foreigners but also to the residents of Brunei. This opens up Brunei's opportunities to invest and construct entertainment and recreational avenues such as parks, hotels, integrated shopping malls, and parking lots to cater to the rising consumer demand domestically by the residents of Brunei. This will allow the industry and the stakeholders to grow not just amidst the pandemic but even beyond the future.

COVID-19 has propelled various sustainable and structural changes along with its long-term economic footprint in Brunei economy, in terms of economic diversification, supply chain logistics, and altering consumer demand structure and lifestyle. The pandemic highlighted the opportunity for the businesses, sectors, and government to prioritise dynamic policies to facilitate and operationalise new growth prospects.

References

Ahmad, N. (2018). Attitudes towards family formation among young adults in Brunei Darussalam. *Pakistan Journal of Women's Studies: Alam-e-Niswan*, 25(1): 15–34. doi:10.46521/pjws.025.01.0052.

Borneo Bulletin. (22 December 2020). Panic buying of chicken could become self-fulfilling prophecy. *Borneo Bulletin Online*. https://borneobulletin.com.bn/2020/12/panic-buying-of-chicken-could-become-self-fulfilling-prophecy/.

CEIC Data. (n.d.). Brunei: Govt revenue: Oil and gas revenue. Retrieved on 5 January 2021 from https://www.ceicdata.com/en/brunei/government-revenue-and-expenditure/govt-revenue-oil-and-gas-revenue.

CSPS. (2021). *Brunei Economic Outlook 2021*. Centre for Strategic and Policy Studies, Bandar Seri Begawan.

Chung, N. (25 June 2020). Tourism players hoping for lifeline from Singapore, Brunei travel. *Free Malaysia Today*. https://www.freemalaysiatoday.com/category/nation/2020/06/25/tourism-players-hoping-for-lifeline-from-singapore-brunei-travel/.

Department of Economic Planning and Statistics. (2020). Brunei Darussalam Statistical Yearbook 2019. In Brunei Darussalam Statistical Yearbook 2019.

Kwek, A. (2016). USDA foreign agricultural service, global agricultural information — Brunei.

Ministry of Finance and Economy. (2020a). Quarterly gross domestic product fourth quarter 2020 and annual 2020.

Ministry of Finance and Economy. (2020b). Towards a dynamic and sustainable economy: Economic blue print for Brunei Darussalam.

Ministry of Health. (2020). *UNDER SECTION 62A INFECTIOUS DISEASES ACT CHAPTER 204. 3/2020*, 1–3.

Othman, A. (31 March 2020a). Keeping the food supply chain on lock. *Borneo Bulletin Online.* https://borneobulletin.com.bn/2020/04/keeping-the-food-supply-chain-on-lock/.

Othman, A. (13 May 2020b). Brunei aviation industry loss lowest in ASEAN. *Borneo Bulletin Online.* https://borneobulletin.com.bn/2020/05/brunei-aviation-industry-loss-lowest-in-asean/.

The Scoop. (30 January 2020). Bruneian tourists spent $1.16bn in Malaysia last year — The Scoop. https://theworldnews.net/bn-news/bruneian-tourists-spent-1-16bn-in-malaysia-last-year-the-scoop.

Ullah, A. A., and Kumpoh, A. A.-Z. A. (2019). Diaspora community in Brunei: Culture, ethnicity and integration. *Diaspora Studies,* 12(1): 14–33. doi: 10.1080/09739572.2018.1538686.

World Health Organisation. (2020a). *Novel Coronavirus (2019-nCoV) Situation Report — 11.* 8. Retrieved from https://n9.cl/4xtow.

WHO. (1 October 2020b). The best time to prevent the next pandemic is now: Countries join voices for better emergency preparedness. World Health Organisation. Retrieved from https://www.who.int/news/item/01-10-2020-the-best-time-to-prevent-the-next-pandemic-is-now-countries-join-voices-for-better-emergency-preparedness.

WHO. (29 December 2020c). Weekly epidemiological update. Retrieved on 29 December 2020 from https://www.who.int/publications/m/item/weekly-epidemiological-update-29-december-2020.

Wong, J., Chaw, L., Koh, W. C., Alikhan, M. F., Jamaludin, S. A., Poh, W. W. P., and Naing, L. (2020). Epidemiological investigation of the first 135 COVID-19 cases in Brunei: Implications for surveillance, control, and travel restrictions. *The American Journal of Tropical Medicine and Hygiene,* 103(4): 1608–1613. doi:10.4269/ajtmh.20-0771.

Wong, J., Koh, W. C., Alikhan, M. F., Abdul Aziz, A. B. Z., & Naing, L. (2020). Responding to COVID-19 in Brunei Darussalam: Lessons for small countries. *Journal of Global Health,* 10(1), 1–4. https://doi.org/10.7189/JOGH.10.010363.

Appendix: Timeline of COVID-19 Policies

Brunei's most significant success was its government's swift response to mitigate the coronavirus's spread. This is the timeline of Brunei's COVID-19-related policies[1]:

---

[1] This set of policies is a concise set of policy information retrieved from daily press conferences broadcasted by Ministry of Health on national television.

21 January 2020: Use of thermal scanning at Brunei International Airport. Imposed travel restrictions from high-risk countries such as Italy and Iran, and the Hubei, Zheijiang, and Jiangsu regions of China (Ministry of Health, 2020).

4 February 2020: Self-isolation of 14 days imposed for individuals returning from affected countries.

9 March 2020: 1st COVID-19 case detected

10 March 2020: Individuals with signs of infection taken to the National Isolation Centre for further testing. A Quarantine Order under the Infectious Diseases Act Chapter 204 requires the individuals to undergo mandatory isolation. Violators may be fined up to BND 10,000 or imprisoned for not more than 6 months or both.

12 March 2020: Closure of all schools, vocational, technical, and higher education institutions as well as tuition schools and music schools.

16 March 2020: Ban on leaving the country for all citizens and residents of Brunei.

17 March 2020: Entry ban into Brunei extended to the rest of Europe, including the United Kingdom.

18 March 2020: Prohibition of (1) Islamic Friday and Five Daily prayers in mosques, (2) Restaurants, cafes, and food courts (3) Stalls and markets, (4) Museums, galleries, and libraries, (5) Cinemas.

23 March 2020: Prohibition of all foreign nationals from entering or transiting in Brunei through Land, Sea, and Air Control Posts and no restrictions for local or foreign companies to enter or exit the country to trade or deliver goods.

5 April 2020: All individuals will be required to undergo self-isolation in facilities provided by the government and will no longer be allowed to undergo self-isolation in their own homes.

7 May 2020: 141 COVID-19 cases detected

16 May 2020: Introduced the "BruHealth" App, which tracks the movement and accessibility of its residents to public places and business premises by scanning a BruHealth QR code. It provides the authorities with information to facilitate contact tracing and monitor room capacity of 30% to ensure social distancing.

Level 1 reduction of social distancing measures by imposing certain conditions on (1) Driving schools; (2) Gyms and fitness centres; (3) Sports facilities (indoor and outdoor); (4) Golf courses; (5) Restaurants, cafés, and food courts, and (6) Stalls and markets.

29 May 2020: Level 1 reduction of social distancing measures; all mosques will be opened for the public to perform their Friday Prayers while still practising social distancing.

5 June 2020: Additional Level 1 reduction of social distancing measures; tuition schools and music schools, whereby only one-on-one classes are allowed.

15 June 2020: Additional Level 1 reduction of the social distancing measures; (1) senior citizens activity centres; (2) Museums, galleries, and libraries; (3) Internet cafés.

Reduction of the social distancing measures from Level 1 to Level 2; (1) Driving schools; (2) Gyms and fitness centres; (3) Sports facilities (indoor and outdoor); (4) Golf course; (5) Restaurants, cafés, and food courts, and (6) Stalls and markets. Commencement of Islamic Friday and Five Daily Prayers in mosques and prayer rooms.

18 June 2020: Reduction of the social distancing measures from Level 1 to Level 2; (1) Schools; (2) Vocational, technical, and higher education institutions; (3) Tuition schools and music schools.

14 August 2020: Reduction of the charges for the RT-PCR COVID-19 swab test imposed on pre-permitted foreigners entering the country from BND 1,000 to BND 350.

17 August 2020: Reduction of the social distancing measures from Level 1 to Level 2; (1) Arcades and Playgrounds (indoor and outdoor).

Reduction of the social distancing measures from Level 2 to Level 3; (1) Swimming pools; (2) Cinemas; (3) Activity centres for the elderly; (4) Mass Gathering limited to 200 people.

Reduction of the social distancing measures from Level 3 to Level 4; (1) Special needs classes; (2) Child care centres; (3) Museums, Galleries, and Libraries.

7 September 2020: Increasing the capacity for Mass Gathering from 200 people to 350 people.

24 December 2020: A new variant of the COVID-19 virus found in the UK. Essential travellers travelling into Brunei required to disclose proof of a negative COVID-19 test taken 72 hours before departure and required to complete up to 14 days of mandatory self-isolation on arrival and only be released based on a negative COVID-19 test result done in Brunei.

31 December 2020: 157 COVID-19 cases detected

About the Authors

Gamini Premaratne holds a Master's Degree in Policy Economics and a Ph.D. degree in Economics with specialisation in Econometrics from the University of Illinois at Urbana-Champaign, USA. He has served as a faculty member in the Department of Economics at National University of Singapore and also as a statistician at the Department of Census and Statistics. Currently, he is working as a faculty member at the School of Business, Universiti Brunei Darussalam. His research interests include behavioural finance, volatility and spillover models, financial markets, macroeconomic modelling, and risk management. He has published locally and internationally refereed journal articles and book chapters, including in *Journal of Financial Econometrics*, *Journal of Statistical Planning and Inference*, *Communication in Statistics*, *Energy Economics*, *Handbook of Asian Finance*.

Aishath Shahudha Abdulla is currently a Ph.D. student in Economics at School of Business and Economics, Universiti Brunei Darussalam. She also obtained her Bachelor's degree in Business (Double major in Economics and Accounting and Finance) with First Class Honours from

Universiti Brunei Darussalam. Her research interests are in the areas of risk management, interconnectedness, and financial stability. She has taught Business Statistics, Econometrics, Principles of Economics, and Monetary Economics.

Farah A'liyah Haji Amer Hishamuddin is a Fixed Income credit analyst at BIBD Asset Management (under the licence of BIBD Securities Sdn Bhd). She holds a Bachelor of Science Degree in Economics and Econometrics with First Class Honours from the University of Bristol.

Chapter 2

Cambodia's Response to COVID-19 and its Socioeconomic Dimensions

Júlia Garcia-Puig*

Open Development Cambodia, Phnom Penh, Cambodia
*julia@opendatacambodia.net

Abstract

Cambodia is among the countries with the lowest incidence rate of reported COVID-19 cases. However, the global economic turmoil is generating deep economic and social implications within its borders. This chapter discusses the emerging socioeconomic challenges along with the government intervention in response to the new scenario. The macroeconomic analysis covers the main channels whereby the Cambodian economy is deteriorating and discusses how the country's rebound is subject to the performance of its major allies. Likewise, the chapter delves into the microeconomic effects, emphasising the subsequent social ramifications, especially among the most vulnerable demographics. It is argued that the current government measures are insufficient to mitigate the growing poverty levels and needs of the population.

*Corresponding author.

Keywords: Cambodia; COVID-19; construction; garment and footwear industry; gender; household indebtedness; policy response; socioeconomic inequality; tourism sector; unemployment; vulnerability.

1. Introduction

Cambodia announced its first case of COVID-19 in 27 January 2020, prior to the World Health Organization's (WHO's) declaration of a global pandemic. At the outset, Cambodia's proximity to China set alarm bells ringing and raised fears over the spread of the virus. As of March 2021, Cambodia remained among the countries with the lowest number of reported cases, with an incidence rate of 13.36 per 100,000 (Johns Hopkins Coronavirus Resource Center, 2021). Nevertheless, serious concerns remain over the capacity of the healthcare structure to address an eventual large-scale nationwide health emergency.

Despite the success in containing the spread of the virus, Cambodia's sound economic growth and development advances were abruptly disrupted by the external demand shocks derived from the global economic contraction. The new scenario has diminished the country's growth perspectives for the upcoming years, hindering the fulfilment of well-being and social development targets. At the very beginning of the pandemic, the slowdown of the Chinese economy had an immediate impact on Cambodia, given the latter's high dependency on their economic and commercial ties. In contrast with the initial perspectives, however, the fast rebound of the Chinese economy will be key for the recovery of Cambodia. In the meantime, two of Cambodia's main economic partners, namely the European Union (EU) and the United States of America (USA), are fully immersed in deep health, economic, and social crises. Hence, the new context is likely to accelerate Cambodia's shift towards a more regional approach for its economic and commercial ties.

In the first place, the chapter provides an overview of the health and economic policy measures adopted by the Royal Government of Cambodia (RGC) in response to the pandemic. The following section describes the changes in the macroeconomic outlook by focusing on the performance of the main industries and drivers of Cambodia's economic growth. The last section discusses the microeconomic and social ramifications and its particularly high incidence on different vulnerable demographics.

2. The Government Intervention

2.1 *Health measures to contain the spread*

The prompt activation of the Cambodia Early Warning Response system (CamEWARN) and the capacity provided by the Global Influenza Surveillance and Response System (GISRS) enhanced the coordination between relevant healthcare actors and the monitoring of epidemiological data. Information reported by health centres, referral and specialty hospitals, was centralised under the Communicable Disease Control (CDC) Department.

In parallel, the Ministry of Health (MoH) scaled up the Rapid Response Teams (RRTs) to increase capacity of the free national 115 health hotline to 10,000 daily calls. Clinical testing was centralised in two labs — the Institute Pasteur Cambodia (IP-C) and the National Institute of Public Health. The U.S. Naval Medical Research Unit-2 Detachment provides surge capacity while all other testing and clinical facilities were put at the government disposal.

Social distancing measures, the closure of leisure and entertainment venues, the banning of mass gatherings — including religious celebrations — and the nationwide closure of schools complemented mandatory quarantines for specific population groups, namely returning migrant workers from Thailand and garment workers. Interprovincial mobility within the country was restricted and national celebrations postponed, including Khmer New Year. Since cases have been primarily imported, the government established strict entry requirements and put a halt on international flights from the most-affected countries.

2.2 *Relief packages*

An effective coordination between line Ministries and relevant government agencies enabled a prompt implementation of emergency measures and relief packages intended to overcome the prevailing deficiencies in social protection, healthcare coverage, and safety nets. Specific interministerial bodies to manage the COVID-19 response were established, including a working group to control the prices and supplies of basic commodities and a task force responsible for budget policy on financing and social assistance. Monetary and banking policies were assigned to a multidisciplinary Working Group, co-chaired by the Ministry of Economy and Finance (MEF) and the National Bank of Cambodia (NBC). In parallel, international aid and development organisations have closely cooperated with the RGC in providing ongoing technical assistance and improving its resource capacity.

Fiscal measures sought to avoid bankruptcies, strengthen the sustainability of businesses, and ensure the capacity of the private sector to resume operations upon the restoration of regular conditions. Tax reliefs, reduced withholding taxes during business suspension, and tax exemptions of the ownership transfer tax along with improvements on the ease of doing business have especially benefitted the worst-hit and largest sectors of the economy, namely tourism, garment, travel goods, footwear, and exports. Aviation companies with registered airlines in the country enjoy tax exemptions as well. Firms' access to financing was facilitated; USD 200 million were allocated for working capital and investment loans, capital injections to the Rural Development and Agriculture Bank, and low interest loans for Small Medium Enterprises (SMEs) (Royal Government of Cambodia, 2020).

Cambodia's Central Bank, the NBC, loosened its monetary policy to ensure sufficient liquidity levels in the banking system. Increases in the Capital Conservation Buffer were delayed and the interest rate on the Liquidity Providing Collateralised Operations and the Negotiable Certificates of Deposit was cut. Reserve requirements for banking and financial institutions were reduced to 7% for both the Khmer riel and foreign currencies.

Key social policy measures included a USD 40 wage subsidy and training programmes for garment and tourism laid-off workers, two of the worst-hit sectors and main drivers of economic growth. A breakthrough for Cambodia's social protection schemes consisted of direct financial support to vulnerable families, provided for the first time at nationwide scale. The prompt deployment of this cash transfer programme was possible by scaling up the national poverty identification system, the IDPoor, which registers and monitors low-income families across the country. Due to the ongoing deterioration of economic conditions, increases in the informal activity and the return of migrant workers, the IDPoor system requires more frequent updates to capture the increasing amount of vulnerable households.

Finally, in the legal sphere, a highly controversial Law on National Administration in the State of Emergency was drafted by the government and approved by the National Assembly and the Senate in April 2020. The law grants "extraordinary powers" to the government in the event of "tumultuous chaos to national security and public order" (Article 4). The fact that these provisions are vague and ambiguous immediately raised concerns over the government using this new law as a tool to facilitate government surveillance and control of information. Notably, this law was passed amidst an ongoing deterioration of freedom of expression and human rights during recent years. The space for free speech has been shrinking in recent years as renewed crackdowns on political opponents, media outlets, journalists, activists, and internet users, have led to new waves of information blockages, shutdowns, and arrests (Freedom House, 2021).

2.3 *Resource mobilisation and public revenues*

The COVID-19 response entailed a significant revenue mobilisation to cover the dramatic surge in public spending. The budget for health-related measures, including testing, treatment, and containment accounted to USD 60 million. The largest budget allocations for social and economic measures consisted of: (i) USD 400 million in social assistance, of which USD 300 million were directed to the IDPoor cash transfer programme and USD 100 million to the work programme; (ii) USD 64 million in wage subsidies and training for laid-off workers; (iii) USD 600 million in low-interest loans to specialised banks and; (iv) USD 50 million to SMEs in the manufacturing and agricultural sector, respectively (United Nations, 2020).

In parallel, the major sources of public revenues have been severely affected by the widespread economic repercussions as well as by the tax relief measures introduced, which are worth USD 200 million approximately. The slowdown in construction demand and garment exports is particularly harmful, as these two represent the largest contributors of indirect and direct government revenues, respectively (The World Bank Group, 2020a). As a result of the growing spending needs and the shrinking of public revenues estimated for 2020 and 2021, public savings will diminish, the fiscal deficit is estimated to increase to 7–12% of the GDP, and the population will grow by close to 40% in the upcoming years (Asian Development Bank, 2020b).

Importantly, part of the earmarked budgets for development policies were reoriented to address COVID-19. Coupled with the ongoing deterioration of socioeconomic indicators, the emerging scenario obstructs the fulfilment of Cambodia's ambitious national plans, which are largely guided by the National Strategic Development Plan 2019–2023 (NSDP) and the Rectangular Strategy-Phase IV. The NSDP provides the macroeconomic framework under which the outlined policies and priority actions are to be pursued by the different line Ministries and government divisions. In turn, the Rectangular Strategy — grounded on the principles of Growth, Employment, Equity, and Efficiency — guides the implementation strategy of the NSDP. The RS is the cornerstone to the government's agenda to promote a sustainable development and reduce poverty levels. Likewise, the current situation raises concerns over the capacity to meet the Cambodian Sustainable Development Goals (CSDGs) and to sustain progress towards becoming a middle-income country by 2030.

3. Economic Consequences

3.1 *Shocks on the main drivers of economic growth*

Cambodia's sound economic performance — averaging 7.7% annual growth rate over the last two decades — has been driven by three key sectors, namely tourism, industrial production and construction (see Figure 1) (World Bank Open Data, 2021a). Grounded on an export-oriented growth model and strong external demand, Cambodia has become highly

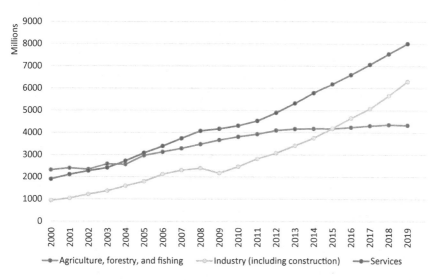

Figure 1: Value-added by sector at constant prices 2010 USD.
Own elaboration. Source of the data: The World Bank Open Data (2021b, 2021c, 2021d).

reliant on the dynamism of the global economy and the stability of its main economic and commercial partners, most of which are among the most-affected countries by the pandemic. Hence, Cambodia's vulnerability to external shocks has severely affected its major contributors to economic growth.

3.1.1 *The tourism and hospitality sector*

With international mobility at a standstill, tourism and hospitality are the worst-hit sectors, interrupting over two decades of consistent growth. A 90% drop in airport traffic brought the number of visitors well below the 6.61 millions of 2019, hindering the target of 12 million set by the Ministry of Tourism for 2025 (Data for Cambodia, 2020). Cambodia registered a sudden fall in arrivals, prompted by its high reliance on Chinese tourists, who accounted for 35.7% of total foreign visitors in 2019. Table 1 shows the most relevant countries of origin of tourists in Cambodia and the evolution in the year prior to the pandemic. Notably, Cambodia has been receiving a growing number of tourists from its neighbouring countries, such as Vietnam and Thailand (Ministry of Tourism, 2019).

Table 1: Major countries of origin of tourists in Cambodia (2019) and yearly change (2018–2019).

Country of Origin	Share of Total Arrivals (%)	Yearly Change (2018–2019) (%)
China	35.7	16.7
Vietnam	13.7	13.6
Thailand	7.1	22.0
Lao PDR	5.5	−14.6
Korea (ROK)	3.9	−15.5
United States of America (U.S.A.)	3.8	−0.8
Japan	3.1	−1.3
Malaysia	3.1	0.9
France	2.5	−3.9
United Kingdom (U.K.)	2.5	0.5

Own elaboration. Source of the data: Ministry of Tourism (2019).

The paralysis of the largest contributor to the economy (26.4% of the GDP in 2019) has significantly driven down growth estimations for the upcoming years and threatens the overall stability of the economy (World Travel and Tourism Council, 2020). For the time being, fiscal support — including tax cuts for determined businesses and the exemption of renewal fees for tourism licenses in 2021 — has not prevented the closure of thousands of tourism-related businesses and the subsequent surge in unemployment. The recovery of the sector is contingent on the evolution of the virus and the lifting of travel restrictions at the global level. Even in the case of a fast resumption of tourism, there are growing concerns over the resilience of businesses to withstand the current crisis.

3.1.2 *The garment and footwear industry*

Low wages, favourable economic conditions and regulations, and Cambodia's strategic position induced a fast expansion of the industrial activity in recent years, underpinned by the garment and footwear production, which accounted for 60% of exports and manufacturing value-added

(International Labour Organization, 2020) and 17% of GDP growth in 2019 (The World Bank Group, 2020a). However, the garment production model, based on the specialisation in cut-make-pack (CMP) and low-value processes, makes the sector highly vulnerable to external shocks. The industry relies on foreign financing and raw material imports from neighbouring countries, which were restricted due to air and land transportation bans.

The major external demand shocks and supply chain disruptions led to widespread order postponements, cancellations, and worker layoffs. By mid-April 2020, over 130 garment and footwear factories had partially or fully suspended their production (The World Bank Group, 2020a) and in June, as many as 25% of factories had no orders. Besides, the major markets for Cambodian exports are among the worst-hit countries by the pandemic, where strict measures and lockdowns have driven down consumption. The total value of garment exports to the European Union, the United States, and Japan fell by over 20% year-over-year (YoY) in the first half of 2020 (International Labour Organization, 2020).

Additionally, the consequences of the pandemic have been exacerbated by the European Union's (EU's) partial withdrawal of the "Everything But Arms" (EBA) agreement, which came into effect on 12 August 2020, and whereby Cambodia lost trade preferential access to the EU market. Under the Generalised Scheme of Preferences (GSP), the EBA grants Least Developed countries with full duty-free, quota-free access into the EU, conditional upon the respect of human rights. The withdrawal is estimated to compromise 20% of Cambodia's exports to the EU, largely garment, footwear, travel goods, and sugar products (European Commission, 2020).

Even though this is a partial and temporary measure, the restoration of EBA is not expected in the foreseeable future as it is conditional on improvements in freedom of expression and human rights in the country. This entails a significant deterioration of Cambodia's trade deficit, standing at USD 8 billion[1] in 2019, which pressures the country to diversify its production and develop ties with new commercial partners.

---

[1] In 2019, the value of Cambodia's exports and imports were USD 14.53 and USD 22.19 billion, respectively.

3.1.3 *Construction and real estate*

In the previous decade to the COVID-19 pandemic, the construction and real estate sectors experienced a boom through which they became the largest contributors to Cambodia's GDP growth (35.7% in 2019). The expansion of capital inflows fuelled the dynamism of the construction and real estate activity as these sectors receive over half of total Foreign Direct Investment (FDI) project value. As reflected in Figure 2, the tourism and garment sectors receive a significantly lower share of FDI (The World Bank Group, 2020a).

Chinese investments are predominant, accounting for half of the total USD 2,845 million in FDI received in 2019. Therefore, China's slowdown at the outset of the pandemic caused a sharp reduction of capital inflows. Overall, Cambodia experienced a 40% contraction of total approved FDI in the first quarter of 2020, which particularly affected the construction and real estate sectors (The World Bank Group, 2020a). In turn, the shock in the construction sector triggered a reduction of construction material imports by the first quarter of 2020 as seen in Figure 3. Nevertheless, the number of approved construction permits issued during that period continued to grow.

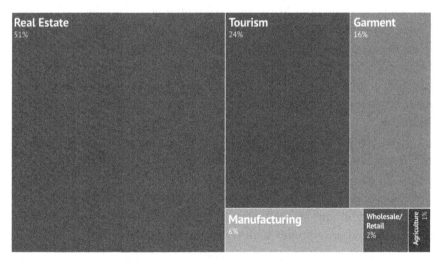

Figure 2:   Distribution of approved FDI project value by sector (2019).

Own elaboration. Source of the data: The World Bank Group (2020a).

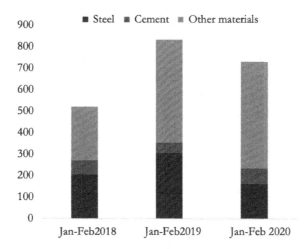

Figure 3:   Value of construction material imports to Cambodia (in billions of Riels).
Source: The World Bank Group (2020a, p. 18).

Despite the moderate impact in the job market — compared to more labour-intensive sectors — the decline in construction and real estate activity severely affect public revenues. Given its recent dynamism, the indirect taxes generated in these two sectors have become one of the major government sources of funding. In the current situation, when public expenditure for health and social measures is on the rise, the contraction of revenues puts further pressure on the public sector. In addition, the enlarging financial gaps are exposing the underlying vulnerabilities of a highly speculative and unregulated sector, for which the government has been repeatedly urged to take action in the last years, especially with regard to construction licences, safety and working conditions, the quality of construction material, and law enforcement.

3.2 *Risks for the financial and banking sectors*

Even though for the first half of 2020 financial stability was preserved and the banking industry remained resilient and profitable, with sizeable capital buffers and low non-performing loans (NPL) ratios, the prolongation of the crisis and the widespread uncertainty that shape the global scenario threaten the macroeconomic and financial stability of Cambodia.

The good momentum of the financial and banking sector in recent years was in large part facilitated by the capital channelled through a growing presence of foreign financial institutions and favourable external economic conditions, in parallel to structural reforms and strong national growth. Hence, the escalating global financial instability can trigger the multiple risks of the sector, rooted in rapid credit growth, insufficient regulation, cross-border and risk-based supervision, liquidity risks, over-reliance on foreign capital, and excessive levels of credit concentration (International Monetary Fund, 2019).

Strong international markets are crucial to ensure robust capital inflows into the Cambodian banking sector, as it is dominated by branches and subsidiaries of foreign commercial banks. A prolonged reduction of FDI will amplify the slowdown of the construction and real estate sectors and generate a rise of defaults and non-performing loans, liquidity issues, and a fall in investors' confidence and prices. To avoid this, the NBC reduced the reserve requirement ratio to 7% for both foreign and local currencies and advised financial institutions to restructure loans and reschedule repayments[2]. Besides, the risk of insolvency and defaults in the private sector is on the rise. In particular, due to the drop of tourists arrivals and the fall in industrial exports, real estate prices and demand, along with the predicted large impacts of the EBA withdrawal (International Monetary Fund, 2019).

4. Distributional Impacts and Socioeconomic Implications

4.1 *The disruption of labour markets and the drop in incomes*

The first symptoms of the macroeconomic contraction led to an immediate shrinking of employment and a deterioration of working conditions. The estimated 1.76 million jobs at risk in a labour market that employs 9.3 million people threatens to drive up unemployment to unprecedented rates

---

[2] By the end of August 2020, USD 3.6 billion in loans had been restructured.

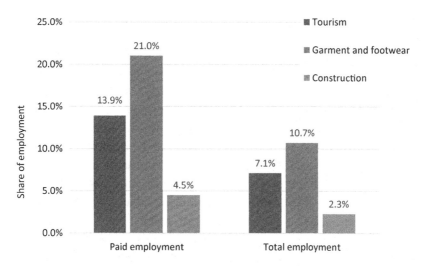

Figure 4: Contribution to employment of the three largest drivers of economic growth in 2019.

Source: The World Bank Group (2020a, p. 4).

along with increased informality and vulnerability (The World Bank Group, 2020a). In addition, the low collective bargaining coverage and trade union membership, with a unionisation rate of 10%, hinders workers' leverage to negotiate better conditions (International Labour Organization, n.d.).

The sectors that have boosted employment growth in recent years (see Figure 4), doubling the share of wage workers up to 50% of total employment in less than a decade, have now turned into the major sources of job destruction (World Bank Open Data, 2021e). Overall, informal and low-skilled workers have faced the sharpest surge in unemployment (Future Forum, 2020).

Tourism and garment workers — who combined account for 35% of total paid employment — have experienced the largest impact among wage workers (The World Bank Group, 2020a). Six months into the pandemic outbreak, at least 433 factories and tourism-related businesses had suspended their activity, displacing 135,000 garment and 17,000 tourism sector workers, respectively (Open Development Cambodia, 2020). In contrast, the capital-intensive construction and real estate sectors will generate less unemployment as they employ 4.5% of wage workers (200,000). Workers who maintain their jobs face wage cuts, reduced working hours, and deteriorated labour conditions. As a result, there have been increasing compensation disputes and widespread workers' demands for out-of-work allowances, wage payment delays, and benefits.

The rise of unemployment and the deterioration of economic conditions have significantly shrunk opportunities for informal workers, who rely on the overall dynamism and well-being of the economy. In fact, it is estimated that every wage worker in the garment industry stimulates demand and consumption to support up to six informal workers (*The Phnom Penh Post*, 2020). Informality in Cambodia accounts for half of total employment and is present across all sectors, including workers in tourism, industrial production, and construction. However, certain vulnerable populations (women, indigenous peoples, youth) and professionals (drivers, street vendors, hairdressers, garbage collectors, domestic workers, and farmers) are overrepresented in the informal economy.

Despite the consequences for the agricultural sector in terms of unemployment have been milder, rural populations face a decline in incomes and increased financial struggles. On the one hand, the overall slowdown of the economy and food chain disruptions have driven up indebtedness of poor rural households, with limited savings and alternatives to address such abrupt shocks. On the other hand, the destruction of employment has particularly affected rural households, as the garment and tourism industries largely employ rural workers. Besides, migrant workers have seen their capacity to support their families through remittances reduced.

Ensuring the resilience of rural populations is crucial given that even after years of industrialisation and shifts of agrarian workers to non-agricultural activities, Cambodia remains a rural country (76% of the population) and agriculture accounts for 31% of total employment (World Bank Open Data, 2021f). Largely based on small and medium-scale production and family-owned businesses, the sector is characterised by low productivity levels, limited diversification, informality, and specialisation in low value-added products. Hence, the sector has limited capacity to absorb the laid-off workers from other industries.

Like in other countries across the region, labour migration remains a fundamental pillar of the Cambodian economy. Remittances sent by the

1.2 million Cambodian migrant workers amount to USD 1.5 billion and benefit 9% of households. The economic slowdown suffered by the main destinations of labour migrants in the region — namely Thailand, the Republic of Korea, Japan, Singapore, Hong Kong, Malaysia, and Saudi Arabia — left millions of migrant workers unemployed overnight. The resulting financial struggles combined with the lack of social protection, the announcement of border closures, and the high sense of uncertainty translated into large waves of migrants going back to their countries of origin. The return of Cambodian workers, mostly from Thailand, and the income declines of those who stayed overseas, is predicted to result in a 15.4% fall in remittances, corresponding to USD 231 million by the end of 2020 (Asian Development Bank, 2020a).

4.2 *Increased household indebtedness*

The sharp fall in incomes amplified the fragility of the microfinance sector and generated rampant indebtedness among households. Initially built by development and nonprofit organisations, the Cambodian microlending sector is, nowadays, one of the largest and most profitable systems world-wide. The USD 10 billion in outstanding microloans represent over one-third of the country's GDP. The sector is oversaturated; there are 2.7 million microloans with an average loan size of USD 3,800 in a country of 3.3 million households (Thomson Reuters Foundation, 2020). Besides, the fact that land titles are usually required as collateral is especially wor-risome for the farmers whose land represents not only their house but also their source of livelihoods. This adds to the increasing pressure faced by rural populations, where 40% of households are indebted (National Institute of Statistics Ministry of Planning, 2018).

The response of the government to ensure the effective restructuration of loan repayments has been insufficient and the system faces increasing instability. As the capacity of borrowers to repay loans decreases, the risks of default and repayment delays continue to grow. Hence, COVID-19 has evinced the preexisting malfunctioning, over indebtedness, and structural risks of the sector. Generalised low levels of financial literacy and a lax regulation underpin the lack of consumer protection. Multiple borrowing practices are commonplace and employed to cover other existing loans and living expenses. Borrowers and human rights organisations have repeatedly denounced coercive and predatory practices, abusive high interest rates, and exceeding loan sizes.

The performance of small businesses is in the spotlight, as they tend to have less liquidity and more limited financing alternatives. The decline of reported monthly sales was sharper for micro firms and SMEs — 52% and 51%, respectively — compared to the 37% of large firms in June 2020 (The World Bank Group, 2020b). MSMEs[3] with less than 10 employees are the backbone of local economies; they account for 80% of enterprises in Cambodia and are critical for job creation (International Labour Organization, 2019).

4.3 *Exacerbation of vulnerability*

The economic and social ramifications of the COVID-19 crisis have materialised across the country, geographies, and sectors; but the poor and most vulnerable households have been disproportionally affected. The downturn in the poverty headcount estimates — increasing from the 9.6% baseline up to 17.6% by the end of 2020 – could drive 1.3 million people below the poverty line (United Nations Development Programme, 2020).

The Cambodian social protection system, limited in scope and capacity, has not prevented the poor from facing higher income instability and indebtedness. Social protection is in its early stage of development, lagging behind other countries in the region in terms of coverage and government spending rates. Despite progress towards the expansion of contributory and non-contributory schemes, access to government assistance of vulnerable populations remains low. In 2019, 6.2% of the total population benefitted from a social protection scheme while coverage of vulnerable people stood at 4.3% (International Labour Organization, 2020). As a result, non-governmental organisations remain the backbone of social assistance provision for vulnerable and poor population.

Hence, coverage remains limited and concentrated on the formal sector, largely excluding the informal sector where poor workers cluster. In

---

[3]The size of firms are defined as follows; micro firms have less than five employees; SMEs between 5–99, and large firms, more than 100.

total, only 2.6 million workers benefit from the National Social Security Fund (NSSF) with injury, sickness, and maternity benefits as well as vocational training programmes (International Labour Organization, n.d.). The COVID-19 relief packages need to be expanded and sustained in the longer term, including the USD 40 wage subsidy to garment and tourism laid-off workers and the direct USD 10–50 payments to 600,000 families through the IDPoor scheme.

Left with limited alternatives and pushed by increasing distress, impoverishment, and risk of land seizures, vulnerable households tend to resort to negative coping strategies. MFI borrowers struggling with debt repayments have reduced their food and electricity consumption, sought additional loans and sold property (CATU, CENTRAL, LICADHO, 2020; Future Forum, 2020). Vulnerable households have as well resorted to taking loans from informal moneylenders at abusive terms and removing children from school. Activity in the informal sector is on the rise, which entails a rise in unstable employment, a lack of legal protection, and poor working conditions.

Women have been disproportionally affected by the crisis in multiple forms as their participation in the labour force is highly concentrated in low value activities and as much as 58% of female employment was considered vulnerable before the COVID-19 outbreak (World Bank Open Data, 2021g). The slowdown of the garment sector has particularly affected women as they account for the majority of workers in such industry. Despite the majority of businesses in Cambodia being female-led, these mostly consist of unregistered micro enterprises, which have been highly impacted by the economic shocks. As a consequence, the wage gap between men and women, which currently stands at 20%, is on the rise.

Combined with school closures, women have faced increased childcare responsibilities and domestic workload. Besides, the pandemic has also increased domestic violence towards women. Income pressures are as well likely to restrict access to healthcare services and aggravate women's health status, already shaped by higher malnutrition rates than men and a strong prevalence of maternal mortality. Besides, learning difficulties posed by the closure of schools and mobility restrictions hinder progress towards gender equality in education. Compared to men, women have lower literacy levels (85.1% and 70.9%, respectively) and complete less years of formal school education (3.8 years for women and 5.6 for men) (International Labour Organization, 2019).

Over three million students were affected by the 3-month nationwide closure of schools and other successive school shutdowns at local level. As in many other countries, school shutdowns evinced the consequences of persisting large socioeconomic inequalities. The expansion of internet and mobile phone use in Cambodia has been rampant in recent years; with 9.7 million users, internet penetration stands at 58%, with a 15% increase compared to 2019 (Simon Kemp, 2020). However, a wide digital divide prevails and disconnected households cluster in rural areas.

Despite the efforts of the Ministry of Education, Youth, and Sports (MoEYS) to facilitate distance learning and provide online educational materials, the closure of schools resulted in a halt on learning of a large part of the three million students across the education system. Challenges included a lack of equipment and tools, limited digital educational resources in Khmer language, and low levels of digital literacy among students, teachers, and families. In addition, the economic hardships faced by disadvantaged families induced school drop-outs in favour of child labour, for which Cambodia is deemed to be a high-risk country.

School drop-outs and the temporary closure of educational institutions deprive children of the school meals on which one-third of the students from poor families rely. A significant decrease in the levels of access to food have been recorded throughout the country. This exacerbates the existing high prevalence of malnutrition, especially in rural areas, risking the unhealthy growth and development of children (Ministry of Education, Youth and Sport, 2021). Overall, 14% of the total population suffers from severe food insecurity and 15% of undernourishment. As for children under five years old, the figures are 24% for underweight and 32% for stunting (34% and 24% in rural and urban settings, respectively).

The low levels of digital connectivity and economic resources among indigenous communities have hampered the adaptation to distance learning of indigenous children and youth. COVID-19 has considerably amplified the vulnerability faced by indigenous groups through a fall in incomes, isolation, low access to healthcare, food shortages, and the deterioration of living conditions. These communities mainly rely on agriculture and local markets, and are significantly excluded from social security schemes, with less than 30% of indigenous people employed in the formal sector. These groups suffer some of the highest poverty levels in the country, with a higher propensity to landlessness, malnutrition, illiteracy, and limited access to health and education services (Balvedi Pimentel *et al.*, 2020).

5. Conclusion

Albeit the relatively low incidence of COVID-19 has not obliged Cambodia to fully cease internal activity, external demand shocks have severely deteriorated its economy at both macro and micro levels. The reactivation of the country's core economic pillars — tourism, trade, and external financing — as well as the sustainability of the current account deficit and growing external debt, are tightly dependent on the behaviour of Cambodia's economic partners, with the main focus on China.

As a result of the severe lockdowns and measures adopted by the Chinese government at the outbreak of the pandemic, the health crisis was acute but shorter than expected. Despite its fast-expanding debt rates, China registered a 6.5% GDP growth in the last quarter of 2020. The rebound of the Chinese economy contrasts with the prolonged ongoing crisis of other major economies, mainly the EU and the U.S.A., where many sectors remain largely paralysed. This scenario, combined with the partial EBA withdrawal, is likely to prompt Cambodia's economic reliance on China, while enhancing a more regional approach. On the one hand, regional travel restrictions are likely to be eased sooner than intercontinental bans. On the other hand, the expansion of Chinese capital inflows and commercial relations with Cambodia will continue to grow. Indeed, the strengthening of economic relations in recent years has resulted in the Greater China region — which includes Hong Kong SAR and Taiwan — representing over half of total FDI received by Cambodia.

At the dawn of the emerging post-COVID-19 scenario fraught with uncertainty, instability, and dependency on external conditions, Cambodia must prioritise the expansion of mitigation measures and contingency plans to strengthen the resilience of the most-affected populations. The insufficient social protection schemes, combined with a lack of safety nets and savings, hinders the capacity of vulnerable households to mitigate income shocks. Preexisting disparities to access health services, education, jobs, and finance have deteriorated and propitiated a long-term setback of socioeconomic development indicators. At the same time, the implications of the growing debt-driven migrations, food insecurity, deterioration of health status, landlessness, and indebtedness are yet to be quantifiable in the long run.

In parallel to the COVID-19 crisis, Cambodia suffers from long-standing and structural issues that require a diversification of its commercial partners for both imports and exports, a move towards higher value-added industrial activities and increases in human capital investment. Hence, along with the exceptional circumstances, the government is pressed to consolidate progress under the National Social Protection Policy Framework 2016–2025 (NSPPF). The NSPPF framework guides the construction of a comprehensive and sustainable system with an adequate provision of social assistance (emergency response, human capital development, vocational training, and welfare for vulnerable populations) and social security (pensions, health insurance, unemployment benefits, employment injuries, and disability benefits).

Despite social protection and contingency strategies being a priority in Cambodia, the government lacks the capacity and financial resources to provide a comprehensive, large-scale response that can be sustained in time. So far, the external technical and financial assistance provided by international development stakeholders, including a number of U.N. agencies, has supported the response to the health emergency as well as its socioeconomic consequences, such as the implementation of distance learning. Moreover, the COVID-19 crisis has turned into a geopolitical playground whereby global leaders seek to expand their dominance. This is a favourable opportunity for China to further expand its increasing role in Southeast Asia. As part of this strategy, China donated 600,000 COVID-19 vaccine doses to Cambodia in February 2021. Irrespective of the external conditions, the primary focus of the Cambodian government at the moment is to maximise the allocation of its limited public resources. The administration needs to implement effective contingency plans that avoid a collapse of the economic activity while protecting the most vulnerable populations. The complexity of the issue requires finding the balance between addressing the most acute needs, sustaining the production capacity and productivity levels, and mitigating the mid and long-term socioeconomic consequences.

References

Asian Development Bank. (2020a). COVID-19 impact on international migration, remittances, and recipient households in developing Asia [online]. Retrieved on 12 November 2020 from https://www.adb.org/sites/default/files/publication/622796/covid-19-impact-migration-remittances-asia.pdf.

Asian Development Bank. (2020b). Debt Sustainability Analysis (DSA). Retrieved on 29 October 2020 from https://www.adb.org/sites/default/files/linked-documents/54195-001-sd-01.pdf.

Balvedi Pimentel, G., Cabrera Ormaza, M., and Cayul, P. (2020). The impact of COVID-19 on indigenous communities: Insights from the indigenous navigator. *The International Work Group for Indigenous Affairs (IWGIA) and the International Labour Organization (ILO)*. https://www.ilo.org/wcmsp5/groups/public/---dgreports/---gender/documents/publication/wcms_757475.pdf> [Accessed 24 November 2020.

CATU, CENTRAL, LICADHO. (2020). Worked to debt over-indebtedness in Cambodia's garment sector. Retrieved on 1 November 2020 from https://www.licadho-cambodia.org/reports/files/230Worked%20to%20Debt%20Joint%20Briefing%20Paper_ENG_30062020.pdf.

Data for Cambodia. (2020). Data for Cambodia. Retrieved on 21 November 2020 from https://www.dataforcambodia.org.

European Commission. (2020). Commission decides to partially withdraw Cambodia's preferential access to the EU market. Retrieved on 29 October 2020 from https://trade.ec.europa.eu/doclib/press/index.cfm?id=2113.

Future Forum. (2020). Effect of Covid-19 on wage workers. Covid-19 economic impact study. Retrieved on 29 November 2020 from https://www.futureforum.asia/publications/covid-19-economic-impact-study/.

Freedom House. (2021). Cambodia: Freedom in the world 2021 country report | freedom house. Freedom House. Retrieved on 27 March 2021 from https://freedomhouse.org/country/cambodia/freedom-world/2021.

International Labour Organization. (2019). Decent Work Country Programme (DWCP) 2019–2023. Retrieved on 9 November 2020 from https://www.ilo.org/wcmsp5/groups/public/---ed_mas/---program/documents/genericdocument/wcms_711728.pdf.

International Labour Organization. (2020). Research brief. p. 2. Retrieved on 29 November 2020 from https://www.ilo.org/wcmsp5/groups/public/---asia/---ro-bangkok/documents/briefingnote/wcms_758626.pdf.

International Labour Organization. (n.d.) Social protection. Retrieved on 29 November 2020 from https://www.social-protection.org/gimi/ShowCountry Profile.action?iso=KH.

International Monetary Fund. (2019). Cambodia: 2019 article IV consultation; Press release; Staff report; and statement by the executive director For Cambodia. Retrieved on 29 September 2020 from https://www.imf.org/en/Publications/CR/Issues/2019/12/23/Cambodia-2019-Article-IV-Consultation-Press-Release-Staff-Report-and-Statement-by-the-48912.

Johns Hopkins Coronavirus Resource Center. (2020). COVID-19 map — Johns Hopkins Coronavirus Resource Center. Retrieved on 28 March 2021 from https://coronavirus.jhu.edu/map.html.

Ministry of Education, Youth and Sport. (2021). Cambodia COVID-19 joint education needs assessment 2020. Retrieved on 27 March 2021 from https://www.unicef.org/cambodia/media/4296/file/Cambodia%20COVID-19%20Joint%20Education%20Needs%20Assessment.pdf.

Ministry of Tourism. (2019). Tourism statistics report. Phnom Penh: Royal Government of Cambodia. Retrieved on 25 October 2020 from https://seishiron.com/wp-content/uploads/2019/07/CAM122019.pdf.

National Institute of Statistics Ministry of Planning. (2018). Cambodia socio-economic survey 2017 . Phnom Penh. Retrieved on 29 September 2020 from https://www.nis.gov.kh/nis/CSES/Final%20Report%20CSES%202017.pdf.

Open Development Cambodia. (2020). Socio-economic impact of COVID-19 on Cambodia. Open Development Cambodia (ODC). Retrieved on 29 October 2020 from https://opendevelopmentcambodia.net/profiles/socio-economic-impact-of-covid-19-on-cambodia/.

Royal Government of Cambodia. (2020). Guidance of the royal government of Cambodia on the additional measures to support the private sector and workers seriously impacted by the COVID-19 pandemic and to recover and promote economic growth after the end of this pandemic.

Simon Kemp. (2020). Digital 2020: Cambodia. Retrieved on 12 November 2020 from https://datareportal.com/reports/digital-2020-cambodia.

The Phnom Penh Post. (2020). Job losses, pay cuts, force Cambodians into bad debts. Phnom Penh. Retrieved on 8 October 2020 from https://www.phnompenhpost.com/special-reports/job-losses-pay-cuts-force-cambodians-bad-debts.

The World Bank Group. (2020a). Cambodia economic update. Cambodia in the time of COVID-19. The World Bank Group. p. 5. Retrieved on 29 October 2020 from http://documents1.worldbank.org/curated/en/165091590723843418/pdf/Cambodia-Economic-Update-Cambodia-in-the-Time-of-COVID-19-Special-Focus-Teacher-Accountability-and-Student-Learning-Outcomes.pdf.

The World Bank Group. (2020b). From containment to recovery. East Asia and Pacific economic update. Retrieved on 2 November 2020 from https://open-knowledge.worldbank.org/bitstream/handle/10986/34497/9781464816413.pdf.

Thomson Reuters Foundation. (2020). Land to lose: Coronavirus compounds debt crisis in Cambodia. Retrieved on 29 November 2020 from https://longreads.trust.org/item/cambodia-coronavirus-compounds-debt-crisis.

United Nations. (2020). UN Cambodia framework for the immediate socio-economic response to COVID-19. Retrieved on 11 November 2020 from https://reliefweb.int/sites/reliefweb.int/files/resources/KHM_Socioeconomic_Response-Plan_2020.pdf.

United Nations Development Programme. (2020). COVID-19 economic and social impact assessment in Cambodia. United Nations Development Programme. p. 6. Retrieved on 13 December 2020 from https://www.kh.undp.org/content/cambodia/en/home/library/covid-19-economic-and-social-impact-assessment-in-cambodia.html.

World Bank Open Data. (2021a). GDP growth (annual %) — Cambodia | Data. Retrieved on 24 November 2020 from https://data.worldbank.org/indicator/NY.GDP.MKTP.KD.ZG?locations=KH.

World Bank Open Data. (2021b). Agriculture, forestry, and fishing, value added (constant 2010 US$) — Cambodia. Retrieved on 30 November 2020 from https://data.worldbank.org/indicator/NV.AGR.TOTL.KD?locations=KH.

World Bank Open Data. (2021c). Industry (including construction), value added (constant 2010 US$) — Cambodia. Retrieved on 30 November 2020 from https://data.worldbank.org/indicator/NV.IND.TOTL.KD?locations=KH.

World Bank Open Data. (2021d). Services, value added (constant 2010 US$) — Cambodia. Retrieved on 30 November 2020 from https://data.worldbank.org/indicator/NV.SRV.TOTL.KD?locations=KH.

World Bank Open Data. (2021e). Wage and salaried workers, total (% of total employment) modeled ILO estimate) — Cambodia. Retrieved on 30 November 2020 from https://data.worldbank.org/indicator/SL.EMP.WORK.ZS?locations=KH.

World Bank Open Data. (2021f). Employment in agriculture (% of total employment) (modeled ILO estimate) — Cambodia. Retrieved on 29 November 2020 from https://data.worldbank.org/indicator/SL.AGR.EMPL.ZS?locations=KH.

World Bank Open Data. (2021g). Vulnerable employment, female (% of female employment) (modeled ILO estimate) — Cambodia. Retrieved on 19 November 2020 from https://data.worldbank.org/indicator/SL.EMP.VULN.FE.ZS?locations=KH.

World Travel and Tourism Council. (2020). Recovery scenarios 2020 & economic impact from COVID-19.

Acknowledgement

The author would like to acknowledge the valuable contributions made by Thy Try, Executive Director/Editor-in-Chief of Open Development Cambodia (ODC). ODC is the leading open data platform in Cambodia, envisioning a sustainable, democratic, and participatory development of the Mekong region. ODC is an initiative from the East West Management Institute (EWMI) and was legally registered as a local non-governmental organisation in 2011. Its mission is to improve the data ecosystem by ensuring access to information, and promoting evidence-based decision-making and good governance.

About the Author

Júlia Garcia-Puig is an economist specialised in development, governance and social accountability, socioeconomic inequality, and open data. Júlia holds a Master's degree in International Development from the Barcelona Institute of International Studies (IBEI). Her experience combines academic research with development work, with a focus on leveraging open data and ICT to promote public access to information, good governance, and equality in Southeast Asian contexts. Based in Cambodia since 2018, she currently works as a Research and Strategy Officer at Open Development Cambodia (ODC) and as a Consultant for development institutions. She can be contacted at julia@opendatacambodia.net.

https://doi.org/10.1142/9789811228476_0003

Chapter 3

COVID-19 and the Economy: How Indonesia Responded

Aris Ananta,*[,§] Windhiarso Ponco Adi Putranto[†,¶] and Ahmad Irsan A. Moeis[‡,‖]

*Department of Economics
Faculty of Economics and Business
Universitas Indonesia, Indonesia
[†]Statistics-Indonesia (Badan Pusat Statistik), Indonesia
[‡]Directorate General of Budget,
Ministry of Finance of Indonesia, Indonesia
[§]arisananta@ui.ac.id
[¶]windhiarso@bps.go.id
[‖]irsan.moeis@kemenkeu.go.id

Abstract

As in all other countries in the world, the COVID-19 pandemic has shattered many aspects of life in Indonesia. The pandemic has caught everybody by surprise, unprepared to adapt to and mitigate the new crisis. This

*Corresponding author.

chapter attempts to show how Indonesia responded to the economic issues during the pandemic: how the government responded to relieve the economic suffering of the people, how individuals coped with the crisis, how business behaved to survive (including the use of e-commerce), and how resilient the macro-economy was. It is based on many scattered surveys, mostly conducted by *Badan Pusat Statistik* (BPS — Statistics Indonesia), on COVID-19. The data are mostly until end of December 2020. The discussion is preceded with the trend of the pandemic and change in population mobility. The chapter concludes that 6 months after the start of the pandemic, people's mobility resumed closer to levels before the pandemic, and the economy was already improving, even as the number of daily infected cases kept rising. Some people and some businesses enjoyed economic opportunities during the pandemic, particularly those who could use online activities and practise tight health protocols.

Keywords: Economy and health; population mobility; individual behaviour; business response; government policy.

1. Introduction

Starting as a health crisis, COVID-19 has become an economic crisis. A trade-off between economy and health is often debated. One side argues that health is number one, because economy will not operate without health. Rising number of sick people overcrowds the budget and human resources, in addition to losing human productivity. Another view argues that economy is number one. Without the economy constantly moving, there will be no money to finance the health sector, and there will be no money to feed people. People may also ask whether they should face the risk of being infected to earn money, or face the risk of being hungry with no infection. The trade-off appears because of the assumption that economy can be growing only because of the freedom of mobility of the population.

This chapter does not attempt to solve this debate. However, it contributes some insights to the debate with the Indonesian experience. It aims to describe and analyse what has happened in the Indonesian economy: how individuals coped with the economic crisis, how businesses managed the crisis, and what the government did to relieve the burden of the people and help to recover the economy. As the pandemic is not expected to have finished at the time of the writing, this chapter is an on-going analysis until the date at the end of writing, January 2021. Furthermore, most recent data collected were for December 2020.

The data are based on existing scattered datasets, mostly published by *Badan Pusat Statistik* (BPS — Statistics Indonesia) and other institutions such as Ministry of Finance, Task Force on Managing COVID-19, and National Population and Family Planning Board (*Badan Kependudukan dan Keluarga Berencana Nasional* — BKKBN). As the pandemic presents difficulties in conducting in-person interviews with probabilistic sampling, many of the datasets used in this chapter were collected with non-probabilistic samples. The non-probabilistic samples include those with big data, small and large online surveys. Each section of this chapter uses different sources of data and briefly describes the data used. The analysis is also enriched with some virtual personal observation through social media and direct virtual contact. Moreover, the coverage of each dataset varies. Caution should then also be exercised when interpreting the dynamics of the individuals and businesses over time. Nevertheless, the data may provide some insights on what was going on in Indonesia's economy during the pandemic.

The second section of the chapter shows the trend of infection in Indonesia until 3 January 2021. The third examines population mobility, which is closely related to the spread of the virus. The fourth section reveals what the government did to minimise the economic burden of the people, especially through its social safety net mechanism. The fifth section examines the economic conditions of the individuals and what they did to cope with the crisis. The sixth section focuses on the business sector — how the business had been surviving. This section includes a discussion on the digitalisation of the commerce during the pandemic. The seventh section analyses what happened to the macro-economy, particularly in terms of economic growth during the pandemic. The chapter is concluded in the eighth section.

2. Trend of COVID-19

As the pandemic resulted in both health and economic crises, the government established the "Committee on Managing COVID-19 Disease [*Komite Penanganan* Corona Virus Disease, 2019]", reporting directly to the President of the Republic of Indonesia. This committee is assisted by two Task Forces (*satgas-satuan tugas*). The first is "COVID-19 Response Acceleration Task Force [*Gugus Tugas Percepatan Penanganan* COVID-19]", and the second is "National Economic Recovery Task Force [*Gugus Tugas Pemulihan Ekonomi Nasional*]". The statistics used in this section are cited from *Analisis Data COVID-19 Indonesia. Update per 03 Januari 2021* [Analysis of COVID-19 Data in Indonesia. Update per 3 January 2021], prepared and published by the *Satuan Tugas Pengangan* COVID-19 [COVID-19 Response Acceleration Task Force]. This is the official data on the statistics on the virus, collected from daily registrations around Indonesia by the Task Force.

The first COVID-19 virus infection was officially announced on 2 March 2020. The economic shutdown was implemented during 15 March 2020 until 4 June 2020 to reduce the spread of the virus. The economic shutdown was known as "Large Scale Social Restriction" [*Pembatasan Sosial Berskala Besar*]. It was not a complete lockdown of the economy, as there was no strict penalty for not following the guidelines. The government asked the people to at least do the following three things: wear facial mask, wash hands, maintain physical distance/avoid crowds and stay at home. The shutdown period was then followed by the "adaptation to new habits" period, practically meaning relaxation of the shutdown, since 5 June 2020, though it continued with implementation of the health protocols.

The number of daily new infections has been fluctuating with a rapidly rising trend throughout 2020. The daily number of infections reached the "peak" at almost 5,000 in the third week of September 2020. This is partly because of a "long holiday" in the period 15–23 August 2020. The weekend was on 15 and 16 August; 17 August is Indonesia's independence day; 20 August (Thursday) is Islamic New Year. Then 21 August (Friday) is decided by the government as a collective leave (*cuti bersama*) day. Then, 22 and 23 August was another weekend. Therefore, people might have crowded the public areas during this "long holiday".

The number of daily new infections then declined to below 3,000 in the first week of November 2020, before it rose again to another "peak" at 8,369 on 3 December 2020. There was also a long holiday during 27–30 October 2020, with 27 and 28 October as the weekend. 29 October is the birthday of the Prophet of Muhammad SAW and then 28 and 30 October were decided as collective leave. The continuing rapid increase in November is probably because of the occurrence of some politically related large crowds in Jakarta and West Java, attended by people from many areas outside Jakarta, since 10 November 2020.

The next peak is 14,518 on 30 January 2021. Since then, the number has been fluctuating with a declining trend, reaching 6,825 on 17 March 2021. By the time of the writing, it is still not clear whether it is a real decline or an under-coverage of the testing.

As of 3 January 2021, the number of people infected is concentrated among young people, especially those aged 31–45 (31.24%), compared to people aged 60 and over (11.45%). Structurally, Indonesian population has a much larger number of young people than older people, therefore it is not surprising that those infected were concentrated among the young people. Furthermore, the young people are more mobile, and therefore they are more likely to be exposed to the COVID-19. The younger generation may not pay much attention to the danger of the virus. On the other hand, the older people may have been much more careful.

On the other hand, on 3 January 2021, the percentage of death (number of deaths over total number of cases) was particularly very high (11.88%) among people aged 60 years old and over, especially men. It is very likely that the deaths were attributed to the existence of co-morbidities. The number of deaths may be under-estimated as some causes of death may have been classified as the co-morbidities. The second largest percentage (4.33) was much lower than the first one, found among people aged 46–59. The third largest was only 1.33% among people aged 31–45. For the remaining ages, the rates were below 0.66%, except for babies (below 2 years old, 1.29%).

In other words, young people are more likely to be exposed to the COVID-19 than the older people. However, when infected, older people are much more likely to die than the young people.

Indonesia is a large archipelagic country. On 3 January 2021, the highest incidence rate (number of total cases per 100,000 population) was found in the province of Jakarta (1,745), much larger than the second one (785) in East Kalimantan, followed by North Kalimantan (616), West Papua (528), and West Sumatra (429). Other than Jakarta, none of the provinces in the Island of Java were included in the five largest incidence rates. The five lowest incidence rates were found outside Java Island: East

Nusa Tenggara (41), West Kalimantan (58), Lampung (72), Jambi (95), and West Nusa Tenggara (110.13).

The highest mortality rate (per 100,000 population) was found in the City of Semarang, the capital of the province of Central Java (51), followed by Central Jakarta (47), City of Surabaya (46), City of Mojokerto (42), and City of Balikpapan (39).

3. Population Mobility

The statistics in this section is based on a non-probabilistic sample of Big Data, as reported in *Analisis Big Data di Tengah Masa Adaptasi Kebiasaan Baru* [A Big Data Analysis during the Period of Adaptation of New Norms], prepared and published by *Badan Pusat Statistik* (July 2020). The data are navigated through smartphones, showing the daily movement of the users. Using Google mobility index, *Badan Pusat Statistik* measures people's mobility during the shutdown (15 March 2020 to 2 June 2020) and part of the adaptation periods (June–July 2020), compared to the baseline of average daily population mobility during 3 January–6 February 2020, before the pandemic was officially announced. A positive index means higher population mobility compared to the one during the baseline; the higher the index, the higher is the mobility from the baseline. A negative index means lower population mobility than the one during the baseline; the higher the absolute value, the less is the mobility compared to the baseline.

Table 1 shows some results from the survey, indicating people's mobility in visiting six places: retail sales and recreation, daily needs

Table 1:   Google mobility index.

	Retail Sales & Recreation	Daily Needs Shopping	Parks	Transit Stations	Workplaces	Home
Mar-20	−13.5	−3.5	−15.6	−19.8	−10.10	6.70
Apr-20	−38.8	−21.1	−36.8	−56.8	−33.00	17.00
May-20	−37.8	−12.5	−35.1	−55.7	−34.00	17.00
Jun-20	−24.7	−6.6	−22.7	−43.2	−21.00	12.50

Source: Compiled from *Badan Pusat Statistik* (July 2020).

shopping, parks, transit stations, workplaces, and home. The Google mobility index was negative for five activities outside home and positive for staying at home during the shutdown. It implies that mobility in the five activities had been down during the shutdown, but staying at home had been much higher compared to the baseline.

The largest decline in mobility is seen in transit stations such as bus stops and train stations. This may reflect people's avoidance of public transportation. April and May 2020 show the largest decline, but the decline becomes smaller in June 2020, the start of the adaptation period. The second largest decline is observed in visiting parks. Again, the highest decline is seen in April and May 2020. April and May 2020 are also the months with largest decline in population mobility to places for retail sales and recreation; as well as workplaces.

As shopping for daily needs is essential for people's lives, the smallest decline in the mobility index is seen on visit to places to shop for daily needs. The government also allowed people to visit these places. Yet, the largest decline is seen in April. After that, the decline keeps becoming smaller.

On the other hand, the mobility index during the pandemic was positive for staying home, meaning that people stayed at home more than during the baseline period. Consistent with the data on mobility outside home, the highest increase in mobility is seen in the months of April and May 2020.

As calculated by *Badan Pusat Statistik*, on average, there is a positive correlation between restriction in population mobility and decline in provincial income during April–June 2020. For example, activity in the province of Bali was about 50% lower than before the pandemic, and the regional domestic product declined by 11%. On the other hand, provinces without severe mobility restrictions enjoyed economic growth: Aceh, Sulawesi Tengah, and Lampung. However, the impact of mobility restrictions on economic growth was relatively small in Jakarta, Yogyakarta, Riau Islands, and Banten.

However, as reported by the *Badan Pusat Statistik*, (data for monthly index for July 2020 has not been available in Table 1), during the implementation of the relaxation of the shutdown (June–July 2020), the daily activities by the end of July had been almost "normal", almost reaching the level before the pandemic, especially for activities like daily shopping, retail and recreation, and visiting parks. Mobility for transit had been rising too, but still much lower than before the pandemic. The index for activity at home remained positive, though slightly lower than during the pandemic, and still much larger compared to the baseline.

4. Government Fiscal Policies

This section describes some fiscal policies made to lessen people's suffering from the pandemic and to recover the economy. The data in this section are cited and compiled from 2020 National Budget, Republic of Indonesia. Managing immense unanticipated economic shock because of the pandemic, the government of Indonesia made an extraordinary effort and response. This uncertain and challenging time has been made a momentum to strengthen the fundamentals of the economy through numerous collaborative fiscal, monetary, and financial policies. These policies are together known as the National Economic Recovery Program (NERP). The economic recovery programme is currently coordinated by the Coordinating Ministry of the Economy, where the task force is led by the Ministry of State Enterprises, and the budgeting is prepared by Ministry of Finance.

The NERP aims to synergise fiscal, monetary, and finance policies in managing health issues and stabilise the economy during the pandemic. Through the NERP, the government allocated budget as Rp 695.2 trillion, equivalent to 4.2% of GDP in 2020. The budget is allocated for six specific components in the year 2020: social safety net, small and medium enterprises (SMEs), Incentive for Business, Line and Ministerial government budget for local governments, health, and corporation. The largest one is social safety net, amounting to Rp 203.9 trillion or 29.33% of the total budget. It aims at households' members who are unemployed, poor, and belong to vulnerable groups. This is supposed to relieve the burden of those in need. It is also supposed to raise aggregate demand among low-income societies. The three largest allocations for social protections are basic needs (21.38% from the budget for social protection), *Program Keluarga Harapan* (PKH) — the Family Hope Programme (18.34%), and

Social Assistance for Outside Jabodetabek region[1] (15.89%). These three sub-components form more than half of the budget for social assistance.

The government has been much more effective in managing the current economic crisis than the 1998 crisis. Social safety net system had been much better prepared. The government has used and expanded the existing social safety net programmes. For example, the basic needs (*Sembako*) programme is a transformation of in-kind food assistance (*Bantuan Pangan Non Tunai* — BPNT). This has changed many times earlier, from market operation programme (*Program Operasi Pasar Khusus* — OPK), rice for poor society (Raskin), and rice for family welfare (Rastra). In the basic need programme, the money is sent directly to the account of the recipient. The money is given not only for rice and eggs, but also for carbohydrates, proteins, vitamins, and other essentials which can be bought from local markets.

PKH (*Program Keluarga Harapan* — Family Hope Programme) is also an existing programme. It is a conditional cash transfer programme, started in 2007, with the main aim to reduce poverty. During the pandemic, the government increased the budget, paying on a monthly basis instead of every 3 months. The number of recipients rose to 10 million families from 9.2 million before the pandemic.

The second largest allocation is Rp 123.46 trillion, or 17.76% of the total budget, to support SMEs. This includes funding for re-construction, interest subsidy, guaranteeing working loan, waiving tax for SMEs, and investments for cooperatives.

The third is Rp 120.61 trillion (17.35%) as tax incentive to support the business environment. This incentive includes deferment of import tax payment for 6 months in 19 manufacturing sectors; and acceleration of VAT refunds in 19 manufacturing sectors.

The fourth largest allocation is Rp 106.11 trillion (15.26%), allocated through ministerial lines and local governments. This allocation is supposed to create job opportunities through a labour intensive programme and provide financial support for local governments. Village Fund (*Dana Desa*) is one of the programmes. It is an existing programme used to

---

[1] Jabodetabek is a megapolitan region including Jakarta, the capital of Indonesia, and its surrounding areas.

mitigate the economic impact of COVID-19. The programme was introduced in 2014 and has been implemented since 2015.

The village fund follows the Government Regulation in Lieu of Law No. 1/2020 on State Financial Policy and Financial Stability. This law is to minimise the negative impact of the COVID-19 on employment in villages. Target beneficiaries are decided through a community-based programme (*musyawarah*) by promoting best practices and relevance to the needs of the village. The focus is on underprivileged and marginalised communities.

There are six priorities in the village fund programme: creating employment opportunities through self-management (where the village communities decide and implement their own activities) and cash for activities; strengthening a sense of togetherness, mutual work, and village community participation; improving village community empowerment both in terms of quality and quantity; increasing access for underprivileged women, children, and marginalised groups to basic education and health services; reducing number of unemployed, half under-employed, and the poor; and expanding social and economic activities in villages.

The fifth largest budget under NERP is Rp 87.55 trillion (12.59%) to manage health issues. This is to finance all activities in containing the spread of COVID-19, including incentives for paramedic, health insurance, and tax incentives for procurements of medical equipment for medical staff dealing directly with COVID-19 related persons.

Lastly is Rp 53.57 trillion (7.71%) for cooperative financing, including budget for labour-intensive programmes and loans for investments.

However, availability of the budget is just a beginning step to manage the economy. The next challenge is to disburse the money. Almost 2 months (end of July) after the government started to relax the shutdown, the disbursement of the government budget was still minimal. The largest disbursement was 39.39% budget for social protection system, followed by 24.47% budget for SMEs. The third was 13.43% to support the business environment. The fourth was 12.90% for budget disbursements through ministerial lines and local governments. The disbursement for health, the source of the crisis, was only 7.78%. There was no disbursement at all for the budget supposed to help corporate financing.

There are four possible explanations for the very low disbursement of the budget though the daily infection kept rising rapidly and the economy was suffering. First, the pandemic came to the people and countries all over the world, including Indonesia, as a shock for which they had been unprepared. Therefore, the regulation and bureaucracy had not been able to act quickly and efficiently. In other words, adaptive regulation and efficient bureaucracy to execute the NERP had not existed yet. Second, there was principal–agent problem in the NERP budget allocation. Ministry of Finance as Chief Financial Officer who allocates the budget cannot control the ministerial lines, local governments, and institutions who receive and execute the NERP budget. The execution of the NERP budget depends on the capability of the executors. Furthermore, the capability varies widely among the executors. Third, availability of data was a classic issue in Indonesia, creating social conflict and lack of accountability in implementing the NERP. Fourth, the policy to manage demand side did not meet the policy in managing supply side. The demand might increase, but it was still not easy to increase the production. There was lack of policy coordination.

Nevertheless, by the end of 2020, there had been an improvement in the implementation of the new normal, resulting in an increase in disbursement to 83.4%.

5. Individual Responses

5.1 *During shutdown*

The discussion in this sub-section is based on results from a survey conducted in the middle of the shutdown, 19 April–3 May 2020, on individual and family responses to the COVID-19. It is an online, non-probabilistic survey, conducted by *Badan Kependudukan dan Keluarga Berencana Nasional* (BKKBN — the National Population and Family Board) and *Institut Pertanian Bogor* (IPB — Bogor Agriculture Institute). The results are published as *Laporan Penelitian Survey Daring. Kondisi Keluarga Pada Masa Pandemi COVID-19* [Report on an Online Survey: Family Conditions during COVID-19 Pandemic].

Table 2:   Changing conditions: Early pandemic and before pandemic.

Condition	Improving	Same	Worsening	Total
Job	1.8	31.2	67.0	100.0
Finance	1.3	30.9	67.7	99.9
Food Sufficiency	1.0	47.7	51.3	100.0
Health	0.7	75.6	23.7	100.0
Interaction/Communication with Core Members	2.3	74.4	23.3	100.0
Interaction/Communication with Extended Family	1.6	57.4	41.0	100.0

Source: BKKBN and IPB (2020).

The survey was collected from 20,640 respondents, with about half of them located in the Island of Java. The age structure is mostly below 60. About 86% have high school or tertiary education. It is a young and educated sample. About a quarter of the respondents has monthly family income below Rp 1.5 million (USD 107). Another quarter had 1.5 to 3.0 million, 22.6% had 3.0–4.5 million, 15% had 4.5–6.0 million, and 13.3% had 6.0 million and above.

Table 2 shows that after more than 1 month of the pandemic, the majority (around 75%) perceived that their health condition and communication with core family remained the same compared to before the pandemic. Only a very tiny percentage said their conditions improved. About a quarter of them said the conditions worsened. However, the communication with extended family is different. Only 56.3% said that the condition did not change; and 42.4% said it is worsening.

On the other hand, the pandemic hit the jobs and financial condition of the families. A large majority (around 68.0%) said that their conditions worsened. The remaining said there was no change. Also, a very tiny percentage said the conditions were improving. A smaller percentage (slightly higher than half) said they had insufficient amount of food.

How did they react to the conditions impacting their jobs and finances? Table 3 indicates that the majority reduced their spending to cope with the worsening job and finance conditions of their families. The

Table 3: Consumption expenditure during shutdown: Early and before pandemic.

	Yes	No	Total
Saving/Reducing Consumption	79.9	20.1	100
Using Saving/Selling Jewellery to Finance Daily Life	50.6	49.4	100
Borrowing/Asking for Basic Needs from Family/ Neighbours/Communities/Government	19.8	80.2	100
Open New Business	19.3	80.7	100
Perceived Sufficient Financial Needs	55.7	44.3	100
Accepting Current Condition	97.7	2.3	100
Perceived Happy Family	80.8	19.1	99.9

Source: BKKBN and IPB (2020).

Table 4: Obedience to health protocols.

	Yes	No	Total
Wearing Mask outside the House	94.7	5.2	99.9
Physical Distancing	90.3	9.7	100
Going outside only for Urgent Needs	76.5	23.5	100
Washing Hands before Eating and Touching Face	96.1	3.9	100
Not Meeting outside the House with >5 Persons	92.3	7.7	100

Source: BKKBN and IPB (2020).

second largest percentage of the respondents financed their life by using their saving/selling jewellery. Only about one-fifth borrowed/asked for basic needs from family, neighbours, communities, or government. About one-fifth opened new businesses to support their financial needs. Moreover, only slightly higher than half of the respondents perceived that financial needs had been sufficiently met. Yet, almost all accepted their conditions, and a large percentage perceived that their family was happy.

Table 4 reveals that in the early part of the pandemic, people were likely to apply health protocols, with more than 90% following the protocols. The lowest percentage is in "going outside only for urgent needs". It should be noted that the information does not mention the quality of the practice such as whether they wore the mask correctly.

6. During Relaxation of Shutdown

6.1 *People's behaviour*

The discussion in this section is based on a non-probabilistic survey on individual behaviour during the relaxation of restriction period. The survey was conducted online by *Badan Pusat Statistik* (2020a). The results are published as *Perilaku Masyarakat di Masa Pandemi COVID-19. Hasil Survey Perilaku Masyarakat di Masa Pandemi COVID-19 (7–14 September 2020)* [Society Behaviour during COVID-19 Pandemic. Results of Survey of Society Behaviour during COVID-19 Pandemic, 7–14 September 2020].

It uses a convenient, voluntary, and snowballing sample. It collected 90,967 respondents, aged 17 years old and above. Female respondents formed 55.23 % of the sample. Most (41.77%) were aged 31–45. The second largest (27.37%) is 46–60; and the third (27.24%), 17–39. Older persons consist of only 3.62%. The highest educational attainment (61.36%) is at least undergraduate degree. This is also a young educated sample. Moreover, civil servants form 27.93% of the sample.

As reported in the survey, more than half (52.84%) of the respondents said that their consumption expenditure was higher compared to during the early part of the pandemic (April–June 2020); 14.91 constant, and 32.25 worsened. The pattern was the same for male and female respondents.

The civil servants seemed to perform better than non-civil servants. Among all respondents, 70.60% still worked, and 22.81% did not work. However, excluding civil servants, only 59.89% worked, higher percentage (31.65%) did not work, implying that the civil servants were more likely to remain working during the pandemic. See Table 5.

Table 5:   Working status in percentage: Relaxation of shutdown.

	Total	Without Civil Servants
Working	70.60	59.89
Not Working	22.81	31.65
Working from Home	4.59	5.68
Fired	2.00	2.78

Source: *Badan Pusat Statistik* (2020a).

Table 6: Obedience to health protocols.

	Percentage	
	Male	**Female**
Wearing Mask outside the House	88.5	94.8
Physical Distancing	68.7	77.5
Avoiding Crowd	71.1	81.2
Washing Hand with Soap for 20 Seconds	69.5	80.1
Using of Hand Sanitiser/Disinfectants	70.5	83.6
Not Shaking Hands	75.3	87.2

Source: *Badan Pusat Statistik* (2020a).

Table 7: Implementation of health protocols in public areas: Relaxation of shutdown.

	Physical Distancing	**Hands Washing**	**Mask Wearing**	**Temperature Checking**
Public Services	82.08	80.76	94.83	77.27
Places of Worship	73.07	75.23	85.64	41.85
Work Places	72.62	82.56	94.35	94.35
Mall/Plaza/Shopping Centre	66.97	77.68	93.44	84.75
Traditional Market	47.16	51.41	82.62	21.21

Source: *Badan Pusat Statistik* (2020a).

In terms of health protocols, Table 6 shows that female respondents seemed to have done better than the male respondents. The best performance is in terms of wearing masks; and the worst is in physical distancing. Among male respondents, only 68.7% followed physical distancing; others (except wearing masks) were below 80.0%. This pattern may indicate poor implementation of health protocols.

Table 7 shows that implementation of health protocols among the public was not good. The traditional market was the worst location, performing the worst in each of the health protocols. On the other hand, public service was the best, except in temperature checking. It should be noted that there is no information on the quality of the health protocols.

The report also shows perception of respondents on how likely they might be infected. It finds that the higher the education, the more they perceived that COVID-19 is infectious and dangerous. On the other hand, 17.0% of respondents said that it is impossible or almost impossible to get infected. The youngest group (aged 17–30) had the highest percentage (20.2%) of those perceiving that they would not get infected. They might perceive they were sufficiently immune. The second highest percentage is seen among the older people (>60 years), with 17.4%. Nevertheless, by the end of 2020, personal observation indicates that older people were more worried about the infection, probably because they already learned that they were more vulnerable when infected with the virus.

6.2 *Online activities*

The discussion in this section is based on Big Data, reported by *Badan Pusat Statistik* (December 2020b), titled *Kajian Big Data sebagai Pelengkap Data dan Informasi Statistik Ekonomi* [Big Data Analysis as a Supplement and Information to Economic Statistics]. As other Big Data sets, the sample is non-probabilistic. The report on Big Data (*Badan Pusat Statistik*, December 2020) is based on information from MarketPlace in Indonesia. It shows that there had been an increase in online transactions during the first quarter to second quarter and third quarter of 2020. Measured monthly, August 2020 reached the highest volume of transactions. It should be noted that the data recorded was only until September 2020. April 2020 recorded the smallest volume of transactions in MarketPlace after the virus was first announced on 2 March 2020 (See Table 8).

The consumption pattern also changed. During the first two quarters of 2020, the highest transaction was on health and beauty care, but it was household goods during the third quarter. The report also shows some interesting transaction items in the MarketPlace: sports, health, and food/drink.

In the area of sports, there had been a shift in the preference: from domination of sport accessories and sport clothes in the first month of 2020 to bicycles and their accessories. Food supplement was the most preferred health item. However, during June–September 2020, medical

Table 8: Volume of online transaction through MarketPlace: January–September 2020 (in million rupiah).

Month	Volume
Jan	29
Feb	130
March	122
April	101
May	141
June	179
July	185
August	280
Sept	199

Source: *Badan Pusat Statistik* (December 2020b).

devices such as facial masks, thermometers, oxygen tubes, and other first aid kits at home had been the most wanted items. This trend may accompany the rising trend of the infection.

As many markets and supermarkets did not open during the pandemic, people used online transactions to buy food. The online sales had been dominated by prepared food, instant food, frozen food, snack, and powder drink.

7. Business Behaviour

7.1 *All firms*

The discussion in this section is based on a publication by *Badan Pusat Statistik* (2020b) *Analisis Hasil Survei Dampak COVID-19 terhadap Pelaku Usaha* [Analysis on Results of Survey on Impact of COVID-19 on Business Behaviour]. The data were collected during 10–26 July 2020, during the relaxation of the shutdown, with 34,559 respondents (firms). It covers all employment, but excludes government, household activities, employers, and international organisations. Method of data collection is computer-assisted web and self-interviewing/online, a combination of probabilistic and non-probabilistic sampling. The probabilistic sampling was based on Statistical Business Register Frame in 2020, collecting information from 24,000 respondents. The purpose is to provide early signs on what businesses had been doing until the time of the survey. This probabilistic sampling is enriched with non-probabilistic, voluntary, sampling to better represent the respondents.

The report mentions that the large-scale mobility restriction reduced the percentage of respondents who were working, with only 58.95% of the respondents still working compared to before the pandemic. Almost a quarter (24.31%) reduced their capacity (working hours, number of workers, or number of machines); some (5.45%) used a hybrid between work-from-home and working as usual; a smaller percentage (2.05%) used work-from-home for all employees. Interestingly, a tiny percentage (0.49%) worked more than before the pandemic. On the other hand, the pandemic collapsed 8.76% of the respondents.

Table 9 indicates how the economic sectors have been hit by the pandemic, especially through the shutdown. Sectors which involved a lot of face-to-face interaction suffered the most. Education service was the

Table 9:   Percentage of firms still operating as usual: 10–26 July 2020.

Water and Waste Management	77.86
Agriculture and Farm	76.63
Real Estate	76.54
Electricity and Gas	73.65
Trade and Vehicle Repair	69.06
Mining and Quarrying	66.81
Financial Services	66.33
Transportation and Storage	58.29
Accommodation, Food, and Drink	51.91
Other Services	50.5
Manufacturing	49.42
Construction	47.81
Education Service	27.29

Source: *Badan Pusat Statistik* (2020b).

worst, having the smallest percentage of firms who were still operating during the interview. Three other services also suffered. Only at most half of them still operated as usual. They were construction, manufacturing, and other services. The best performance, with high percentages still operating as usual, was seen in sectors dealing with essential goods/services and involving less person-to-person interaction such as water and waste management, agriculture and farm, real estate, and electricity and gas.

In terms of income, the three worst sectors experiencing declining income were: accommodation, food, and drink, with 92.47% of the firms experiencing declining income. The second highest percentage was seen among "other services" (90.90%) and transportation and warehousing (90.34%). The best was real estate, where only 59.15% of them experienced declining income. The second best is electricity and gas, with 67.85%, followed by water and waste management (68.00%).

One way to cope with the crisis is to diversify the business, by doing the usual business but adding new products, new designs, new ways of doing business, and/or new locations. As an illustration from personal observation, a respondent in hotel business shifted to concentrate more on catering as people did not visit the hotel and, on the other hand, people still consumed food and drink during the pandemic. He sold snack online and this had been a promising business as people staying home demanded for snacks.

Another illustration is a publisher of primary and high school books. During the pandemic he shifted to sell health equipment needed during the pandemic, such as facial masks, hand sanitisers, disinfectants, gloves, and equipment to wash hands. The publisher also produced more religious, especially Islamic, books.

Among the respondents surveyed by the *Badan Pusat Statistik*, about 15% diversified their businesses. There were three sectors with the highest percentage of firms diversifying into other businesses: manufacturing (21.97%); accommodation, food, and drink (19.88%); and retail and vehicle repair (16.71%). They might also shift to different sectors. Nevertheless, only about 5% of the respondents changed to new sectors completely. This may be because working in new sectors is more challenging than diversification of the business.

One respondent from personal observation said they could not shift to new sectors, as they had been doing the existing business so long that it was the only field they knew anything about. The respondent used online marketing, but that did not help much. They did not move to new sectors partly because their existing business was still going on, though suffering.

Another illustration is of a person who worked in tourism. She managed to shift the business, from tourism to selling chicken noodles (*mie ayam*). She shifted to a new business (of opening a small "resto" for chicken noodles) probably because there was no hope to survive in the tourism sector. These noodles were cheap and a favourite of many people.

It seems that most businesses realised the importance of being healthy in order to keep them surviving during the pandemic. A respondent in personal observation mentioned the importance of keeping the employees healthy. First, it is for the benefit of the employees and employers. Second, if one or two employees become infected, the business will be closed for about two weeks, implying large losses.

In the survey conducted by *Badan Pusat Statistik*, most of the firms followed the health protocols, by conducting physical distancing, providing equipment to wash hands (water, soap, and hand sanitiser), and requiring the employees to wear masks. The three largest sectors with highest percentages of implementing health protocols were health services (95.92%), education services (95.02%), and financial services (94.61%). Furthermore, larger firms were more likely to follow the health protocols than the small firms (see Table 10).

Table 10: Percentage of firms practising health protocols: 10–26 July 2020.

	Large Firms	**Small Firms**	**Total**
Physical Distancing	95.92	79.47	81.91
Hand Washing	97.35	80.23	81.87
Mask Wearing	97.23	83.96	85.88

Source: *Badan Pusat Statistik* (2020b).

The survey by *Badan Pusat Statistik* also reveals that only 5.76% started using the internet during the pandemic. Almost half (46.5%) did not use the internet. Another half (47.75%) had been using the internet since before the pandemic. They experienced rising income, about 1.14 times their income before the pandemic.

A high percentage (about 80%) used the internet for marketing. A high percentage (62.64%) of those who used internet did not change their business. Some (27.45%) diversified their businesses, and 9.9% had new business/sectors.

On the other hand, the government also helped and facilitated the use of digital technology for SMEs, reducing the possibilities of digital divide. This digital technology is to help the economy grow, particularly the SMEs, while avoiding the spread of the virus by reducing in-person contact. Furthermore, digital technology also helps to widen the geographic market of SMEs.

The government has created its own digital platform for buying products and services needed by the government. It creates its own MarketPlace, a platform for right vendors and right customers. It is different from an online store, where there is only one vendor. MarketPlace consists of many vendors, similar to a shopping mall. The owner simply provides the platform, similar to providing spaces in a mall. The vendors provide all goods and services to sell.

One example of MarketPlace created by the government is PaDI *(Pasar Digital* — Digital Market) platform to buy goods and services supplied by SMEs and bought by state enterprises (https://info.padiumkm.id/about), established on 17 August 2020. This platform is expected to help SMEs and create transparency among state enterprises. All transactions are virtual. It should be noted, however, that a large firm may create several smaller firms to be eligible to be classified as an SME. Therefore, this large firm can utilise the MarketPlace owned by the government. During the pandemic, government expenditure plays an important role in keeping the economy going.

Another MarketPlace created by the government is SIPlah *(Sistem Informasi Pengadaan Sekolah)*, focusing on goods and services needed for online teaching (https://siplah.kemdikbud.go.id/). Unlike PaDI, SIPlah collaborates with private MarketPlace. The third MarketPlace created by the government is *Bela Pengadaan*, a platform for vendors to sell goods and services needed by state ministries and institutions, with a maximum value of Rp 50 million (about USD 360). This platform can be seen here, https://kepo-pbj.lkpp.go.id/backend/web/uploads/documents/Program_Bela_Pengadaan_1595.pdf.

Societies also started using digital technologies. This technology often breaks societies' tradition. For example, people have been used to enjoying person-to-person communication in traditional markets. With the digital technology, people miss the joy of person-to-person interaction, including the activity of bargaining. However, during the pandemic, society and traders have been forced to have new traditions/norms. They shifted to online markets. Farransahat *et al.* (2020), for example, showed how a traditional market "Pasar Sambilegi" in the city of Yogyakarta could survive without jeopardising health by using a digital platform, www.pasarsambilegi.id.

This programme was conducted by three parties. First is the association of traders in Pasar Sambilegi market. Second is the local government. Third is support and training from academics in Universitas Gadjah Mada, mostly from Faculty of Social and Political Science and Faculty of Economics and Business. This programme has then been replicated in Kolombo market, at Condong Catur *kelurahan*/village, Yogyakarta. This platform, pasarkolombo.id, is funded by the Village Fund from the government. See further discussion in Section 4.

7.2 *E-commerce*

This sub-section focuses on e-commerce, mostly based on *Statistik E-Commerce 2020* (*Badan Pusat Statistik*, December 2020a). The survey was conducted from 1 January until 31 August 2020, with 17,063 units of e-commerce covering all provinces in Indonesia by *Badan Pusat Statistik*. The sample is businesses which used internet to receive orders or sell goods and services during 2019. It uses the listing in *Statistik E-Commerce 2019* as the pandemic had not permitted *Badan Pusat Statistik* to have a complete listing in 2020. The analysis in the report is based on 16,277 e-commerce business in 2019. The weaknesses of these data collections are that some entities were already out, and some new entities were not

Table 11: Changes in businesses conditions: In percentage of number of firms, 1 January–31 August 2020.

	Income	# of Workers	Distribution of Goods
Lower	85.83	85.01	76.91
Same	9.59	10.36	19.58
Higher	4.58	4.62	3.51
Total	100.00	99.99	100.00

Source: *Badan Pusat Statistik* (December 2020a).

recorded. *Badan Pusat Statistik* defines electronic commerce (e-commerce) as any sales and purchases of goods and services through computer network with a specific aim to receive orders. However, payment can be made online or in person.

The survey finds that most e-commerce surveyed were non-formal, with the following features: majority used instant message and social media as means of selling; total income or only from e-commerce was below Rp 300 million; most (73.05%) of the payment was by cash-on-delivery method; more than half (52.81%) used direct delivery of goods and services. Almost half (48.42%) of the e-commerce during 2020 (until end of August) was in "wholesale and retail trade" as well as "car and motor-cycle repair and maintenance". "Food, drink, and grocery", fashion, and cosmetics were the three largest consumption items among the e-commerce businesses.

The survey shows that income, volume of activities (measured by number of workers), and distribution, declined during the pandemic, lower in August 2020 than in the survey in 2019. As shown in Table 11, most of the businesses (85.83%) listed in 2019 suffered a decline in income in 2020; most of the business (85.01%) suffered a decline in number of workers employed; and 76.91% suffered in distribution of the goods.

There are some possible explanations. First is that the income of people was stable or declining during the pandemic. Purchasing power remained constant or declined. Second, there were more e-commerce entities. Hence, price and sales declined. *Badan Pusat Statistik* (July 2020), using Big Data from MarketPlace Website for Indonesia, indicates that number of e-commerce entities initially went down during the shutdown, but it then rose from April.

During the pandemic (April–June 2020), compared to January–March 2020, there was a sharp increase in consumption of health and beauty care products, followed by household goods, female clothes, food and drink, health, and vouchers. There was a sharp decline in spending for souvenirs and parties, followed by photography, books, and stationeries, and Muslim fashion.

The *Badan Pusat Statistik* report also shows that reduction in income is seen in almost all e-commerce businesses with more than 100 workers. Higher number of workers was associated with more likelihood of suffering from declining income. A similar pattern is seen on volume (number of workers): the higher the number of workers hired, the more likely were the firms to suffer a decline in number of workers. However, the pattern is slightly different in distribution of goods. The firms most likely to suffer in distribution of goods were those with 29–99 workers, not those with more than 100 workers. However, excluding the 100 workers and more, the correlation remains positive, the higher the number of workers hired, the more likely were the firms to suffer in distribution of goods.

Table 12 shows that there were five industries most likely to suffer during the pandemic, either in income, number of workers, or distribution of goods. The five industries were "transportation and storage", corporate services, "accommodation, food, and drink", other services, and construction. Almost all (96.02%) e-commerce businesses working in transportation and warehousing suffered from declining income, followed by 94.21% in corporate

Table 12: Five largest industries suffering during the pandemic.

Declining Income	Declining # of Workers	Worsening Distribution of Goods
Transportation and Warehousing (96.02)	Transportation and Warehousing (96.02)	Transportation and Warehousing (90.76)
Corporate Service (94.21)	Corporate Service (94.602)	Corporate Service (86.68)
Accommodation, Food, and Drink (91.81)	Accommodation, Food, and Drink (91.17)	Construction (83.33)
Other Services (89.86)	Other Services (89.25)	Accommodation, Food, and Drink (80.62)
Construction (86.11)	Construction (88.89)	Other Services (79.92)

Source: *Badan Pusat Statistik* (2020a).

services and 91.81% in "accommodation, food, and drink". A similar pattern is seen with volume (number of workers). However, the probability of suffering from declining distribution of goods was not as large as in income and volume. The highest percentage suffering from worsening distribution of goods was only 90.76%, also among transportation and warehousing. This is followed by corporate services (86.68%). The third is however not "accommodation, food, and drink", but construction (83.33%).

Among those who used internet to start new businesses, the largest new sectors were: education service (19.40%), manufacturing (7.9%), "retail and repair of motor vehicle and motorcycle" (7.3%), and "accommodation, food, and drink" (7.1%).

8. Macro-Economy

8.1 *GDP growth*

Before the COVID-19 pandemic, Indonesia's economy had not been favourable. As seen in Table 13, during 2017–2019, before the pandemic, the GDP growth rates measured quarter over quarter (q-to-q) had been fluctuating. The rates can be negative or positive. At the end of 2019, just shortly before the start of the global and Indonesian pandemic, the q-to-q growth was already negative. This decline perhaps reflects the decline in global demand, including tourism as the pandemic had affected other countries, especially China. On the other hand, the year-on-year (y-on-y) growth rates had always been positive, above 5.0%, except in the fourth quarter of 2019, just before the pandemic, barely reaching 5.0%. Yet, per capita GDP had kept rising during 2017–2019, before declining during the pandemic (2020). However, calculation of per capita GDP with 2010 constant prices reveals a decline in per capita GDP in 2018 because of weakening Indonesian currency.

The q-to-q growth became worse in the first quarter of 2020, when more countries in the world had been hit by the pandemic. The decline rose from 1.74% in the last quarter of 2019 to 2.41% in the first quarter of 2020. In the second quarter, when the pandemic became worse in Indonesia, the decline was more severe, 4.19%. These three consecutive q-to-q growth rates resulted in a y-on-y decline in the second and third

Table 13:   GDP growth rates: 2017–2020.

Year		GDP Growth (%)		Per Capita GDP (Current USD)
		y-on-y	q-to-q	
2017	Quarter I	5.01	–0.30	3,877
	Quarter II	5.01	4.01	
	Quarter III	5.06	3.19	
	Quarter IV	5.19	–1.70	
2018	Quarter I	5.07	–0.41	3,927
	Quarter II	5.27	4.21	
	Quarter III	5.17	3.09	
	Quarter IV	5.18	–1.69	
2019	Quarter I	5.06	–0.52	4,174
	Quarter II	5.05	4.20	
	Quarter III	5.01	3.05	
	Quarter IV	4.96	–1.74	
2020	Quarter I	2.97	–2.41	3,912
	Quarter II	–5.32	–4.19	
	Quarter III	–3.49	5.05	
	Quarter IV	–2.19	–0.42	

Source: *Badan Pusat Statistik* (2021b).
Data on per capita GDP (2018–2020) are cited from *Badan Pusat Statistik* (2021a).
Data on per capita GDP (2017) are cited from *Badan Pusat Statistik* (February 2020).

quarters of 2021, making Indonesian economy fall into recession. The brighter side was that the decline in the third quarter was only 3.49%, lower than 5.32% in the second quarter. Furthermore, from a lower base, the q-to-q in the third quarter of 2020 was already positive at 5.05%.

8.2 *GDP composition*

8.2.1 *By expenditure*

Table 14 indicates that, in the first quarter of 2020, q-to-q expenditure declined in all components of GDP, with the largest decline seen in

Table 14: GDP growth rates by expenditure: 2020.

	First Quarter		Second Quarter		Third Quarter		Fourth Quarter	
	q-to-q	y-on-y	q-to-q	y-on-y	q-to-q	y-on-y	q-to-q	y-on-y
Economic Growth	−2.41	2.97	−4.19	−5.32	5.05	−3.49	−0.42	−3.40
Household Consumption	−1.99	2.83	−6.51	−5.51	4.69	−4.05	0.49	−3.61
Non-Profit Household Consumption	−2.29	−5.09	−0.78	−7.76	0.79	−1.97	0.22	−2.14
Government	−44.01	3.75	22.32	−6.90	16.94	9.76	27.15	1.76
Investment	−7.89	1.70	−9.71	−8.61	8.45	−6.48	4.19	−6.15
Export	−6.38	0.23	−12.81	−11.66	11.67	−11.66	2.41	−7.21
Import	−11.89	−2.19	−14.16	−16.96	−0.01	−23.00	16.28	−13.52

Source: First and second quarters are cited from *Badan Pusat Statistik* (August 2020).
Third and fourth quarters are cited from *Badan Pusat Statistik* (2021a).

government spending (44.01%). It can be noted that the state budget was prepared in 2019. The pandemic has shattered the details of the budget. Many activities were cancelled, resulting in the large decline in government spending in the first quarter. This is in contrast to the decline in other components, below 10% except import (11.89%).

However, with rapidly rising number of daily infections in the second quarter of 2020, the government expenditure rebounded with q-to-q growth at 22.33% in the second quarter and 16.94% at the third quarter. This large increase may indicate the rising government's social assistance, health expenditure, and economic expenditure to manage the crisis.

On the other hand, the rebound of the government expenditure in the second quarter was not accompanied by rebound in other expenditure components. Indeed, the decline in q-to-q for household expenditure was worse in the second quarter of 2020, when the pandemic started to rise rapidly. Yet, the household expenditure rebounded in the third quarter. Investment also declined in the first two quarters of 2020, rebounding only in the third quarter. A similar pattern was seen in exports. On the other hand, the growth in import expenditure kept declining though with a very

Table 15: GDP growth rates by industry: 2020.

	First Quarter		Second Quarter		Third Quarter		Fourth Quarter	
	q-to-q	y-on-y	q-to-q	y-on-y	q-to-q	y-on-y	q-to-q	y-on-y
Economic Growth	−2.41	2.97	−4.19	−5.32	5.05	−3.49	−0.42	−3.40
Agriculture	9.46	0.02	16.24	2.19	1.01	2.16	−20.15	2.59
Mining	−0.73	0.45	−3.75	−2.72	1.72	−4.28	1.65	−1.20
Manufacturing	−1.17	2.06	−6.49	−6.19	5.22	−4.31	−0.38	−3.14
Electricity	−5.66	3.85	−7.89	−5.46	8.30	−2.44	0.94	−5.01
Water	−0.89	4.56	1.28	4.56	1.51	5.94	3.11	4.98
Construction	−6.92	2.90	−7.37	−5.39	5.72	−4.52	3.48	−5.67
Wholesale	−1.38	1.60	−6.71	−7.57	5.67	−5.05	−0.87	−3.64
Transportation	−6.37	1.29	−29.22	−30.84	24.28	−16.71	5.08	−3.64
Accommodation	−3.54	1.95	−22.31	−22.02	14.77	−11.81	5.86	−8.88
Information and Communication	2.97	9.80	3.44	10.84	3.13	10.72	0.99	10.91
Finance	5.34	10.62	−10.32	1.03	2.59	−0.95	5.61	2.37
Real Estate	0.49	3.79	−0.26	2.30	0.97	1.96	0.07	1.25
Business Services	−2.28	5.39	−14.11	−12.09	1.92	−7.61	2.66	−7.02
Gov Administration	−8.54	3.16	−2.65	−3.22	1.52	1.82	8.95	−1.55
Education	−10.39	5.89	−0.68	1.21	5.62	2.41	7.83	1.36
Health	1.09	10.39	−4.15	3.71	13.73	15.29	5.78	16.54
Other Services	−1.19	7.09	−15.12	−12.60	5.05	−5.55	2.24	−4.84

Source: First and second quarters are cited from *Badan Pusat Statistik* (August 2020).
Third and fourth quarters are cited from *Badan Pusat Statistik* (2021a).

small decline in the third quarter. The small decline was perhaps because the amount of import in the second quarter was already low.

8.2.2 *By industries*

Table 15 shows that in the first quarter of 2020, q-to-q economic growth declined in all industries, except agriculture, finance, information and communication, health, and real estate. The two largest declines were seen in construction (–6.92%) and transportation (–6.37%). Agriculture had the best, highest growth (9.46%). This is the time when the pandemic started hitting some countries seriously, but not Indonesia. Indonesia just observed it in early March, by the end of the first quarter.

The q-to-q growth decline by industries became worse in the second quarter of 2020. The three worst hit industries were transportation (minus 29.22%), indicating the impact of shutdown, followed by accommodation (minus 22.31%), and business services (minus 14.11%). The best performance was still in agriculture, with a positive q-to-q at 16.24%. Interestingly, health sector also declined. Finance declined with 10.30%.

The rebounding of the q-to-q growth in the third quarter was seen in all industries. The highest growth rates were in transportation (24.28%) and accommodation (14.70%). This may be the result from relaxation of the restriction in June 2020. However, value-added in health industry also increased, a big jump to 13.73%.

8.3 *Employment*

As reported in *Keadaan Ketenagakerjaan Indonesia 2020* [Condition of Employment in Indonesia in 2020], published by *Badan Pusat Statistik* (November 2020), labour force participation rate almost remained stable, from 67.53% in August 2019 to 67.77% in August 2020. On the other hand, unemployment rate rose from 5.23% in August 2019 to 7.07% in August 2020. Furthermore, among the employed people, there was decline in the percentage of fully employed people, from 71.04% to 63.85%. In other words, people were as likely to join the labour force in August 2020 (during the pandemic) as in August 2019 (before the pandemic). However, employment opportunities may have declined and they might not find the desired jobs, resulting in higher unemployment rate and smaller percentage of those working full time.

It should be noted that there is no unemployment benefit in Indonesia, implying that those who were not employed and those who were not fully employed may have support from own savings, spouse/family members, communities, or government social assistance. The government social assistance may have been very useful for the lowest income group.

9. Concluding Remarks

COVID-19 pandemic affects economic growth through three channels. First is the direct effect through health sectors. People become sick and die. Lots of money is needed to treat the sick people. Money used to treat the sick people can actually be used for more productive programmes/ activities. Second is the opportunity cost of those who become sick. Because when people are sick or die, productivity declines. Third is through mobility restriction to minimise the spread of the virus. The mobility restriction hinders people from working as usual, resulting in declining labour supply; and consumers are unable/afraid to go out, resulting in declining aggregate demand for goods and services, and in turn, declining demand for labour.

This chapter finds that rising number of infections went together with rising short-run population mobility and economic growth in the first semester of 2020. By the end of August 2020, population mobility had come closer to "normal" (before the pandemic), particularly during "long holidays". This high population mobility is consistent with the data on continuously rising number of daily infection cases.

The economy had shown promising signs. In the third quarter of 2020, the q-to-q economic growth was already positive, and the decline in y-on-y economic growth was already lower than that in the second quarter. This promising economic growth was observed along with rising population mobility and number of daily infections of COVID-19. The following are some possible explanations.

First, some sectors of the economy, especially those with online activities as the core, may have flourished during the pandemic. Online technology helped raising household consumption and improving small and medium scale enterprises. In other words, the pandemic may have provided excellent economic opportunities for them. Second, civil servants, with fixed income, may have fared better than those in private sectors with uncertainty of the future. Third, government expenditure (including social assistance) may have helped raise aggregate demand, too. Fourth, application of health protocol among large firms, producing high value-added, may have maintained the economic activities, too.

Yet, the pandemic has not changed the structure of national income very much, either by expenditure or industry. Until the third quarter of

2020, the Indonesian economy has been dominated (more than 60.0%) by the following industries: manufacturing; agriculture, forestry, and fishing; construction; and mining and quarrying. In terms of expenditure, the economy was dominated by household expenditure (almost 60.0%), followed by investments, exports, and government expenditure.

In short, some people suffered economically, but others enjoyed economic prosperity. Some were happy, some were sick. Economic activities may resume as before the pandemic, but the infection may be untreatable. There are then two possible solutions to continue being healthy and prosperous economically. One is that people should be prepared with new emerging norms related to digital technology, including the use of robot and artificial intelligence, to reduce person-to-person interaction. Second is that population mobility can be promoted as long as the people continue practising health protocols well and follow healthy life styles; and government/societies can provide cheap, effective, and rapid testing of COVID-19 and deliver cheap, effective, and safe vaccines.

References

Badan Pusat Statistik (BPS). (February 2020). *Pertumbuhan Ekonomi Indonesia Triulan IV-2019*. [Indonesia Economic Growth. Fourth Quarter of 2019]. Jakarta: Badan Pusat Statistik.

Badan Pusat Statistik (BPS). (July 2020). *Analisis Big Data di Tengah Masa Adaptasi Kebiasaan Baru.* [Analysis of Big Data during Adaptation to New Norm Period]. Jakarta: Badan Pusat Statistik.

Badan Pusat Statistik (BPS). (August 2020). *Pertumbuhan Ekonomi Indonesia Triwulan II-2020*. [Indonesia Economic Growth. Second Quarter of 2020]. Jakarta: Badan Pusat Statistik.

Badan Pusat Statistik (BPS). (November 2020). *Keadaan Ketenagakerjaan Indonesia 2020*. [Employment Condition in Indonesia 2020]. Jakarta: Badan Pusat Statistik.

Badan Pusat Statistik (BPS). (December 2020a). *Statistik E-Commerce 2020.* [2020 E-commerce Statistics]. Jakarta: Badan Pusat Statistik.

Badan Pusat Statistik (BPS). (December 2020b). *Kajian Big Data sebagai Pelengkap Data dan Informasi Statistik Ekonomi.* [Analysis on Big Data as Supplement to Data and Information on Economic Statistics]. Jakarta: Badan Pusat Statistik.

Badan Pusat Statistik (BPS). (2020a). *Perilaku Masyarakat di Masa Pandemi COVID-19. Hasil Survey Perilaku Masyarakat di Masa Pandemi COVID-19,*

7–14 September 2020. [Society Behaviour during COVID-19 Pandemic. Results of Survey on Society Behaviour during COVID-19 Pandemic]. Jakarta: Badan Pusat Statistik.

Badan Pusat Statistik (BPS). (2020b). Analisis *Hasil Survei Dampak COVID-19 terhadap Pelaku Usaha.* [Analysis on Results from Survey on Impact of COVID-19 on Business Behavior]. Jakarta: Badan Pusat Statistik.

Badan Pusat Statistik (BPS). (2021a). *Pertumbuhan Ekonomi Indonesia Triwulan IV-2020.* [Indonesia Economic Growth. Fourth Quarter of 2020]. Jakarta: Badan Pusat Statistik.

Badan Pusat Statistik (BPS). (2021b). *Pertumbuhan Ekonomi. Produk Domestik Bruto.* [Economic Growth. Gross Domestic Product]. Jakarta: Badan Pusat Statistik.

Badan Kependudukan dan Keluarga Berencana National (BKKBN) and Institute Pertanian Bogor (IPB). (2020). *Laporan Penelitian Survey Daring. Kondisi Keluarga Pada Masa Pandemi COVID-19.* [Research Report on Online Survey. Family Situation during COVID-19 Pandemic].

Farransahat, Matahari, Acniah Damayanti, Hempri Suyatna, Puthut Indroyono, Rindu Sanubari Mashita Firdaus. (2020). *Pengembangan Inovasi Sosial Digital: Studi Kasus Pasarsambilegi.id.* [Development of Digital Social Innovation: Case Study in Pasarsambilegi.id]. *Journal of Social Development Studies*, 1(2): 14–26.

Satuan Tugas Penanganan COVID-19, Republic of Indonesia. (2021). *Analisis Data COVID-19 Indonesia. Update per 03 Januari 2021.* [Data Analysis on Indonesia COVID-19. Update per 3 January 2021]. Jakarta: Satuan Tugas Penanganan COVID-19, Republic of Indonesia.

About the Authors

Aris Ananta is an economist-demographer with a multi-disciplinary perspective. He is professor at the Faculty of Economics and Business, Universitas Indonesia. Previously, he spent 2 years (1999–2000) as senior fellow at the Department of Economics, National University of Singapore. He then focused on conducting socio–political–economic issues in Southeast Asia as senior research fellow at Institute of Southeast Asian Studies, Singapore, during 2001–2014. Currently, he is also visiting professor at Centre for Advanced Research, Universiti Brunei Darussalam; and adjunct researcher at the Demographic Institute, Faculty of Economics and Business, Universitas Indonesia. He is also the President of Asian Population Association, 2019–2021. He received his undergraduate degree in economics from Universitas Indonesia. He obtained his master's in Socio-Economic Statistics from George Washington University in 1979. He earned his Ph.D. in Economics from Duke University in 1983. He was appointed as professor in Population Economics in 1995 at Universitas Indonesia. His current research interest includes economic approach to ageing population, population mobility, people disabilities, welfare, and COVID-19; as well as statistics on ethnicity. His current regional interests include Indonesia, Brunei, Southeast Asia, and Asia.

Windhiarso Ponco Adi Putranto is an economist-statistician, working in Statistics Indonesia (*Badan Pusat Statistik* — BPS) since 1995. He is a deputy director of Statistical Indicator at Directorate of Analysis and Statistical Development. He works in developing SDGs Indicators and Social–Economics Statistical Indicators. With 26 years of experience working at BPS, he has been working in various areas as a statistician. Among them are National Accounts, Industrial Statistics, Statistical Modelling. Most recently he has become a member in the BPS COVID-19 Statistical Taskforce working group. His task is developing of statistical business process during the pandemic, such as conducting several rapid surveys in 2020. He obtained his doctoral degree in Economics from Faculty of Economic and Business, Universitas Indonesia in 2018. He earned his master's degree in Computer Science from Chiba University Japan in 2004 and finished his undergraduate degree in Statistics from Academy of Statistics in Jakarta, Indonesia. His research interest includes political economy, regional development economy, and public policy.

Ahmad Irsan A. Moeis is an economist-accountant. He is a senior budget analyst at Directorate General of Budget, Ministry of Finance of Indonesia. He is also chief of the Expert Council for Indonesia Budget Analyst Association. Currently, he is responsible for ensuring sustainability of the financing social security programme in Indonesia. He received his doctoral degree in Economics from the Faculty of Economics and Business, Universitas Indonesia, in 2018. His dissertation is titled "An Inquiry into a Just and Financially Sustainable Pension System: An

Illustration with Indonesia's Data". His master's degree is in Planning and Public Policy from Universitas Indonesia, received in 2012. He finished his undergraduate study in Budgeting from PKN-STAN (State Accountancy School). His research interests are related to issues on social welfare, social protection, and pension system.

https://doi.org/10.1142/9789811228476_0004

Chapter 4

The Impact of the COVID-19 Pandemic on Malaysia's Economy

Dzul Hadzwan Husaini*[,‡] and Hooi Hooi Lean[†,§]

Faculty of Economics and Business
Universiti Malaysia Sarawak, Malaysia
[†]*Economics Program*
School of Social Sciences
Universiti Sains Malaysia, Malaysia
[‡]*dzulhadzwan85@gmail.com; hdhadzwan@unimas.my*
[§]*hooilean@usm.my; learnmy@gmail.com*

Abstract

The COVID-19 global infection has been recognised as an alarming pandemic threat in Malaysia since the second week of March 2020. The government was forced to hastily implement the Movement Control Order (MCO) to prevent the growing spread and terrifying health threat of COVID-19. The necessary lockdown measures drastically slowed down the economic growth of the country and caused an adverse impact on many industries, businesses, and households. Multiple stimulus packages have since been announced by the government towards securing

---

[‡]Corresponding author.

and recovering the economy from the resultant effects of the pandemic. The stimulus packages were intended to provide coverage for both the welfare of consumers (demand side) as well as the producers (supply side). The objectives of this chapter are as follows:

(1) To describe and discuss the impacts of the devastating COVID-19 pandemic based on selected macroeconomic indicators.
(2) To review the existing economic policy on combating and mitigating the effects of the pandemic.
(3) To propose some significant improvements and necessary modifications on the general economic policy.

We conclude that the severe adverse impact of the pandemic on the macroeconomy is very significant and extremely "game-changing". However, it shows some improvement with the implementation of the various stimulus packages throughout the year of 2020. We suggest that the government focuses on fine-tuning and strategising the economic policy that aims to encourage a sustainable growth in domestic spending, and consumer and producer confidence in its efforts of stimulating the economy.

Keywords: COVID-19 pandemic; macroeconomy; stimulus packages; Malaysia.

1. Introduction

The inevitable spread of the COVID-19 virus to Malaysia started on 25 January 2020. Since then Malaysia was hit by three consecutive waves of COVID-19 before the end of 2020. The first COVID-19 wave of the deadly virus occurred in Malaysia from 25 January to 16 February 2020. The second wave happened from 27 February to 30 June 2020, and mainly involved a religious gathering held at a mosque in Seri Petaling, a suburb of Kuala Lumpur (Rampal and Liew, 2021). It was under control until the first week of March 2020, when the number of active cases recorded was less than 100. The first death caused by COVID-19 happened on 17 March 2020. The situation was recognised as a full-blown pandemic in Malaysia since the second week of March 2020. The number of accumulative cases had by then increased dramatically up to more than 2,000 within 3 weeks. As of 15 April 2020, the number of COVID-19 cases had stood at 5,182 accumulatively. To prevent the spread of COVID-19, a maiden Movement Control Order (MCO) was declared and implemented from 18 March 2020 to 3 May 2020 under the Prevention and Control of Infectious Diseases Act 1988 (Act 342). The number of accumulative cases up to 3 May was 6,298 by then. Statistically, the implementation of the MCO was undeniably most effective in controlling the deadly spread of COVID-19 infections in Malaysia.

The initial MCO was subsequently replaced by the Conditional Movement Control Order (CMCO) that ran from 4 May 2020 to 9 June 2020. The CMCO regime relaxed certain more drastic restrictions to allow the economy to resume somewhat. As of 9 June 2020, the cumulative cases were recorded at 8,336. Within the first 48 days of the CMCO period, 2,038 new cases were recorded. A further relaxation of the lock-down measures by the subsequent Recovery Movement Control Order (RMCO), an even more lenient form of the control measures, was experienced from 10 June 2020 to 6 November 2020. The RMCO relaxed the stringent Standard Operating Procedures (SOP) even further than that of the CMCO and allowed interstate travel. Almost all business sectors were allowed to resume almost full operations albeit with ever-present restrictions and new normal practices. Unfortunately, within the first 149 days of the RMCO implementation, there were 29,851 new cases that had been logged, representing an unacceptable and alarming "spike" in infections. It is widely believed that the resumption of near-normal economic and social activities had greatly contributed to and resulted in the rising number of daily infections at that time. This number of cases signalled the undisputed conclusion that Malaysia was by then heading into the third wave of COVID-19 infection.

The eventual third wave of COVID-19 began on 8 September 2020 and the government once again implemented the CMCO on 7 November 2020. Nevertheless, the new CMCO was implemented selectively only in certain states/districts that have a high number of new infection cases, such as Sabah, Selangor, Kuala Lumpur, Putrajaya, Terengganu, Johor, Penang, Kedah, and Sarawak (Kuching City only). From 7 November 2020 to 15 December 2020, the new cases were recorded at 47,261. The detailed statistical content of the MCO, CMCO, and RMCO, respectively, are summarised in Table 1.

Table 1:   Summary information of MCO, CMCO, and RMCO.

Regulation	Content	Period	Number of New Cases
MCO	• All types of gathering activities are prohibited (including sport, recreation, and religious activities) • Business premises should be closed, except for supermarkets, public markets, grocery stores, and convenience stores selling everyday necessities • Restrictions on the entry of all tourists and foreign visitors into the country • To close all government and private premises except those involved in essential services • To close all schools, colleges, and universities • Interstate travel is prohibited	18 March 2020 to 3 May 2020	5,508
CMCO (1)	• All types of gathering activities (including sport, recreation, and religious activities) are allowed if they follow the SOP • Business premises can open with some operation time adjustment • All government and private premises can open if they follow the SOP • Interstate travel is prohibited	4 May 2020 to 9 June 2020	8,336
RMCO	• All types of gathering activities (including sport, recreation, and religious activities) are allowed if they follow the SOP • Business premises can open with some operation time adjustment • All government and private premises can open if they follow the SOP • Interstate travel is allowed	10 June 2020 to 6 November 2020	29,851
CMCO (2)	• All types of gathering activities (including sport, recreation, and religious activities) are allowed if they follow the SOP • Business premises can open with some operation time adjustment • All government and private premises can open if they follow the SOP • Interstate travel is prohibited (Until 6 December 2020)	7 November 2020 to current	47,261

The implementation of the MCO/CMCO/RMCO, while "flattening" the curve of infections, undeniably slows down the economic growth in the country as a result. It imposes an adverse and drastically dampening impact on many industries, businesses, and household incomes. It is expected to cause a negative growth of exports, a high unemployment rate, a high number of small and medium enterprises' (SMEs) shutdowns, lower purchasing power, and a drastic decrease of aggregate income. Other than the tourism sector which arguably suffered the most and was the very first industry to be affected, many SMEs have also suffered from business disruption and insufficient cash flow, and the overall supply chain broke down or at least suffered from massive disruptions. The Department of Statistics Malaysia (DOSM) observed that the COVID-19 pandemic had changed the Malaysian consumption and spending behaviour. Total household expenditure dropped significantly to RM 2,868 per month during the MCO, compared to a pre-COVID-19 figure of RM 6,398 per month. Once these figures were further analysed into the different income groups, it was noted that the B40 and M40 groups reduced household spending by approximately 50%, whereas the T20 group's household spending dropped by almost two-thirds of their previous household expenditures.[1]

Many international and domestic economic and financial institutions revised their forecasts to a lower GDP growth for the Malaysian economy for the year 2020. In the beginning of the world's second wave of COVID-19 infection, the World Bank forecasted that the economic growth of Malaysia would be at –0.1% in 2020. The International Monetary Fund (IMF) forecasted the economic growth of Malaysia at only 1.7%. Bank Negara Malaysia (BNM) had foreseen a contraction of the Malaysian economic growth at between –2.0% to 0.5% in 2020, compared to a 4.3% growth in 2019.[2] However, in the third quarter of 2020, the World Bank revised the economic growth forecast for the country at 3.5% to 5.5%.

---

[1] B40 refers to the households that earn an income below RM 4,000 per month. M40 refers to the households that earn a monthly income between RM 4,000–RM 8,000. T20 refers to the households that earn an income of more than RM 8,000 per month.

[2] https://www.theedgemarkets.com/article/world-bank-lowers-malaysias-2020-gdp-forecast-49-contraction.

Subsequently, BNM also further revised the nation's economic growth forecast to 5.5%. Meanwhile, the IMF later revised its forecast for Malaysia's economic growth to 6%, which is higher than the forecasts of any of the other global or domestic financial institutions.[3]

The major causes for most people's concerns are the output loss caused by the COVID-19 pandemic, the MCO, and commodity supply disruptions. However, the government optimistically forecasts the economic growth will reach 1.5% after considering the execution of the RM 260 billion of the Economic Stimulus Package (ESP). The ESP is expected to ease the burden of society in general, and the business community in particular, caused by the lockdown.

Given the concerns arising from multiple waves of COVID-19 outbreaks, it is crucial and timely to examine whether the actual economic impact of COVID-19 was as devastating as predicted. Which sectors were affected more, and why? It is important to address such issues more definitively through the published national statistics. It is also prudent to evaluate the actual effect of COVID-19, with the remedial effects of the stimulus countermeasures and compare this with the predictions made at the time before the data were available. Hence, it will lead the policymakers and the stakeholders to have a clearer picture and adequate information especially on the scenario after the pandemic. Consequently, a more accurately targeted offset policy could be devised and improvement needs on the current policy can be identified and taken up towards achieving economic recovery.

Generally, this chapter examines the impacts of the COVID-19 pandemic on the macro economy of Malaysia throughout the year of 2020. The objectives of this chapter are as follows:

(1) To describe and discuss the impacts of COVID-19 pandemic based on selected economic indicators.
(2) To review the existing economic policy on the effects of the pandemic.
(3) To propose some significant improvements on the economic policy for adjustment and adoption in the post-COVID-19 regime.

---

[3] https://www.freemalaysiatoday.com/category/nation/2020/10/14/imf-expects-malaysias-gdp-to-increase-7-8-next-year/#:~:text=KUALA%20LUMPUR%3A%20The%20 International%20Monetary,the%20previously%20estimated%203.8%25%20contraction.

The chapter is organised as follows. The next section discusses selected macroeconomic indicators in Malaysia for the years of 2019 and 2020. Section 3 deliberates on the current economic policy in combating the pandemic. The last section concludes with some policy recommendations.

2. Important Economic Indicators in 2019–2020

2.1 *Gross domestic product (GDP)*

Table 2 reports the quarterly growth rate of GDP by sector from 2019:Q1 to 2020:Q3. The impact of the COVID-19 pandemic can be seen in 2020:Q1, when the quarterly GDP growth decreased by about 7.02%. It became even worse in 2020:Q2, when it was recorded at –15.86% due to the imposition of the MCO. After that, the GDP has shown signs of improvement in Q3 with an increase of about 21.34% from the previous quarter. It was driven by the actions taken by the government in relaxing the implementation of MCO that consequently allowed many businesses to restart their operations. In the meantime, an increase in purchasing power driven by the one-off cash aid to households and the 6-month loan repayment deferment were the major push factors for the GDP growth in 2020:Q3. Unfortunately, the third wave of the pandemic infections that started in September 2020 caused another adverse impact episode on the economic growth in Q4.

At the sectoral level, the accommodation sector was affected the most when in 2020:Q1 and 2020:Q2 its quarterly growth rate was at –15.49% and –77.02%, respectively. However, it increased to 1.33% in Q3. The accommodation sector is most central to the tourism industry. The sector includes all organisations and businesses that offer rooms or places to stay for travellers like hotels, service apartments, chalets, homestays, camping facilities, etc. A place to stay is an essential service or facility for most travellers. Hence, a resultant low number of travellers due to lockdown measures in place has a very drastic direct impact on the accommodation sector.

The gloom in the travel and accommodation industries are next followed by the decline in the motor vehicles, transport and storage; and construction sectors with the growth rate at –44.42%, –42.09%, and

Table 2:   Quarterly GDP growth (2019Q1–2020Q3).

Sector	2019Q1	2019Q2	2019Q3	2019Q4	2020Q1	2020Q2	2020Q3
Total	−4.42	2.21	3.25	2.67	−7.02	−15.86	21.34
Agriculture	−5.31	−1.51	15.41	−12.34	−8.42	8.99	13.54
Mining and quarrying	−5.52	1.29	−11.15	13.67	−4.21	−17.28	0.03
Manufacturing	−4.64	4.44	1.16	2.27	−6.11	−15.94	0.28
Construction	1.55	−3.59	5.59	−2.29	−7.39	−41.92	0.67
Electricity and gas	2.08	3.92	0.56	−1.24	1.65	−14.08	0.11
Water, sewerage, and waste management	0.58	−0.63	3.13	2.99	0.1	2.3	0.02
Wholesale trade	−12.29	9.45	10.49	−0.12	−14.42	−15.8	0.33
Retail trade	−6.03	−0.51	4.2	10.2	−10.64	−22.9	0.28
Motor vehicles	−13.12	2.39	25.07	−6.21	−19.14	−44.42	1.51
Food and beverage	−3.6	2.01	2.11	10.32	−10.32	−32.22	0.14
Accommodation	−5.63	4.22	6.64	1.92	−15.49	−77.02	1.33
Transport and storage	−2.24	1.98	2.39	4.67	−11.01	−42.09	0.55
Information and communication	3.63	3.36	1.56	−1.79	3.52	1.55	0.02
Finance	−0.28	0.08	2.71	3.35	−1.94	−11.85	0.21
Insurance	−0.15	−6.35	2.94	7.15	3.24	−9.18	−0.02
Real estate	0.47	2.01	1.93	0.65	−4.4	−30.85	0.22
Business services	−0.99	4.46	−1.62	7.55	−5.13	−22.73	0.08
Private health services	−0.71	7.11	−0.9	0.39	−4.24	−14.51	0.15
Private education services	−4.77	3.96	7.19	−0.16	−6.29	−13.51	0.12
Other services	2.08	0.22	2.06	1.31	−2.84	−22.93	0.16
Government services	−10.95	1.36	4.54	9.84	−10.35	0.58	0.06

Source: Economic Planning Unit (2020). Authors' own calculation on 31 October 2020.

–41.92% in 2020:Q2, respectively. Nevertheless, these three sectors recorded a positive growth at 1.51%, 0.55%, and 0.67% in Q3, respectively. Tellingly, the MCO also has a direct adverse impact on these sectors as the activities in these sectors are fully involved with physical movements of people and/or goods. Luckily, the adverse impact on these sectors does not drag on for a long time with the subsequent relaxation of the MCO.

There are a few sectors that are not affected much by the COVID-19 pandemic, i.e. the agriculture sector, the water, sewerage, and waste management sectors, the information and communication sectors, and government services sectors. The agriculture sector performed the best with an increase of 8.99% in 2020:Q2 and 13.54% in Q3. The sewerage and waste management sector has shown an increase of about 2.3% in 2020:Q2 and 0.02% in 2020:Q3. The information and communications sector has shown an increase of about 1.55% in 2020:Q2 and 0.02% in 2020:Q3. The government services sector has shown an increase of about 0.58% in 2020:Q2 and 0.06% in 2020:Q3. In general, we understand that these sectors do not rely much on physical movement. Thus, the implementation of the MCO did not have an adverse impact on their businesses.

Basically, the agriculture sector was not affected at all as the retail and wholesale businesses for agricultural products are allowed to operate as usual during the MCO because they provide necessities and essential goods for the people. Water, sewerage, and waste management sector is categorised as essential goods as well and it does not involve retail trading activity. The implementation of MCO has shifted many economic and social activities online. The development of the digital economy needs the support from the information and communication sector in providing the facilities for digitalisation and consequently pushes up the demand for information and communication products in the market.

2.2 *International trade*

Table 3 and Figure 1 report monthly statistics of import, export, and trade balance from January 2019 to September 2020. Overall, in 2019, the export and import were recorded at the lowest level in February 2019 with RM 67,683 million and RM 55,567 million, respectively. The highest

Table 3: Monthly import, export, and trade balance (2019M01–2020M09).

Month	Import (million)	Export (million)	Trade Balance (million)
2019M01	73,922	86,341	12,419
2019M02	55,567	67,683	12,116
2019M03	69,681	85,677	15,996
2019M04	74,377	86,228	11,851
2019M05	75,109	84,679	9,570
2019M06	65,630	76,691	11,061
2019M07	73,796	89,765	15,969
2019M08	70,461	81,513	11,052
2019M09	69,438	78,252	8,814
2019M10	73,289	90,861	17,572
2019M11	74,261	80,947	6,686
2019M12	73,880	86,436	12,556
2020M01	72,081	84,114	12,033
2020M02	61,832	74,451	12,619
2020M03	67,805	80,119	12,314
2020M04	68,420	64,787	−3,634
2020M05	52,263	62,650	10,387
2020M06	61,966	82,819	20,854
2020M07	67,383	92,559	25,176
2020M08	65,915	79,130	13,215
2020M09	66,957	88,927	21,971

Source: Economic Planning Unit (2020).

level of export and import was in October 2019 (RM 90,861 million) and May 2019 (RM 75,109 million), respectively. Furthermore, the trade balance was recorded at the highest level in October 2019 with RM 17,772 million. It fell to RM 6,686 million in December 2019, which was the lowest value of trade balance in the year of 2019. The widening lockdowns in many countries and mobility restrictions across the world caused the decline of global demand and supply.

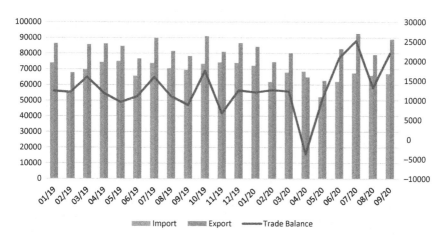

Figure 1: Import, export, and trade balance, 2019–2020.

Source: Economic Planning Unit (2020).

In 2020, during the pre-MCO period (January to March 2020), the trade balance was in a surplus. In April 2020, the trade balance became a deficit (–RM 3,634 million). This is the first time the trade balance has been in a deficit in the past 10 years. It was derived from the occurrence of a decrease of export growth of about 19.12% and an increase of import growth of about 0.91% in April 2020. As the Economic Planning Unit reported, almost all exported products were affected by the pandemic except for electrical, medical and pharmaceutical, iron and steel, and apparel products.

The trade balance went back to a surplus from May 2020 and onward. It increased from RM 10,387 million in May to RM 25,176 million in July. It was derived from an increase of export growth of about 48% from May to July 2020. The value of exports and the country's trade balance in July are the highest since January 2019. One of the reasons that the export growth increased rapidly in this period is that the export of many items that were supposed to be shipped abroad had been postponed for about 1 to 2 months due to the lockdown in April 2020. Interestingly, we note that the trade balance in June, July, and September were higher than those for the same period in 2019.

During this pandemic, the demand for medicinal and pharmaceutical products have been experiencing increasing trends not only in the

Table 4:   Export and import growth for medicinal and pharmaceutical products.

Period	Export	Import
MCO and CMCO (March 2020–May 2020)	1.57%	5.99%
RMCO (June 2020–November 2020)	3.50%	–4.21%

Source: Economic Planning Unit. Authors' own calculation on 31 October 2020.

domestic market but also in the global market (Ayati *et al.*, 2020). Table 4 reports the import and export growth of medicinal and pharmaceutical products during the periods of MCO, CMCO, and RMCO. The export growth for the medicinal and pharmaceutical products was 1.57% from March 2020 to May 2020, while the import growth was 5.99%. During the RMCO period, the export for the medicinal and pharmaceutical products growth was placed at 3.5% from June 2020 to November 2020, which is better than the MCO and CMCO periods. In the meantime, the import growth for medicinal and pharmaceutical products registered at –4.21% on average from June 2020 to November 2020. The statistics tell us that Malaysia imported more medicinal and pharmaceutical products to accommodate the high demand in the domestic market. However, when the spread of COVID-19 infections was under control, the domestic demand declined and Malaysia started to export more medicinal and pharmaceutical products abroad.

2.3 *Inflation*

Table 5 reports the monthly inflation rate from January 2019 to July 2020. In general, the Consumer Price Index (CPI) showed a decreasing trend from March 2020 to April 2020. The sectors that contributed to a decrease of the inflation rate are the food sector, utilities sector, transport sector, education sector, and restaurant and hotels sectors. The MCO and resultant slowing of the economy had driven the market to push down the average price of products and services in these sectors. Many businesses offered lower and discounted prices as an attempt to attract more demand from their customers.

Table 5: Monthly inflation rates (2019M01–2020M07).

Period	Total	Food &Non Alcoholic Beverages	Alcoholic Beverages & Tobacco	Clothing & Footwear	Housing, Water, Electricity, Gas & Other Fuels	Furnishings, Household Equipment & Routine Household Maintenance	Health	Transport	Commun-ication	Recreation Service and Culture	Education	Restaurant & Hotels	Miscellaneous Goods & Services
2019M01	-0.50	0.91	0.00	0.11	0.00	0.17	0.25	-5.47	0.00	-0.09	0.42	0.00	0.36
2019M02	0.25	0.15	-0.06	-0.11	0.50	0.26	0.16	0.45	0.00	0.18	0.42	0.15	-0.09
2019M03	0.25	-0.45	0.06	0.11	0.00	0.26	0.25	2.61	0.00	-0.09	0.08	0.00	0.36
2019M04	0.00	-0.15	0.12	-0.11	0.00	0.00	0.16	0.44	-0.10	0.09	0.00	0.23	0.09
2019M05	0.25	0.30	0.06	-0.11	0.33	0.34	0.00	0.17	0.00	-0.09	0.08	-0.15	0.00
2019M06	0.00	0.08	0.06	-0.11	0.00	0.09	0.16	-0.35	0.00	0.09	0.00	0.23	0.27
2019M07	0.08	0.30	0.00	-0.42	0.00	0.17	0.08	0.17	0.00	-0.09	0.08	0.08	0.36
2019M08	0.25	0.23	0.06	0.00	0.50	0.00	0.16	-0.09	0.00	0.00	0.08	0.15	0.53
2019M09	0.00	-0.22	-0.06	0.00	0.00	-0.09	-0.08	0.09	0.00	0.63	0.42	0.15	0.35
2019M10	0.16	0.08	0.00	-0.32	0.00	0.00	0.08	0.17	1.56	0.00	0.08	0.00	-0.18
2019M11	0.08	0.00	0.06	0.11	0.41	0.09	0.16	0.00	0.00	0.09	0.00	0.08	0.44
2019M12	0.16	0.45	-0.12	-0.11	0.00	0.09	0.00	0.09	0.00	-0.09	0.00	0.15	-0.09
2020M01	0.08	0.15	-0.06	-0.11	0.00	0.00	0.24	0.09	0.00	0.18	0.42	0.08	0.44
2020M02	0.00	0.07	0.06	0.00	0.33	0.09	0.08	-0.96	0.00	0.00	0.08	0.15	-0.09
2020M03	-1.23	-0.07	0.12	-0.11	0.00	0.00	0.32	-8.69	0.00	-0.09	0.00	-0.23	0.44
2020M04	-2.73	-0.15	0.00	0.00	-3.75	-0.43	0.00	-13.46	0.00	0.00	-0.08	0.00	-0.17
2020M05	0.26	0.30	0.06	0.00	-0.08	-0.17	0.00	1.00	0.00	0.00	-0.08	0.08	0.52
2020M06	1.02	0.45	0.06	-0.11	0.00	0.09	0.08	7.81	0.00	0.00	-0.17	-0.38	0.43
2020M07	0.67	0.07	0.12	0.00	0.00	0.26	0.08	4.90	0.00	0.00	0.41	-0.08	0.26

Note: Economic Planning Unit (2020). Authors' own calculation on 31 October 2020.

On the other hand, it also derives from a cheaper energy price as the world oil price was decreasing significantly during this period.[4] A price reduction can be seen clearly in the utilities sector and the restaurant and hotels sectors. Low prices in the utilities sector are due to the subsidy given by the government on the utility bills to assist households and businesses tide over the difficult times. On the other hand, cheaper price in restaurant and hotels sector responded to the initiatives taken by the market players in these sectors by offering a low and competitive price to boost the demand from the market especially in June and July 2020. During this time, the government relaxed the implementation of the MCO and the number of COVID-19 infection cases was by then relatively under control.

2.4 *Employment and unemployment*

Table 6 reports the numbers of employed and unemployed, and the unemployment rate from January 2019 to August 2020. The unemployment rate had shown a rapid increase since March 2020 where it stood at 3.9%. In April and May 2020, the unemployment rate jumped to 5% and 5.3%, respectively. These statistics have clearly shown that the negative impact of the MCO had forced many companies to cut off and retrench a large number of workers in order to sustain their businesses.

The high number of unemployed comprised most of the job losses in the airline and tourism industry. For example, AirAsia is reported to have cut down about 30% of their workers in response to the economic downturn through their retrenchment plan.[5] Malindo Airline also took the same strategy, which affected more than 2,000 of their workers.[6] In line with these unfortunate developments, the Malaysian Trades Union Congress

---

[4] https://www.dosm.gov.my/v1/index.php?r=column/cthemeByCat&cat=106&bul_id=cE9 sL2M3VXFTcGVvOEFOVkVDK1Bwdz09&menu_id=bThzTHQxN1ZqMVF6a2I4RkZ oNDFkQT09.

[5] https://asia.nikkei.com/Business/Transportation/AirAsia-to-slash-workforce-by-30-considers-10-stake-sale.

[6] https://www.thestar.com.my/business/business-news/2020/04/08/70-of-malindo-air-staff-to-take-unpaid-leave.

Table 6: Unemployment rates (2019M01–2020M08).

Month	Employed (Million)	Unemployed (Million)	Unemployment Rate (%)
2019M01	14,992.8	515.6	3.3
2019M02	15,026.8	516.4	3.3
2019M03	15,035.2	521.3	3.4
2019M04	15,089.8	523.3	3.4
2019M05	15,122.5	519.8	3.3
2019M06	15,134.6	521.4	3.3
2019M07	15,179.8	524.8	3.3
2019M08	15,185.8	520.2	3.3
2019M09	15,229.9	521.4	3.3
2019M10	15,265.6	512.1	3.3
2019M11	15,315	513.9	3.3
2019M12	15,286	517	3.3
2020M01	15,317.6	511.7	3.2
2020M02	15,344.5	525.2	3.3
2020M03	15,232.4	610.5	3.9
2020M04	14,933.4	778.8	5
2020M05	14,887.9	826.1	5.3
2020M06	14,990.2	773.2	4.9
2020M07	15,073.4	745.1	4.7
2020M08	15,153.5	741.6	4.7

Note: Economic Planning Unit (2020).

(MTUC) reported that about 30,000 workers in the hotel industry had lost their jobs since the implementation of the MCO.[7]

However, in the third quarter of 2020, most of the restrictions had been eased, interstate travel was allowed, and more businesses were reopened as a result of a declining number of daily COVID-19 infections in the second quarter and early third quarter of 2020. With this release of the

---

[7] https://www.freemalaysiatoday.com/category/nation/2020/05/31/30000-in-hotel-industry-have-lost-jobs-says-mtuc/.

tight hold of the MCO, the total employment numbers started to increase from 14,887.9 million workers in May to 15,153.5 million workers in August. However, the country's economic situation is still not able to bounce back to the high levels as in February 2020, before the first lockdown occurred. It was reported by the Department of Statistics Malaysia that the number of workers employed increased by about 88,000 new jobs to bring the employment population to 8.47 million in Q3:2020.[8] The number of job vacancies increased, too, from the previous quarter to 179,000 in Q3:2020. In addition, there were about 21,000 new jobs created in the private sector in Q3:2020.

2.5 *Business climate*

We use leading, coincident, and lagging indexes as the indicators to discuss the business condition prevailing in Malaysia. Table 7 reports the monthly leading, coincident, and lagging indexes from January 2019 to July 2020. The usage of leading index indicators can designate the possibility of an early signal to any business cycle turning point. It is used to predict the economic direction in an average time period of 6 months ahead. Coincident index examines the current condition of an economy or the current business cycle. Lagging index is used to measure and confirm the performance of any previous economic condition. The base year of these indexes is 2015 = 100. In the case of Malaysia, this index is composed from seven economic components where those changes tend to precede changes in the overall economy. Those seven economic components are real money supply, Bursa Malaysia Industrial Index, real import of semi-conductors, real import of other basic precious and other non-ferrous metals, the number of housing units approved, expected sales value (manufacturing), and the number of new companies registered.[9] A

---

[8] https://www.dosm.gov.my/v1/index.php?r=column/cthemeByCat&cat=480&bul_id=R3
VRSE9iU2U1ZFRpRlh3SDFNSmJwZz09&menu_id=Tm8zcnRjdVRNWWlpWjRlbmtla
Dk1UT09.
[9] https://www.dosm.gov.my/v1/index.php?r=column/cthemeByCat&cat=82&bul_id=dEJ
Rd1hDMG9obGYrWVRhczNpVFVXQT09&menu_id=YmJrMEFKT0p0WUIxbDl1bzZ
ydW9JQT09.

Table 7: Leading, coincident, and lagging indexes, by monthly, 2019–2020.

Period	2019			2020		
	Leading Index	Coincident Index	Lagging Index	Leading Index	Coincident Index	Lagging Index
January	101	113.2	151.9	101.7	115.5	153.6
February	99.2	112.5	154.1	100.9	116.3	153.1
March	99.6	112.3	150.6	95.9	108.3	144
April	101.9	113.2	151.8	96.1	91.4	158.9
May	100.2	113.7	152.3	100.8	101.2	166.9
June	100	113.5	150	104.6	110	167
July	101.4	114.1	152.3	109.2	111.4	169.3
August	100.8	114.6	151.9	—	—	—
September	100.8	114.3	152.4	—	—	—
October	102.3	114.8	153.3	—	—	—
November	101.9	115.1	152.8	—	—	—
December	101.6	115.3	154	—	—	—

Note: Economic Planning Unit (2020).

higher index quantum indicates the economic condition is experiencing a convincing upturn, while a lower index quantum is indicative of an economic decline.

Before the MCO, the three indexes in January 2020 and February 2020 were higher as compared to the same index in January 2019 and February 2019, respectively. It means, the economic prospect is more convincing in the beginning of 2020 as compared to the same period in the year 2019. During the MCO, all the three indexes dropped in March 2020. However, the leading and lagging indexes increased in April 2020. An improvement in April might be a "knee-jerk" response to the implementation of the government's economic stimulus packages. The indexes increased once again in May and onward and might likely be a reactive response to the introduction of the CMCO and subsequently the RMCO. Many significant economic activities were allowed to operate in these periods of time. Surprisingly, the leading and lagging indexes in May–July 2020 are higher than the numbers in May–July 2019.

2.6 *Market sentiment*

We use the CEO confidence index, business conditions index, consumer sentiments index, and retail trade index to discuss the market sentiment. All indexes are based on the survey by the Malaysian Institute of Economic Research. Table 8 reports these quarterly indexes from Q1:2019 to Q3:2020. The CEO confidence index is an indicator to measure how confident the top management of corporates are about the domestic economy. The trend shows that the CEO's confidence in the domestic economy decreased from 93.1 in Q1:2019 to fall to 85.3 in Q4:2019. However, the CEO confidence index registered at 88.4 in Q1:2020, which is higher than in the previous quarter (Q4:2019). The index dropped significantly to the lowest in Q2:2020. This reflected the loss of confidence and the worry caused by the implementation of the MCO since March 2020. There is some improvement in Q3:2020, but it is still smaller than the index value before the imposition of the MCO.

The business conditions Index is indicative of the condition of the business situation in the economy in terms of its current and future prospect for business capacity. This index covered a sample of 350 manufacturing businesses in 11 industries that are operating in Malaysia. The main indicators of this index are production level, new order bookings, sales performances, inventory build-up, and new job openings. The business conditions index was lower in the second half of 2019 than the first half

Table 8: CEO confidence index, by quarterly 2019–2020.

Period	CEO Confidence Index	Business Conditions Index	Consumer Sentiments Index	Retail Trade Index
2019Q1	93.1	94.3	85.6	134.4
2019Q2	90.1	94.2	93.0	138.5
2019Q3	90.2	69	84	141.9
2019Q4	85.3	88.3	82.3	143.1
2020Q1	88.4	83	51.1	137.1
2020Q2	26.9	61	90	108.8
2020Q3	61.5	86.3	91.5	137.6

Note: Economic Planning Unit (2020).

of 2019. In the beginning of 2020, business conditions index was registered at 83 in Q1:2020, which decreased by about 6% from Q4:2019. As the MCO started to be implemented in March 2020, the business conditions index decreased further to 61 in Q2:2020. However, the index increased to 86.3 in Q3:2020. Comparatively, the index value is smaller as compared to the index value in 2019, indicating that the business condition was worse than in 2019 due to the pandemic.

On the other hand, the consumer sentiments index informs the feelings and confidence level of a consumer on their budget constraints and the prospect of the domestic economy, respectively. The survey covers consumer spending trends and sentiments. Consumer sentiments index started to decrease from Q3:2019 to Q1:2020. A low index was in response to the pre-pandemic sentiment in January 2020 and February 2020 and the implementation of MCO in March 2020. However, this index bounced back in Q2:2020. This upward trend may also be a reactive response to the various economic stimulus packages doled out by the government in March and April 2020.

The retail trade index is informative of the retail sector activity in terms of value and volume. It is also an indicator for domestic demand of final goods. In 2019, the retail trade index increased in every quarter. In the beginning of 2020, the retail trade index was registered at 137.1 in Q1:2020, a decrease from 143.1 in Q4:2019. But it was higher than the index value in Q1:2019 if we make a comparison on a year-over-year basis. It means the retail trade performed better in quarter 1 for the year of 2020 than 2019. We can see that the retail trade index dropped significantly to 108.8 in Q2:2020 due to the implementation of the MCO since March 2020. It has undergone some improvement in Q3:2020. However, the index value is still lower than the value in Q3:2019 if we compare on a year-over-year basis.

Overall, the CEO confidence index, business conditions index, and retail trade index showed the lowest in Q2:2020. While the consumer sentiments index was at the lowest index in Q1:2020. We can conclude that the market sentiment on the pandemic and the early stages of the MCO implementation was worse for businesses and economic activities besides social interaction. However, the introduction of various economic stimulus packages manages to improve the market sentiment in Q3:2020 somewhat and mitigates against the ill effects of the pandemic-induced and MCO-caused economic downturns.

3. The Economic Policy on COVID-19 Pandemic

The government decided to follow other countries to implement the MCO which largely entailed the prohibitions and restrictions on gatherings, mass assemblies, commuting, and travelling by the entire population in combating and reversing the spread of the COVID-19 virus in Malaysia. However, the implementation of the MCO and its drastic measures had an adverse impact on economic activities and peoples' well-being. Sufficient coverage of offset policy is very important to ensure the economy can recover well after it resumes operations fully. The government has announced several economic stimulus packages to cushion the adverse impact from the pandemic and the lockdowns.

Chronologically, the government announced the first economic stimulus package valued at RM 20 billion on 27 February 2020. It was before the execution of the MCO. The second announcement of the economic stimulus package valued at RM 250 billion was on 27 March 2020. It was announced during the maiden MCO period. The third announcement of the economic stimulus package valued at RM 10 billion was announced on 6 April 2020. On the other hand, BNM also supported these fiscal measures by promoting the country's monetary expansion by adjusting the Overnight Policy Rate (OPR) and reducing it four times consecutively to provide additional liquidity in the market.

3.1 *First stimulus package*

The first stimulus package was announced on 27 February 2020 by the Pakatan Harapan Government. It was before COVID-19 became a pandemic in Malaysia. RM 20 billion was allocated in this package. This stimulus package focuses more on cushioning the tourism sector and SMEs from the external shock. It involves a direct government spending in the economy and tax reduction. These incentives aimed to improve the businesses' cash flow and increase domestic spending. The stimulus package was expected to trigger the economic growth and increase it from a range of 3.2% to 4.2%.

3.2 Second stimulus package

The second stimulus package aptly named as The PRIHATIN Economic Stimulus Package was announced by the Perikatan National Government on 27 March 2020. This stimulus package has been valued at RM 250 billion. It is more than 11.5 times higher than the first stimulus package. The PRIHATIN is intended to comprehensively cushion the whole economy from the adverse impact of the MCO since its implementation on 18 March 2020. For this round, almost everyone was affected by the lockdown. Cash assistance and electricity bill discounts were provided to firms, households, and individuals. A big sum of the budget (RM 100 billion) was allocated for the loan repayment moratorium programme. However, this programme is not involved with a fiscal commitment. It is to encourage the demand in the market as the purchasing power of consumers is expected to be increased through the implementation of the fiscal stimulus package. It is calculated that when households and businesses have a higher purchasing power, it will eventually encourage more domestic spending. In the end, the domestic businesses are expected to earn more revenue in turn, and consequently, it helps to improve their cash flow.

On the supply side, the government also allocated several budgets for business loans especially for the SMEs via commercial banks and other government agencies. Various responses were received from the people and the industry players expressing that there was a growing demand for some adjustments to be made to some of the features of the stimulus package.

First, the wage subsidy programme.[10] Initially, this programme planned to give a wage subsidy of RM 600 per worker for 3 months. But, many industries players requested for an increase of the subsidy quantum and an extension of the coverage period due to the deep impact suffered from the MCO. Second, there was a strong demand from the SME players to be

---

[10] https://www.pmo.gov.my/2020/03/speech-text-prihatin-esp/.

awarded a business grant instead of a repayable loan in spite of any possible "easy" terms to ease their cash flow during these hard times.[11]

3.3 *Third stimulus package*

In responding to the feedback on the wage subsidy programme and a specific aid for SMEs, the third stimulus package called "PRIHATIN plus" was announced by the federal government on 6 April 2020. This is a mini stimulus package as an extension of the PRIHATIN economic stimulus package. An additional RM 10 billion was allocated. It involves the wage subsidy that increased the amount of incentive to RM 1,200 per worker and the provision of a business grant of RM 3,000 for SMEs. The aim of this stimulus package was to improve the business cash flow for recipient companies both during the MCO and the post-MCO periods. The intention of the stimulus extension programme was to moderate the increase in the unemployment rate through a wage subsidy programme.

3.4 *Fourth stimulus package*

Consequent to the three previous stimulus packages, the federal government subsequently announced another stimulus package that became known as the National Economic Recovery Stimulus (PENJANA) on 5 June 2021, which is a short-term economic recovery plan to extend credit to companies especially SMEs. This initiative is intended as a kickstart measure for Malaysia's economic recovery. In this stimulus package, there are 41 programmes worth RM 35 billion to re-energise the economy. RM 10 billion is a direct fiscal injection by the government. The aims of this stimulus package are to empower the people, propel businesses and stimulate the economy. The time frame to execute all programmes would be from June 2021 to December 2021. There are 11 programmes that the plan targets at empowering the people and businesses with. The government also listed 14 other programmes intended to propel businesses on to a path of recovery and growth. To stimulate the economy, 16 new programmes had been strategised.

---

[11] https://www.bharian.com.my/berita/nasional/2020/03/670224/majikan-perlu-tuntut-program-subsidi-upah.

3.5 *Monetary policy adjustments*

BNM also supported these macro initiates by promoting the monetary expansion, with the Overnight Policy Rate (OPR) being reduced four times to provide additional liquidity in the market. Since March 2020, BNM announced a 0.25% reduction of OPR four times. On March 2020, the OPR stood at 3.25. As of 7 July 2020, the OPR was further reduced to 1.75.[12] A lower interest rate generally leads to a lower investment rate for the depositors. On the other hand, the cost of borrowing becomes cheaper for the borrowers. This monetary policy is expected to encourage more spending in the domestic market as an unattractive lower savings rate will discourage the depositors to save more money in the bank and conversely encourage investments and spending which are hoped to churn the economy faster and fuel growth.

3.6 *Budget 2021*

This national budget is different from other previous annual budgets tabled in previous years not only in terms of size but also in scope and intention. The country's budget for the year 2021 is focused on the fiscal strategy in reviving the economy from the pandemic. Basically, the government allocated a total budget of RM 322.5 billion. About RM 236.5 billion is meant for operational expenditure, RM 69 billion for development and RM 17 billion for the COVID-19 fund. The COVID-19 fund mainly covers the Wage Subsidy Programme, small-scale infrastructure projects, SME soft loans and food security projects. The government estimates the budget deficit will stand at 5.4% of GDP by the end of 2021.

The government also extended the loan repayment moratorium for another 3 months forward. For this round, the targeted groups are the B40 and the SMEs only. On the other hand, the government also allows selected members of the Employees' Provident Fund (EPF) to withdraw their old

---

[12] https://www.bnm.gov.my/interest-rates-volumes?p_p_id=bnm_market_rate_display_portlet&p_p_lifecycle=0&p_p_state=normal&p_p_mode=view&_bnm_market_rate_display_portlet_product=rrm&_bnm_market_rate_display_portlet_monthStart=0&_bnm_market_rate_display_portlet_yearStart=2020&_bnm_market_rate_display_portlet_monthEnd=1&_bnm_market_rate_display_portlet_yearEnd=2021.

age savings to a maximum withdrawal of 10% of their total deposits from their EPF accounts. This programme is intended to reduce the burden of people who are facing an income reduction or have lost their jobs during or as a result of the pandemic. However, many people requested for an amendment to this measure as Malaysia by then was suffering the third wave of the pandemic in Q4:2020.[13] They requested for the loan repayment moratorium programme to be further lengthened and extended for a wider coverage and that the EPF deposit withdrawal should be automatically approved for everyone without any terms and conditions imposed. In addition, the loan repayment moratorium programme should be extended for another 6 months ahead at least instead of just 3 months.

4. Conclusion and Policy Recommendation

The COVID-19 virus infection has been declared a pandemic threat to life and health in Malaysia since March 2020. The government implemented the MCO and lockdown measures to combat the spread of COVID-19. The MCO however gave rise to massive adverse impacts on the economy as it disrupted the daily economic and social activities. Without sufficient and accurate offset policy, the impact of the MCO will drag on longer in the country. Statistically, real economic activity, i.e. output (GDP), inflation rate, unemployment, and trade balance, had shown a trend of decreasing in 2020:Q2. The resultant declining inflation rate was not expected to be an advantage to the consumers' purchasing power because many were left unemployed and/or had had their wages cut. In addition, the index for all market sentiments indicated that the market sentiment on the current economic situation in 2020:Q2 was worse. Throughout the period of 2020, the production and employment were at the lowest point reflecting the necessary draconian measures in the implementation of the MCO in 2020:Q2. However, the production and employment levels were seen to be increasing in 2020:Q3 and 2020:Q4 in response to the implementation of CMCO and RMCO that

---

[13] https://www.thestar.com.my/news/nation/2020/11/12/announcement-on-loan-moratorium-epf-soon.

relaxed many restrictions of MCO. This was also supported by the execution of multiple stimulus packages that aimed to strengthen the business resilience and prepare the economy to grow once the pandemic is over.

Multiple offset policies have been announced by the government in securing and recovering the economy from the pandemic. Generally, there are four main components in the economy, namely private consumption (C), total investment (I), government expenditure (G), and net export (NX). The current situation affected the performance of I and NX. A reduction of interest rate led to a lower rate of return in the capital market. The lockdown had a direct impact on international trade as well. Hence, the I and NX are too weak to trigger the desired economic growth. Therefore, the economy is relying more on the C and G to activate economic growth during this hard time. However, to encourage more C and G, high fiscal commitment is required, especially with the government's fiscal constraints. In this chapter, we recommend several policies that the government can consider in improving the C and G towards economic recovery.

First, the government implemented the 6-month loan moratorium from April 2020 to September 2020. This programme had increased people's purchasing power in the market despite the economic calamity and it provided valuable breathing space for the people. Higher purchasing power in the hands of the consumers in the market will help the producers improve their cash flow. However, this programme will give an adverse impact to the financial institutions and capital markets if the programme takes a longer coverage time period.

The government should introduce a debt restructuring programme for households and corporate entities especially the SMEs after the loan moratorium ends. Debt restructuring programmes are important to avoid a shock on consumer purchasing power after the loan moratorium ends. Instead of giving loan deferment for 6 months, there should be a plan to coordinate a debt restructuring programme which aims to reduce the loan instalment after the moratorium ends. It can be done by extending the period of the loan contract. Debt restructuring programmes should have less bureaucracy, too. These debt restructuring programmes will give a larger multiple effect in the economy at both the demand and supply sides. At the demand side, the purchasing power is still strong to support the domestic demand because the consumers have extra money in their pockets. At the supply side, the producers can enjoy a lower overhead cost as their monthly loan instalments are reduced. Thus, the marginal revenue is expected to increase.

Second, the government should improve the tax system to maximise its revenue from tax collection. Initially, the government has injected a lot of money into the market via fiscal policy. With all the economic stimulus packages, the spending of the government amounted to around 20% of GDP. To finance all these economic stimulus packages, the government depends a lot on domestic borrowings. Hence, it increases the deficit to 6% of GDP. In addition, the commitment on debt in the future is also high. There is a need to improve the tax system in maximising government's tax revenue collection. The Goods and Service Tax (GST) system is one of the options to replace the current Sales and Service Tax (SST) system. We advise the government to reintroduce the GST, however, it should start with a lower rate such as 1%–2%. GST is more efficient than SST. On the other hand, it also diversifies the source of income from levying and relying too much on the oil revenue. The more productive the tax collection system, the more the revenue can be maximised through tax collection. Thus, improving the tax system will reduce the fiscal pressure because the money that had been injected into the economy will be returned to the government.

Third, a 6% service tax has been extended to the foreign digital service providers since January 2020. The digital tax is expected to contribute RM 400 million to the national revenue. An increasing trend of online transactions in the country especially during the lockdown promotes new business opportunities to many people. Hence, we suggest the government may consider extending the digital tax to the domestic users. By extending this tax to the domestic users, the government can be expected to raise more revenue from the digital tax.

References

Bank Negara Malaysia. (2021). Retrieved on 8 February 2021 from https://www.bnm.gov.my/interest-rates-volumes?p_p_id=bnm_market_rate_display_portlet&p_p_lifecycle=0&p_p_state=normal&p_p_mode=view

&_bnm_market_rate_display_portlet_product=rrm&_bnm_market_rate_
display_portlet_monthStart=0&_bnm_market_rate_display_portlet_year-
Start=2020&_bnm_market_rate_display_portlet_monthEnd=1&_bnm_mar-
ket_rate_display_portlet_yearEnd=2021.

Department of Statistics Malaysia. (2020a). Retrieved on 11 December 2020
from   https://www.dosm.gov.my/v1/index.php?r=column/cthemeByCat&
cat=480&bul_id=R3VRSE9iU2U1ZFRpRlh3SDFNSmJwZz09&menu_id=
Tm8zcnRjdVRNWWlpWjRlbmtlaDk1UT09.

Department of Statistics Malaysia. (2020b). Retrieved on 11 December 2020
from   https://www.dosm.gov.my/v1/index.php?r=column/cthemeByCat&
cat=106&bul_id=cE9sL2M3VXFTcGVvOEFOVkVDK1Bwdz09&menu_
id=bThzTHQxN1ZqMVF6a2I4RkZoNDFkQT09.

Department of Statistics Malaysia. (2020c). Retrieved on 11 December 2020
from   https://www.dosm.gov.my/v1/index.php?r=column/cthemeByCat&
cat=82&bul_id=dEJRd1hDMG9obGYrWVRhczNpVFVXQT09&menu_
id=YmJrMEFKT0p0WUIxbDl1bzZydW9JQT09.

Economic Planning Unit. (2020). National Account. Retrieved from https://www.
epu.gov.my/en/socio-economic-statistics/socio-economic/national-accounts.

Free Malaysia Today. (14 October 2020). IMF expects Malaysia GDP to increase
7–8% next year. https://www.freemalaysiatoday.com/category/nation/2020/
10/14/imf-expects-malaysias-gdp-to-increase-7-8-next year/#:~:text=KUALA
%20LUMPUR%3A%20The%20International%20Monetary,the%20
previously%20estimated%203.8%25%20contraction.

Free Malaysia Today. (31 May 2020). 30,000 in hotel industry have lost jobs, says
MTUC. https://www.freemalaysiatoday.com/category/nation/2020/05/31/
30000-in-hotel-industry-have-lost-jobs-says-mtuc/.

Hun, C. J. (29 September 2020). World Bank revises Malaysia's 2020 GDP forecast
to larger 4.9% contraction. *The Edge Markets.* https://www.theedgemarkets.
com/article/world-bank-lowers-malaysias-2020-gdp-forecast-49-contraction.

Kaplan, K. (22 October 2013). Flu shots may reduce risk of heart attacks, strokes
and even death. *Los Angeles Times.* https://www.latimes.com.

Kumar, P. P. (5 June 2020). AirAsia to slash workforce by 30%, considers 10%
stake sale. *Nikkei Asia.* https://asia.nikkei.com/Business/Transportation/
AirAsia-to-slash-workforce-by-30-considers-10-stake-sale.

Parzi, M. N. (28 March 2020). Majikan perlu tuntut Program Subsidi Upah.
Berita Harian. https://www.bharian.com.my/berita/nasional/2020/03/670224/
majikan-perlu-tuntut-program-subsidi-upah.

Rampal, L. and Liew, B. S. (2021). Malaysia's third COVID-19 wave — a paradigm shift required. Medical Journal of Malaysia. 76: 1–4.

Sidhu, B.K. (8 April 2020). 70% of Malindo Air staff to take unpaid leave. *The Star*. https://www.thestar.com.my/business/business-news/2020/04/08/70-of-malindo-air-staff-to-take-unpaid-leave.

The Prime Minister's Office of Malaysia. (2020). Retrieved on 11 December 2020 from https://www.pmo.gov.my/2020/03/speech-text-prihatin-esp/.

The Star. (12 November 2020). Announcement on loan moratorium, EPF soon. https://www.thestar.com.my/news/nation/2020/11/12/announcement-on-loan-moratorium-epf-soon.

About the Authors

Dzul Hadzwan Husaini is currently a lecturer of Economics at the Faculty of Economics and Business, Universiti Malaysia Sarawak, and a Ph.D. candidate at Universiti Sains Malaysia. His research interests include energy economics, energy finance, and business economics. He has published several articles in a few indexed journals.

Hooi Hooi Lean is a professor at the School of Social Sciences (Economics Programme), Universiti Sains Malaysia. She is also an affiliated professor at IPAG Business School, France and Universitas Indonesia. She has published more than 160 articles in many reputed international journals. Her H-index is 45 and there are more than 9,000 citations to her works on Google Scholar. She has been listed as being among the top 2% scientists in the world by Stanford University. Prof. Lean was recognised as one of the Top Research Scientists Malaysia by Academy of Sciences Malaysia in 2018. She received Malaysia's Research Star Award in 2017 from the Ministry of Higher Education Malaysia and Clarivate Analytics; and National Academic Award in 2015 from the Ministry of Higher Education Malaysia. Prof. Lean is a Fellow of East Asian Economic Association. She serves as an associate editor for the *Singapore Economic Review, Frontiers in Energy Research, Malaysian Journal of Economics*, and *International Journal of Economics and Management*. She is also an editorial board member of the *Energy Research Letters, Journal of Asian Finance, Economics and Business,* and *Asian Journal of Economics and Finance.* She is also a member of the editorial advisory board of the *Indonesian Capital Market Review* and the *Labuan Bulletin of International Business & Finance.*

https://doi.org/10.1142/9789811228476_0005

Chapter 5

COVID-19 Pandemic and the Malaysian Tourism

Tze-Haw Chan*[,‡] and Jin Hooi Chan[†,§]

*Graduate School of Business, Universiti Sains Malaysia, Malaysia
†Faculty of Business, University of Greenwich, London, UK
‡thchan@usm.my
§j.h.chan@greenwich.ac.uk

Abstract

This chapter analyses the impacts of the coronavirus pandemic on the Malaysian tourism industry. The discussion starts with general development of global tourism, followed by the drastic changes in Malaysian tourism and the economic conditions before and during the pandemic. With support of updated statistics, this chapter further presents the disastrous strikes on domestic tourism value chain, hotel lines, and the aviation industry. The relevant policy responses and post-pandemic tourism recovery are also discussed for better understanding of the vulnerable ecosystem. This chapter concludes that the recovery is progressive along UNWTO's Scenario 1 (before or by 2023) but subjected to domestic policy efficacy and global responses, especially the availability and affordability of vaccines. This chapter recommends proactive short-term

---

‡Corresponding author.

policy initiatives in preparing the sector and its value chain to be COVID secure, and then launching marketing campaigns. For long-term strategic planning, the government should look into initiating and building capacity of digitalisation in the sector.

Keywords: Pandemic; tourism value chain; hotel; aviation industry; vaccines.

1. Introduction

Globalisation and universal mobility have promoted tourism to become one of the world's largest and rapidly growing service sectors. In 2018, there was a record of 1,400 million international tourists travelling worldwide, a rise of 6% over 2017, according to the World Tourism Organization (UNWTO, 2019). Due to the growth of budget airlines and the rise of digital services, the tourist numbers have far accelerated in recent years as compared to the past decades. For instance, there were only 25 million international tourist visits in 1950, rising to 166 million in 1970, and then 435 million in 1990. The rapidly growing number of travellers has contributed to the global economic growth. It generates foreign exchange, drives regional development, directly supports numerous types of jobs and businesses, and underpins many local communities. A recent report by the Organisation of Economic Co-operation and Development (OECD, 2020) highlighted that tourism directly contributes on average 4.4% of GDP, 21.5% of service exports, and 6.9% of employment in OECD countries.

However, the global tourism industry is facing severe challenges amid the COVID-19 pandemic since all world tourist destinations have imposed some travel restrictions (UNWTO, 2020a).[1] Studies reveal that tourism is among the most severely affected industries by the COVID-19 pandemic (e.g. Khalid *et al.*, 2021; Zhang *et al.*, 2021). World tourism recorded a 74%

---

[1] These include the suspension of foreign and domestic flights, the interstate and intercity travel restrictions, quarantine policy (14-day isolation), essential testing and symptoms monitoring of residents from countries with high risk, to control the spread of COVID-19. However, these measures have severe consequences on the world social and economic dynamics (Akin and Gozel, 2020). They have disrupted and changed the way governments, the global health system, and the world economy operates (Delgado *et al.*, 2020).

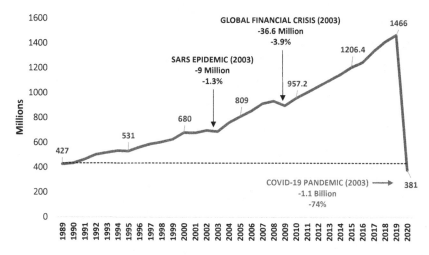

Figure 1: Global crises and world tourism, 1989–2020.

Source: Reproduced from UNWTO (2020a).

decline in international tourist arrivals (Figure 1), which makes it 1.1 billion lesser tourists, almost returning to levels of 30 years ago (UNWTO, 2020b). In comparison, the decline in international tourist arrivals was reported at 4% (2 million) and 0.4% (37 million), respectively, in the 2009 Global Financial Crisis and the 2003 SARS pandemic. This collapse in international tourism resulted in an estimated loss of USD 2 trillion in the world GDP and a USD 1.3 trillion loss in export revenues. Further, the pandemic put 100 to 120 million jobs in the tourism sector at risk, where many of these jobs are in small and medium-size enterprises (UNWTO, 2020).

Among all regions, Asia and the Pacific documented the highest decline in international tourist arrivals (–84%, 57 million), followed by Africa (–75%, 18 million), Middle East (–75%, 16 million), Europe (–70%, 221 million), and Americas (–69%, 69 million) in 2020 (see Table 1).

2. Malaysian Tourism and Economic Development

In Malaysia, tourism revenues have contributed to three high-priority goals: income generation, employment, and foreign exchange earnings.

Table 1: International tourism arrivals by region, 2019–2020.

Regions	2019 (Million)	% Change	2020 (Million)	% Change
Asia & the Pacific	360	4	57	–84
Africa	71	2	18	–75
Middle East	65	8	16	–75
Europe	746	4	221	–70
Americas	219	1	69	–69
Total	**1,461**	**4**	**381**	**–74**

Source: World Tourism Organization, February 2021.

Table 2: Malaysian GDP contribution by sector and economic activity (%), 2000–2019.

	Contribution by Sector and Economic Activity (%)							GDP at Current Price
Year	Agriculture	Mining & Quarrying	Manufacturing	Construction	Services	Import Duties	Tourism Expenditure	(RM mil)
2010	10.4	10.9	24.5	3.4	49.9	1.0	7.1	797,327
2015	8.3	8.8	22.3	4.7	54.7	1.2	5.9	1,176,941
2019	7.3	8.6	21.4	4.7	56.9	1.1	5.7	1,510,692

Source: Tourism Malaysia, Bank Negara Malaysia.

As a service sector, tourism becomes the third biggest contributor to Malaysia's economic growth, after manufacturing and commodities exports (see Table 2). In 2019, it generated about RM 86.1 billion, accounted for 5.7% of the total GDP, and employed 3.5 million people.

In terms of visitor arrivals, Malaysia ranks ninth in the world, and second after Thailand in the ASEAN region in 2019 (Table 3). Malaysia was, previously, the top Southeast Asian country in attracting foreign tourists before Thailand took over the helm from 2015. Based on the Tourism Satellite Account (DOSM), the inbound tourism accounted for about 5.7–7.5% of Malaysian nominal GDP (current price) during 2010–2019. However, there was a slight downward trend of inbound tourism-GDP ratio over the past decade (see Figure 2). Whereas the outbound tourism has accounted for about 2.4–3.0% of nominal GDP. Nevertheless, the number of employed in Malaysian tourism has consistently expanded

Table 3: Visitor arrivals to ASEAN member nations (in person), 2000–2019.

	2000	2005	2010	2015	2016	2017	2018	2019
Brunei	984,093	127,142	214,290	218,213	218,809	258,955	278,136	333,200
Myanmar	270,665	660,206	791,507	4,681,020	2,907,207	3,443,133	3,549,428	4,364,100
Lao PDR	737,208	1,095,315	2,513,028	4,684,429	4,239,047	3,868,838	4,186,432	4,791,100
Cambodia	466,365	1,421,615	2,508,289	4,775,231	5,011,712	5,602,157	6,201,077	6,610,600
Philippines	1,992,169	2,623,084	3,520,471	5,360,682	5,967,005	6,620,908	7,127,678	8,260,900
Viet Nam	2,150,100	3,467,757	5,049,855	7,943,651	10,012,735	12,922,151	15,497,791	18,008,600
Indonesia	5,064,217	5,002,101	7,002,944	10,406,759	11,519,275	14,039,799	15,810,305	16,107,000
Singapore	7,691,399	8,942,408	11,638,663	15,231,469	16,403,595	17,424,611	18,508,302	19,113,800
Malaysia	**10,271,582**	**16,431,055**	**24,577,196**	**25,721,251**	**26,757,392**	**25,948,459**	**25,832,354**	**26,100,800**
Thailand	9,508,623	11,516,936	15,936,400	29,881,091	32,529,588	35,591,978	38,277,300	39,797,400
ASEAN	**39,136,421**	**51,287,619**	**73,752,643**	**108,903,796**	**115,566,365**	**125,720,989**	**135,268,803**	**143,487,500**

Source: ASEAN Secretariat, 2020.

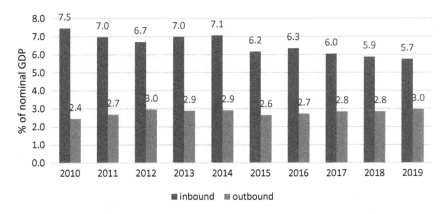

Figure 2:   Malaysian inbound and outbound tourism to GDP, 2010–2019.

Source: Tourism Satellite Account, DOSM.

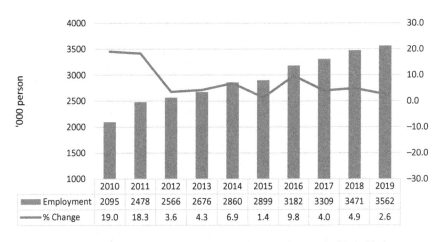

Figure 3:   Employment in the Malaysian tourism industry, 2010–2019.

Source: Tourism Satellite Account, DOSM.

from 2,095,000 to 3,562,000 persons, with a growth of 70%, over 2000–2019 (see Figure 3).

Apart from the ample success of previous "Visit Malaysia Year" (VMY) since 1990,[2] Malaysia was keen to capitalise on the recent upward

---

[2] Prior to 2020, Malaysia has launched four times of "Visit Malaysia Year" (VMY) to promote tourism. These campaigns were previously launched in 1990, 1994, 2007, and 2014, respec-

trend of tourism expansion in ASEAN. Hence, the "Visit Truly Asia Malaysia 2020" campaign was launched again in 2019, in the hope of attracting 30 million visitors and RM 100 billion revenues by 2020. However, the outbreak of COVID-19 and the Movement Control Orders (MCOs) have significantly impacted the tourism industry, leading to total abandonment of this ambitious campaign.

3. Malaysian Tourism in Desolation

Malaysia discovered the first infection case of coronavirus in the southern state at Johor Bahru on 25 January 2020 (Foo *et al.*, 2020). With a total population of 32 million, Malaysia reported an accumulated 300,752 coronavirus cases (273,417 recovered) and 1,130 deaths on 28 February 2021 (Ministry of Health).[3] Table 4 shows summary statistics of coronavirus cases in Malaysia.

A spike in COVID-19 cases was recorded in the middle of March 2020 and consequently contained via the first MCO 1.0 until mid-May, followed by gradual easing of restrictions with Conditional Movement Control Order (CMCO). The number of COVID-19 cases remained low for several months thereafter. The second wave of infection occurred in October 2020, coincidently after the Sabah state (in East Malaysia) election in September. However, the government continued with CMCO and, by 21 November 2020, a relaxed Recovery Movement Control Order (RMCO) was introduced to allow for economic reactivation.

Unfortunately, MCO 2.0 was reimposed on 11 January 2021 due to the third wave of the COVID-19 outbreak and serious concerns on the near-breaking of national healthcare system. By January–February 2021, a total of 187,742 new cases were reported, surpassing the total cases of 113,010 in 2020. A nationwide state of emergency was declared on 12 January 2021 to curb the virus spread. The Parliament and State Legislative assembly sessions were also suspended until 1 August 2021. After the peak of infection cases in January–February, the government downgraded the

---

tively, with different themes and mascots. Tourist arrivals were recorded at 7.4 million, 10.22 million, 20.97 million, and 28 million, respectively, during the past VMYs.

[3] http://COVID-19.moh.gov.my/terkini. The data presented here are until 21 February 2021.

Table 4:   Malaysia's coronavirus statistics, 2020Q1–February 2021.

Date	COVID-19 Tests	Confirmed Cases	Death Cases
2020	**3,189,618**	**113,010**	**471**
Q1	21,381	2,766	43
Q2	610,164	5,873	78
Q3	763,496	2,585	15
Q4	1,794,577	101,786	335
2021 January	1,486,101	101,949	289
2021 February	1,410,591	85,793	370
Grand Total	**6,086,310***	**300,752**	**1,130**

Note: *Total number of COVID tests was recorded until 25 February 2021, while confirmed cases and death cases were updated to 28 February 2021.
Source: Ministry of Health (MOH) Malaysia, Our World in Data. https://ourworldindata.org/coronavirus/country/malaysia?country=~MYS.

MCOs (except for hot spot states like Kuala Lumpur, Selangor, Penang, and Johor) to CMCO from 19 February to 4 March.

The closure of international borders and MCOs, which constrain inter-district and inter-state travels, have affected both national and domestic tourism (DOSM, 2020). According to UNWTO (Table 5), the fall of foreign tourists' arrivals in Southeast Asia is far more than the world average, while the decline of Malaysian foreign tourist arrival is slightly higher than the ASEAN average. By September 2020, Malaysia lost 78% foreign tourist arrivals. The decline was 36% in the first quarter, followed by almost 99% in the second and the third quarters of 2020. Among all, the reduced tourist arrivals from Singapore, China, and Indonesia made up 50% of the total arrivals to Malaysia (Foo *et al.*, 2020). The diminishing trend of the top-3 foreign tourist arrivals to Malaysia is presented in Figure 4, where a severe decline was recorded until March 2020 and then arrivals reached almost zero afterwards. In terms of tourism expenditure, Malaysia recorded RM 12.63 billion during January–September 2020, a decrease of 80.9% as compared to 2019 (Tourism Malaysia, 2020).[4]

---

[4] http://mytourismdata.tourism.gov.my/wp-content/uploads/2021/01/Msia-Tourism-Performance-Fast-Facts-January-September-2020-v.1.pdf.

Table 5: Contractions of international tourist arrivals, 2020.

Tourist Arrivals	Millions			Percentage Change Over Same Period of Previous Year (%)								
	2018	2019	2018/19	2020 (YTD)	Q1	Q2	Q3	June	July	August	September
World	1407	1461	3.7	−71.9	−28.5	−94.6	−78.6	−91.2	−79.6	−76.7	−79.6
ASEAN	135.3	143.5	7.7	−78.0	−35.1	−97.0	−98	−98.1	−98.0	−97.9	−98.1
Malaysia	25.8	26.1	1.0	−78.6	−36.8	−99.7	−99.3	−99.7	−99.2	−99.5	−99.2

Source: UNWTO World Tourism Barometer and MyTourismData. Malaysia Economic Performance (MEP), Department of Statistics Malaysia.

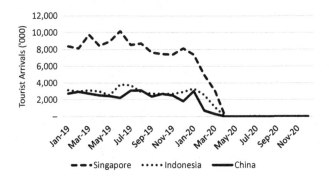

Figure 4: International tourists arrivals to Malaysia by major countries, 2020.
Source: MyTourismData.

The prolonged pandemic and national closure policy have driven the Malaysian economy to its worst annual showing — annual contraction of 5.9%, since the Asian financial crisis in 1997. By year-on-year change, the Malaysian economy contracted by 17.1% in the second quarter, followed by 2.6% and 3.4%, respectively, in the following third and fourth quarters of 2020 (Figure 5). All economic sectors continued to record negative growth except for manufacturing and exports. Being the most important sector, services plunged by 16.2%, 4.0%, and 4.9% in the said quarters. Such a shrinking trend was mainly due to the rigid movement controls and decline in tourism activities with disruption to its supply chain.

To this end, it is clear that the Malaysian tourism industry has been severely disrupted and has diminished the aggregate performance of the Malaysian economy. In the subsequent sections, the author will discuss further about the specific effects of the coronavirus pandemic on the tourism value chain, the hotel sector, and the aviation industry. A discussion on post-pandemic tourism and some conclusions are also offered.

4. Pandemic Effect on Tourism Value Chain

The Tourism Malaysia Agency has conducted annual assessment of foreign tourists via face-to-face interviews and has listed details of tourist expenditure into 12 major components, as shown in Table 6. Based on the

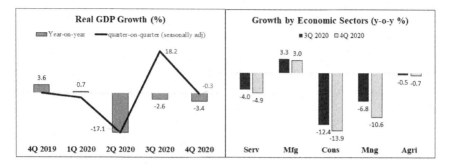

Figure 5: Malaysian real economic growth by economic sectors.
Source: Bank Negara Malaysia Quarterly Report, Q12021.

Table 6: Malaysian tourist expenditure components (RM million), 2015–2020.

RM Mil	2015	2016	2017	2018	2019	2020	2019/20 % Change
Shopping	21634.4	26025.1	26868.0	28101.2	28944.2	4475.2	−84.5
Accommodation	17556.4	20442.5	21034.2	21622.7	20674.4	2955.0	−85.7
Food & Beverage	9262.0	10754.9	10927.9	11274.1	11457.1	1837.7	−84.0
Local Transportation	4561.9	5418.5	4765.6	5132.2	6546.9	913.8	−86.0
Organised Tours	4008.9	4433.3	4026.1	3701.9	5427.0	602.4	−88.9
Entertainment	2488.3	3201.8	3204.4	3028.9	2928.9	564.7	−80.7
Domestic Airfares	2419.2	2545.0	2629.3	2524.1	2239.7	175.7	−92.2
International Airfares	2557.4	3612.3	3368.8	3786.1	4221.0	577.3	−86.3
Medical	2142.7	2955.5	3040.1	2860.6	2928.9	346.5	−88.2
Fuel	622.1	656.8	575.2	588.9	258.4	18.7	−92.8
Sports	207.4	246.3	246.5	252.4	172.3	N/A	N/A
Miscellaneous	1658.9	1806.2	1479.0	1262.0	344.6	165.8	−51.9

Source: Tourism Satellite Account, DOSM.

2019 report, shopping, accommodation, and food and beverages (F&B) ranked among the top-3 expenditures, followed by local transportation, organised tours, entertainment, domestic and international airfares, medical, and lastly fuel, sports, and miscellaneous. In July 2019, the Malaysian government launched the Visit Malaysia Year campaign — Visit Truly Asia Malaysia 2020, with the goal of attracting 30 million tourists and RM 100 billion revenues. The focus will be on ecotourism, arts, and culture. The promotion of tourism was meant to benefit more than 194 industries that are involved in the value chain of the tourism sector (DOSM, Q12020).

Nonetheless, the campaign was ceased due to the pandemic and the tourist arrivals had contracted from 26.1 million (2019) to 4.3 million (2020), causing a drastic drop of 85.3% in tourist revenues from RM 86 billion to RM 12 billion. Table 6 shows clearly that tourism was booming for years before the pandemic struck. The value chain was disrupted and all tourism expenditure components shrank by 80.7–92.8% in 2020. Of all, tourists from Singapore recorded as the highest in total expenditure with RM 2.70 billion (–83.5%), followed by Indonesia with RM 1.95 billion (–77.9%), China RM 1.81 billion (–85.8%), India RM 0.74 billion (–70%), and Thailand RM 0.58 billion (–79.3%).

Evidently, the widespread MCOs (MCO1.0 and MCO2.0) have almost seized the domestic tourism activities.[5] The worst hit sub-sectors are the food and beverages, followed by transportation and storage (DOSM, Q42020).[6] The DOSM did a national survey on March 2020, suggesting that the COVID-19 pandemic has changed Malaysian behaviour in consumption and spending. The total household expenditure dropped significantly to RM 2,868 per month during the MCO, compared to pre-COVID-19 figures of RM 6,398 per month in 2019. Examining further the different income groups, it was observed the B40 and M40 groups reduced their expenditures by approximately 50%, whereas the T20 figure dropped by almost two-thirds.[7] If such a declining trend of

---

[5] During CMCO (May–September 2020), strict MCOs were relaxed. The domestic tourism sector experienced a pick-up. However, after the spike of coronavirus cases in October, the recovery of domestic tourism sector turned back. Until March 2021, there was no sign of recovery in tourism.

[6] https://www.dosm.gov.my/v1/index.php?r=column/cthemeByCat&cat=100&bul_id=Y1 MyV2tPOGNsVUtnRy9SZGdRQS84QT09&menu_id=TE5CRUZCblh4ZTZMODZIbm k2aWRRQT09.

[7] Malaysian households are categorised into three different income groups: Top 20% (T20), Middle 40% (M40), and Bottom 40% (B40).

consumption continues, the sinking demand for tourism activities is inevitable.

5. Pandemic Effect on Hotel Industry

The hotel industry is one of the main pillars of the tourism sector, which employs about 3.6 million personnel and is a key contributor to Malaysia's GDP (Malaysian Associations of Hotels (MAH), 2021). But the COVID-19 outbreak and the following MCOs (MCO 1.0 and MCO 2.0) across the country in March 2020 and January 2021, have put the hotel industry on the verge of collapse.

A total of 170,085 room cancellations were reported during the period of 11 January–16 April 2020 and thereby caused a loss of RM 68 million in the Malaysian hotel industry. The details of the hotel rooms' cancellation and the associated losses during the period are as reported in Table 7. Of all, Kuala Lumpur, Sabah, and Pulau Pinang suffered the largest losses. In addition to room cancellation, the hotel workforce experienced the worst hit. Based on a sample of 54,299 employees associated with Malaysia's hotel sector, 2,041 workers had lost their jobs, 5,054 faced salary-cuts, and further 9,973 employees were forced to go on unpaid leave (Foo *et al.*, 2020).

In addition, the statistics of state-wise foreign and domestic hotel guests in the period of January–September 2020 are presented in Table 8. The hotel sector recorded an average of 34% and 78% drop in domestic and foreign guests, respectively. Tourist hotspots like Kuala Lumpur, Melaka, and Sabah experienced the largest contraction of hotel guests. The drop in the number of guest arrivals to the hotel sector induced a loss of RM 22.7 million from domestic and RM 4.6 million from foreign guests, which can be directly attributed to the national closure policy and movement controls.

Due to the adverse consequences of the pandemic, the hotel industry in Malaysia has been forced to take a number of responses such as retrenchment, bankruptcy, and temporary or permanent closures of the business (see Awan *et al.*, 2020; Mahalingam, 2020a; Chin, 2020a, 2020b). During the MCO 2.0, the number of daily infections had increased

Table 7: Severity of room's cancellation in Malaysia, January–April 2020.

Rank	State	Room Cancellations	Losses Due to Room Cancellations (RM)
1	Kuala Lumpur	55,050	23,021,301
2	Sabah	32,392	11,550,605
3	Pulau Pinang	17,753	8,908,000
4	Selangor	22,929	7,212,048
5	Negeri Sembilan	13,534	6,690,500
6	Johor	18,455	5,636,470
7	Kedah	3239	3,291,500
8	Perak	2403	1,022,289
9	Melaka	4074	690,499
10	Pahang	180	144,628
11	Sarawak	76	22,525
Total		**170,085**	**68,190,364**

Source: Malaysian Association of Hotels (2020).

Table 8: Hotel guests in Malaysia, January 2019–September 2020.

| Locality | Domestic | | % | Foreigner | | % | Total (%) |
	2019	2020	19/20	2019	2020	19/20	19/20
Kuala Lumpur	5,205,761	3,384,538	–35	7,387,197	1,572,097	–79	–61
Putrajaya	219,012	147,996	–32	127,551	20,433	–84	–51
Selangor	1,873,175	1,283,600	–31	1,133,905	289,285	–74	–48
Penang	2,362,571	1,666,948	–29	2,278,943	519,390	–77	–53
Perak	1,880,346	821,117	–56	227,490	53,501	–76	–59
Kedah	1,734,966	1,570,750	–9	1,158,453	374,191	–68	–33
Perlis	118,748	81,622	–31	4,993	980	–80	–33
N. Sembilan	1,418,331	810,262	–43	365,845	62,062	–83	–51
Melaka	2,060,516	955,651	–54	1,112,265	180,079	–84	–64
Johor	3,283,696	2,410,640	–27	1,731,883	416,625	–76	–44
Pahang	5,859,633	4,947,016	–16	2,241,279	498,507	–78	–33
Terengganu	1,230,903	994,382	–19	161,771	18,808	–88	–27

Table 8: (*Continued*)

Locality	Domestic		%	Foreigner		%	Total (%)
	2019	2020	19/20	2019	2020	19/20	19/20
Kelantan	791,671	455,905	–42	39,380	4,216	–89	–45
Peninsular Malaysia	**28,039,329**	**19,530,427**	**–30**	**17,970,955**	**4,010,174**	**–78**	**–49**
Sabah	3,094,361	1,155,289	–63	2,264,068	482,746	–79	–69
Labuan f.t	304,185	210,216	–31	55,399	20,034	–64	–36
Sarawak	2,985,685	1,826,258	–39	408,471	93,963	–77	–43
Whole Malaysia	**34,423,560**	**22,722,190**	**–34**	**20,698,893**	**4,606,917**	**–78**	**–50**

Source: Tourism Malaysia (based on Hotel Survey).

drastically. From March 2020 to January 2021, around 100 hotels closed operations affecting over 7,000 employees (MAH, 2021). In 2020, the hotel industry alone lost RM 6.5 billion and the industry is set to lose on average RM 300 million in revenues for every 2 weeks due to the implementation of MCO 2.0 since early January 2021 (MAH, 2021),[8] even though the industry had earlier set an ambitious target to achieve 33% growth in 2020 (Mahalingam, 2020).

6. Pandemic's Effect on Aviation Industry

The pandemic dealt a severe blow to the aviation industry globally, resulting in a battle for survival in a year dubbed "the worst year in aviation history" by the International Air Transport Association (IATA). IATA estimates that the global airlines would have suffered a loss of USD 118.5 billion (RM 481 billion) in 2020, or USD 66 for every passenger carried, and a further loss of USD 38.7 billion in 2021. The financial status is predicted to improve but not before the end of 2021. To contain the COVID-19 outbreak, many countries across the world are enforcing international travel restrictions. These international travel restrictions are unprecedented and have a significant damaging effect on the tourism

---

[8] https://www.hotels.org.my/press/34167-cry-of-despair-from-the-hotel-industry-hotel-industry-in-serious-need-of-immediate-rescue.

Table 9: Changes of seats and international destinations in ASEAN, 2019–2020.

Airport	2020 Rank	Number of Destinations		% Change	Number of Seats		% Change
		2019	2020		2019	2020	
Bangkok	1	165	60	–63.6	3.11	0.22	–92.8
Manila	2	59	33	–44.1	1.41	0.12	–91.8
Singapore	3	163	44	–73.0	3.97	0.15	–96.3
Jakarta	4	44	33	–25.0	0.97	0.08	–91.2
Ho Chi Minh	5	53	12	–77.4	0.87	0.06	–92.7
Kuala Lumpur	**6**	**129**	**44**	**–65.9**	**2.64**	**0.11**	**–95.8**
Myanmar	7	29	10	–65.5	0.29	0.01	–95.1
Phnom Penh	8	40	21	–47.5	0.40	0.02	–95.5
Vientiane	9	22	5	–77.3	0.14	0.01	–93.5
Bandar Sri Begawan	10	31	5	–83.9	0.13	0.01	–94.0

Source: Reproduced from MAVCOM.

industry (Gössling *et al.*, 2020). The government of Malaysia has also closed borders and restricted international travel, particularly from the high-risk countries.

During January 2020–2021, the airline industry almost stopped its flight operation to and from Malaysia. The plummeted travel demand put the airline industry on the brink of bankruptcy (Foo *et al.*, 2020). Table 9 shows that high numbers of passengers have been reported to change seats and international destinations in ASEAN, including Malaysia. The Kuala Lumpur International Airport's (KLIA) air connectivity ranked sixth among ASEAN in 2020, which is a drop from the third place in 2019. The decline rates of demand due to flight changes were about 91.2–96.3%. In December 2020, Malaysian Aviation Commission (MAVCOM) fore-casted that the revenue-at-risk for Malaysian and foreign carriers operating out of the country is at a higher degree, i.e. RM 14.3 billion and RM 6.7 billion, respectively, compared with the previous estimates of RM 11.3 billion and RM 4.6 billion.

The aviation regulator (MAVCOM), then again, was predicting passenger traffic in 2020 to contract by between 72.8% and 75.7% year on

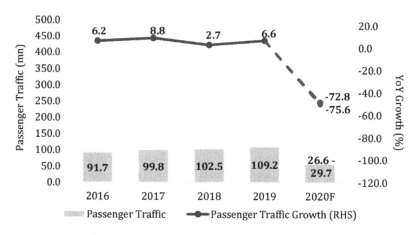

Figure 6: Passenger traffic in Malaysia, 2016–2020.

Source: MAVCOM.

year (y-o-y), which translates into between 26.6 million and 29.7 million passengers (see Figure 6), given the expected lower load factor and longer period of seat capacity recovery by airlines. Major airlines in Malaysia, namely Malaysia Airlines Bhd (MAS), AirAsia Group Bhd and its long-haul affiliate AirAsia X Bhd (AAX), and Malindo Airways Sdn Bhd have also shed thousands of jobs after grounding most of their planes following the MCO in March 2020 to preserve cash flow. AirAsia Japan became the first airline casualty of the pandemic within the AirAsia group to cease operations in the early October 2020. AirAsia, Malindo Air, and Malaysia Airlines have imposed staff salary cuts, ranging from 10% to 100% (Foo *et al.*, 2020). Further, to reduce management cost, Malaysia Airlines has asked their 13,000 employees to take voluntary unpaid leave starting April 2020, when the COVID-19 situation deteriorated (Mustapha *et al.*, 2020). Similarly, AirAsia, a low-cost airline, planned massive lay-offs, including 60% of the cabin crew and pilots (Mustapha *et al.*, 2020).

At the same time, Malaysia Airports Holdings Bhd (MAHB) was also in dire business troubles. MAHB, which manages 39 airports in the country, swung to a net loss of RM 431.17 million for the cumulative 9 months ended on 30 September 2020, from a net profit of RM 507.53 million in 2019. This was mainly due to a significant decrease of 58.6% annual revenue, in tandem with a 65.5% contraction in passenger movements due to global travel restrictions under the pandemic.

7. Scenarios for Post-Pandemic Tourism Recovery

Despite the substantial loss in the tourism sector due to the novel coronavirus pandemic, UNWTO predicts the future prospects of global tourism recovery to be at the second half of 2021, whereas the return to the 2019 levels could take 2.5 to 4 years (UNWTO, 2020a). Experts have considered travel restrictions as the main barrier weighing on the recovery of international tourism, along with slow virus containment and low consumer confidence (UNWTO, 2020a). The three potential scenarios of global tourism recovery proposed by UNWTO are presented in Figure 7. Scenario 1 indicates recovery in 2.5 years (by mid-2023); Scenario 2 indicates recovery in 3 years (by end of 2023); whereas Scenario 3 indicates recovery in 4 years (by end of 2024). The gradual rollout of COVID-19 vaccine will eventually lead to easing of any movement control and thereby has a potential to induce a higher consumer confidence (UNWTO, 2020b). These in turn will help in the gradual normalisation of travel demand and hence recovery of the tourism industry.

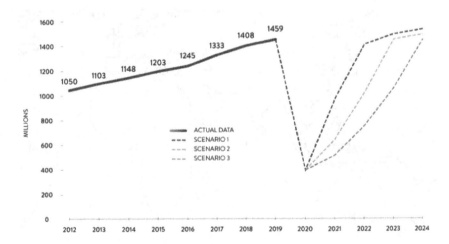

Figure 7: Global international tourist arrivals: Scenarios for 2021–2024 (millions).

Source: UNWTO World Tourism Barometer and Statistical Annex, January 2021.

In Malaysia, financial aid to support the tourism sector takes place in phases. At the early stage of the pandemic, the government announced different incentives such as tax concession, postponement of loan repayment to banks, wage subsidy programme (Foo *et al.*, 2020), discount vouchers of RM 100 per person (Karim *et al.*, 2020), and an RM 30 million fund allocation to the Tourism Board (Medina, 2020). However, these incentives seem insufficient to treat the severe wounds of the tourism industry.

In November 2020, the Ministry of Tourism, Arts, and Culture (MOTAC) responded to market appeals with a Stimulus Recovery Plan (SRP) that aims to restore confidence to travel, revive domestic tourism, and maximise resources. The recovery plan focuses on strategic collaborations and smart partnerships with domestic players like airline companies, tourism-related agencies including services/hospitality, transportation, and private companies as well as collaborations with non-government organisations (NGOs) such as the MAH and Malaysia Budget Hotel Association (MyBHA). Under the SRP programme, airlines, hotels, transport companies, and other operators are to cooperate and offer joint travel packages. Vouchers/discounts/cash rebates will be offered to bring direct impacts on the domestic travel consumptions.

At the same time, domestic tourism programmes are promoted using digital technology through online orders and purchases, mobile applications, and the redemption of cash e-vouchers. This will reduce costs for businesses and visitors and make the country's tourist industry more competitive. All in all, the SRP strategy is to inject resources into domestic tourism and restore the trust of domestic tourists. Less hope was given to international tourists as the international tourism recovery remains slow due to global uncertainties and travel constraints.

The efforts and effectiveness of SRP were unfortunately halted by early 2021, when MCO 2.0 was reimposed on 11 January 2021 due to the third wave of COVID-19 outbreak. What remains positive is the arrival of 312,390 doses of vaccines (Pfizer–BioNTech) in February 2021 that will set into motion the National COVID-19 Immunisation Programme. The first phase of immunisation is scheduled from 26 February–April for frontline personnel, including those from the Health Ministry, Malaysian Armed Forces, Royal Malaysia Police, Civil Defence Force, and Malaysian

Volunteer Department. The second phase is then scheduled from April–August for senior citizens aged 60 and above and vulnerable groups with morbidity issues, as well as persons with disabilities. Finally, the third phase is to be from May 2021–February 2022 for those aged 18 and above.

According to the annual Economic and Monetary Review of Bank Negara Malaysia (March 2021), the Malaysian economy is projected to return to 2019 pre–pandemic levels by the middle of 2021, where annual GDP may expand by 6–7.5%. Similarly, in a statement released on 17 March 2021, the International Monetary Fund projected that the Malaysian economy is set to recover in 2021 with economic growth projected at 6.5%, driven by a strong recovery in manufacturing and construction. It is thus foreseen that when the pandemic eases and economic activities reactivate, earnings in tourism and its value chains will rebound. Market confidence will boost consumption after the restrictive lockdowns are removed, and airline passenger numbers would have recovered gradually. New promotion of tourism programmes could also spur travel demand in both domestic and international segments. If such projection is accurate, we would expect Malaysian tourism to rebuild at a pace aligned with UNWTO's Scenario 1 (before or by 2023). However, the recovery of Malaysian tourism, at the present stage, is still questionable on account of the slow progress of the vaccine programme and possible new waves of infection outbreaks across the states.

8. Conclusion and Policy Implications

The COVID-19 crisis has witnessed a huge contraction in tourism-related sectors due to travel restrictions and travel risk aversion behaviour globally. This chapter has offered estimates on the impacts on Malaysia tourism since the global outbreak of COVID-19. Like other tourism destinations, international travel restriction policy has prohibited the arrival of foreign visitors and thereby shaken the Malaysian tourism sector. Local travel restrictions such as MCOs have dampened domestic economic activities following the suspension of operations by non-essential service providers and a lower operating capacity of manufacturing firms. It further reduces social and recreational activities and hence affects the entire tourism value chain.

At the same time, budget deficits and national debts of Malaysia have enlarged following fiscal expansion to finance the economic stimulus and rescue plans. Yet, encouraging news on vaccines has boosted hopes for tourism recovery, though many challenges remain, as the sector is expected to be in life-support mode until the pandemic retreats and travel restrictions ease. However, it remains unclear on when and to what extent the whole economic, and tourism, activities will be fully recovered, due to the availability, affordability, and effectiveness of vaccines. As of December 2020, over 73 million people have been infected with corona-virus, and more than 1.6 million people have died globally. Vaccines have been developed and are already being distributed in Canada, China, Russia, the UK, the US, and ASEAN, including Malaysia. While such efforts are expected to change the trajectory of the pandemic, the distribution process still faces significant hurdles, including complex logistical challenges. It was reported that about 48% of all vaccine doses administered so far have gone to just 16% of the world's population in high-income countries (Our World in Data, 2021). At the same time, there are estimates that 90% of the population in 67 countries will not be able to receive a COVID-19 vaccine in 2021. In addition, global uncertainties remain high and new waves of the pandemic are rising due to possible virus mutations and policy inefficiency, which will affect the recovery process of tourism and sub-sectors in Malaysia.

Despite the above uncertainties, the tourism sector needs to be prepared for the return of the tourists. The government and the sector have to derive strategies to enhance biosafety measures along the entire domestic and overseas tourism value chains. This should include destinations, restaurants and cafes, and transport facilities such as tour buses and airports. In addition, consideration should be given to speed up the vaccination programme, and the use of vaccine certificate for workers and visitors (or request for extra COVID testing or additional stringent precautions to be imposed on whoever is without a vaccine certificate). While there isn't any global COVID-secure standard, we need to review respective practices in our main markets so that the tourists will have the confidence to visit Malaysia — an important social psychology of tourists (Guan *et al.*, 2021). Having the above in place, we should embark in proactive marketing at key overseas tourism markets.

Other than short-term measures, the government needs to develop a long-term strategic plan to ensure the sector is more resilient and able to withstand future turbulent environments, such as pandemics, wars, or extreme climate change-induced disasters. One of the key strategies is to build up the capacity of digitalisation and its relevant value chains. The sector has to move beyond merely adoption of digital technologies, such as Virtual Realities and artificial intelligence, for marketing purposes. We have to venture into digital content development, novel business models, and profit model innovations, just to name a few, echoing calls from other recent studies (Chan *et al.*, 2020, 2021).

Acknowledgement

This work is partly supported by the United Kingdom Newton Fund Programme, Economic and Social Research Council and Arts and Humanities Research Council UK [ES/P010377/1] and supported by RCUK SEA Newton-Ungku Omar Fund [304/PSOSIAL/650874/E121]. Special thanks to Abdul Saqib for the early draft of the analysis. The authors are also grateful to the anonymous referees of this chapter. Any remaining errors and omissions are our own.

References

Akin, L., and Gözel, M. G. (2020). Understanding dynamics of pandemics. *Turkish Journal of Medical Sciences*, 50(SI-1): 515–519.

Awan, M. I., Shamim, A., and Ahn, J. (2020). Implementing 'cleanliness is half of faith' in re-designing tourists, experiences and salvaging the hotel industry in Malaysia during COVID-19 pandemic. *Journal of Islamic Marketing*. doi: 10.1108/JIMA-08-2020-0229.

Chan, J. H., Chen, S-Y, Piterou, A., Khoo, S. L., Lean, H. H., and Hashim, I. H. M. (2021). An innovative social enterprise: Roles and issues from an arts hub in a World Heritage Site in Malaysia. *City, Culture and Society*, 25 (June 2021): 100396.

Chan, J. H., Hashim, I. H. M., Khoo, S. L., Lean, H. H., and Piterou, A. (2020). Entrepreneurial orientation of traditional and modern cultural organisations:

Cases in George Town UNESCO World Heritage Site. *Cogent Social Science*, 6(1): 1810889.

Chin, C. (16 April 2020a). COVID-19: Eligible hotels in Malaysia to be certified 'clean and safe', says MAH. *The Star*. https://www.thestar.com.my/lifestyle/travel/2020/04/16/COVID-19-eligible-hotels-in-malaysia-to-be-certified-039clean-and-safe039-says-mah.

Chin, C. (1 April 2020b). How the Malaysian hotel and travel industry is helping COVID-19 frontliners? *The Star*. https://www.thestar.com.my/lifestyle/travel/2020/04/01/how-malaysian-hotels-and-travel-companies-are-helping-COVID-19-frontliners.

Delgado, D., Wyss Quintana, F., Perez, G., Sosa Liprandi, A., Ponte-Negretti, C., Mendoza, I., and Baranchuk, A. (2020). Personal safety during the COVID-19 pandemic: Realities and perspectives of healthcare workers in Latin America. *International Journal of Environmental Research and Public Health*, 17(8): 2798.

Department of Statistics Malaysia. (Q1-2020). Economic performance for first quarter 2020. https://www.dosm.gov.my/v1/index.php?r=column/cthemeByCat&cat=100&bul_id=R09wdGZSektvNmw5T1VCeVphNXRqdz09&menu_id=TE5CRUZCblh4ZTZMODZIbmk2aWRRQT09.

Department of Statistics Malaysia. (Q3-2020). Economic performance for third quarter 2020. https://www.dosm.gov.my/v1/index.php?r=column/cthemeByCat&cat=100&bul_id=ZlRNZVRDUmNzRFFQQ29lZXJoV0UxQT09&menu_id=TE5CRUZCblh4ZTZMODZIbmk2aWRRQT09.

Department of Statistics Malaysia. (Q4-2020). Economic performance fourth quarter 2020. https://www.dosm.gov.my/v1/index.php?r=column/cthemeByCat&cat=100&bul_id=Y1MyV2tPOGNsVUtnRy9SZGdRQS84QT09&menu_id=TE5CRUZCblh4ZTZMODZIbmk2aWRRQT09.

Foo, L. P., Chin, M. Y., Tan, K. L., and Phuah, K. T. (2020). The impact of COVID-19 on tourism industry in Malaysia. *Current Issues in Tourism*, 1–5.

Gössling, S., Scott, D., and Hall, C. M. (2020). Pandemics, tourism and global change: A rapid assessment of COVID-19. *Journal of Sustainable Tourism*, 1–20. doi: 10.1080/09669582.2020.1865387.

Guan, J., Chan, J. H., Bi, J., and Qi, X. (2022). Cultural proximity, destination familiarity and tourists' sense of away-from-home (SAFH). *Journal of Destination Marketing and Management*, 23, 100670.

Karim, W., Haque, A., Anis, Z., and Ulfy, M. A. (2020). The movement control order (MCO) for COVID-19 crisis and its impact on tourism and hospitality sector in Malaysia. *International Tourism and Hospitality Journal*, 3(2): 1–7.

Khalid, U., Okafor, L. E., and Burzynska, K. (2021). Does the size of the tourism sector influence the economic policy response to the COVID-19 pandemic? *Current Issues in Tourism*, 1–20.

Mahalingam, E. (26 March 2020). Hotel sector hit by COVID-19. *The Star*. https://www.thestar.com.my/business/business-news/2020/03/26/hotel-sector-hit-by-COVID-19.

Malaysian Association of Hotels (MAH). (4 February 2020). Cry of despair from the hotel industry: Hotel industry in serious need of immediate rescue. https://www.hotels.org.my/press/34167-cry-of-despair-from-the-hotel-industry-hotel-industry-in-serious-need-of-immediate-rescue.

Medina, A. F. (19 March 2020). Malaysia issues stimulus package to combat COVID-19 impact. *ASEAN Briefing*. Retrieved on 29 January 2021 from https://www.aseanbriefing.com/news/malaysia-issues-stimulus-package-combat-COVID-19-impact/.

Mustapha, N. N. S. N., Yazid, M. F. M., and Shamsudin, M. F. (2020). How airline industry may rise post COVID-19 pandemic. *Journal of Postgraduate Current Business Research*, 1(1). http://abrn.asia/ojs/index.php/jpcbr/article/view/100.

OECD. (2020). Tourism trends and policies. Retrieved on 3 February 2021 from https://www.oecd-ilibrary.org/docserver/6b47b985en.pdf?expires=1614750050&id=id&accname=guest&checksum=70C96DB778144C21CFE98CE37B9D4401.

Our World in Data. (2021). Coronavirus (COVID-19) vaccinations. https://ourworldindata.org/COVID-vaccinations.

Tourism Malaysia. (2020). Malaysia tourism performance January–September 2020. https://www.tourism.gov.my/media/view/malaysia-s-tourism-performance-records-negative-growth-of-78-6-from-jan-sep-2020#.

UNWTO. (2019). International tourism highlights, 2019 edition. Retrieved on 25 February 2021 from https://www.e-unwto.org/doi/pdf/10.18111/9789284421152.

UNWTO. (2020a). COVID-19: UNWTO calls on tourism to be part of recovery plans. Retrieved on 29 January 2021 from https://www.unwto.org/news/COVID-19-unwto-calls-on-tourism-to-be-part-of-recovery-plans.

UNWTO. (2020b). International tourist numbers could fall 60–80% in 2020. UNWTO Report. Retrieved on 29 January 2021 from https://www.unwto.org/news/COVID-19-international-tourist-numbers-could-fall-60-80-in-2020.

Zhang, H., Song, H., Wen, L., and Liu, C. (2021). Forecasting tourism recovery amid COVID-19. *Annals of Tourism Research*, 103–149.

About the Authors

Tze-Haw Chan presently serves at Graduate School of Business, Universiti Sains Malaysia. He received his PhD in International Finance, MSc in Financial Economics, and BEcon in the years 2009, 2001, and 1999, respectively. Previously, he has been the recipient of Prime Minister's Perdana Research Fellowship (2009–2012), the founder of the Centre for Globalisation and Sustainability Research (CGSR, 2008) in Multimedia University, and senior data analyst in International Medical University (IMU, 2004–2006). Dr Chan has contributed more than 80 publications in the area of East Asian Economics, International Finance, and Applied Econometrics. He is actively involved with consultation projects funded by both public and private sectors like Malaysia Competition Commission (MyCC), Economic Planning Unit (EPU), World Bank, Intel, Silterra, etc. He has supervised more than 30 MBA and 13 PhD candidates. His profile is made available at ResearchGate, Google Scholar, and Academia.

Jin Hooi Chan is associate professor of Sustainable Strategy, Innovation, and Entrepreneurship at Faculty of Business, University of Greenwich, United Kingdom. As a multidisciplinary researcher, he is also a Chartered Engineer and Chartered Environmentalist, with an extensive international experience. He received a PhD degree in Management Studies from Judge Business School, and an MPhil degree in Sustainable Development at University of Cambridge. His research builds on the study of industrial organisation, industrial policy, strategy, innovation, and entrepreneurship. He is active across multiple geographical regions, such as the UK, Europe, Africa, East and South East Asia, and his interests cover various sectors, e.g. sustainability and environment, tourism, cultural and heritage, creative tech, clean-tech, and e-commerce and digital technologies. He publishes at top-tier academic journals, and his books and book chapters are published by internationally reputable publishers. He also writes for policy and practitioners' outlets. He is Principal Investigator and Co-Investigators for major international research projects funded by UK research councils (ESRC & AHRC), European Union, National Natural Science Foundation of China, and National Social Science Foundation of China.

Chapter 6

Financial Stress of Singapore in the Time of COVID-19

Sook-Rei Tan*,‡, Wei-Siang Wang†,§, and Wai-Mun Chia†,¶

*Business School, James Cook University, Singapore
†Economics Department, School of Social Science, Nanyang
Technological University, Singapore
‡sookrei.tan@jcu.edu.au
§wswang@ntu.edu.sg
¶aswmchia@ntu.edu.sg

Abstract

This study extends the existing literature on the use of financial stress index (FSI) to assess the financial condition of Singapore during the COVID-19 crisis. Specifically, a high-frequency FSI is constructed to provide timely analysis which is imperative given the pandemic is still lingering across the globe. There are two main uses of the FSI. First, we use FSI to detect episodes of financial stress and investigate whether Singapore's financial system is facing frailty during the pandemic.

---

*Corresponding author.

145

Second, we use a vector autoregression (VAR) model to analyse the comovement between FSI, COVID-19 indicators, and global financial factors, which shed light on the main drivers underlying Singapore's financial stress since the COVID-19 outbreak. Our findings suggest that (1) excessive stresses were detected during 9 March–21 April 2020, a period that corresponded to the evolution of COVID-19 into a global pandemic as well as the beginning of Singapore's Circuit Breaker period; and (2) the dynamics of Singapore's FSI is more due to the global financial factors than it is to the severity of the domestic COVID-19 condition.

Keywords: Financial stress; financial markets; COVID-19.

1. Introduction

On 11 March 2020, the World Health Organization (WHO) officially declared COVID-19 outbreak as a global pandemic. The COVID-19 crisis transcends beyond a public health issue and has created huge impacts on financial, economic, and social facets. To contain the spread of the coronavirus disease, governments around the world have implemented various preventive measures, such as border control, lockdown, and social distancing that aim to lower mobility and face-to-face contact between people. The unprecedented scale of the disease outbreaks and the worldwide quarantine measures have caused disruptions to almost all business activities which have subsequently led to an upsurge of financial and economic uncertainty and influenced lives of millions of people.

While the economic downside may take a longer time to fully manifest, global financial markets showed signs of tremendous instability when the pandemic first surfaced. For instance, March 2020 marked the record-breaking crash in stock markets — a 26% plunge in Dow Jones Industrial Average (DJIA) occurred within barely 4 trading days, which was the largest fall since the 2008 Global Financial Crisis (GFC) (Mazur *et al.*, 2020). On 20 April 2020, oil prices of the United States (US) turned negative for the first time in history (BBC News, 2020). Figure 1 plots the daily equity flows of six emerging market economies (EMEs)[1] for a 90-day period after three major global financial events. The three events

---

[1]The series is computed by taking the difference between value of equity purchases and value of equity sales by foreigners.

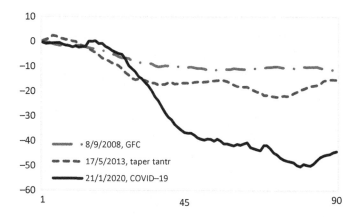

Figure 1: Cumulative daily net equity outflows (in USD billion) from EMEs (India, Indonesia, Philippines, Sri Lanka, Taiwan, Thailand) for a 90-day window during the GFC, Taper Tantrum, and COVID-19.

Source: CEIC, author's calculation.

include the GFC in 2008, the Taper Tantrum resulted from the US Federal Reserve's announcement of Quantitative Easing tapering in 2013, and the ongoing COVID-19 pandemic. The figure shows that withdrawal of equity flows from EMEs during the COVID-19 crisis was much more severe than that of the GFC and Taper Tantrum periods. This implies that financial vulnerabilities of EMEs are likely to aggravate following the adverse capital flow shocks as investors shift their investments towards safer assets, a phenomenon known as flight to quality.

Even though most financial asset prices have already rebounded from the pandemic-induced crashes, experts warned of the increased disconnection between financial market valuations and real economic fundamentals during the COVID-19 period (Jones, 2020; Igan *et al.*, 2020). Given the misty global economic outlook, Singapore as a highly open economy and regional financial hub in ASEAN region is particularly susceptible to external disturbances.

In fact, Singapore's economy has been highly integrated into the world and had previously been confronted with multiple challenges originated from abroad. Most saliently, Singapore was among several Asian countries that were gravely hit by the Severe Acute Respiratory Syndrome (SARS), the predecessor to the current COVID-19 disease caused by the

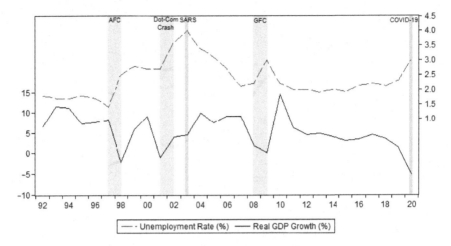

Figure 2:   Overall unemployment rate (right-axis). GDP in chained (2015) dollar, year-on-year growth rate (left-axis).

Source: Singapore Department of Statistics, Manpower Research & Statistics Department.

SARS-related coronaviruses in 2003. As a comparison, Figure 2 shows the overall unemployment rate and real gross domestic product (GDP) growth of Singapore during 1992–2020 that covered multiple regional or global crises, including 1997–1998 Asian Financial Crisis (AFC), 2001–2002 Dot-Com bubble crash, 2003 SARS outbreak, 2008–2009 GFC, and 2020 COVID-19 outbreak. The increase in annual unemployment rate during COVID-19 was on par with GFC, while the decline in real GDP growth was the largest compared to all the precedents, signalling profound economic impact of the COVID-19 pandemic. Such economic uncertainty has led investors to cast doubt on financial resilience in the near future albeit the economy is in mild recovery in early 2021 (Khanna, 2021).

Against such a backdrop, a real-time monitoring and an early warning indicator of financial stress is imperative for policymakers to gauge the domestic financial condition in order to avert or mitigate a potential financial crisis. Financial stress level can also be served as an additional yardstick to determine sign of recovery and appropriate timing to tighten any stimulus packages that are put in place to mitigate the adverse effect of the pandemic on the domestic economy. Thus, leveraging the daily dataset for several key financial sectors, we aim to construct a high-frequency Financial Stress Index (FSI) to give a first-hand analysis of the financial frailty of Singapore.

The objectives of the study are twofold. First, we will identify episodes of financial stress during the early pandemic period (1 January and 21 August 2020) with the daily FSI we constructed for Singapore. Second, using a vector autoregression (VAR) model, we investigate the relationship between Singapore's FSI and two main variables, namely COVID-19 indicators (as represented by daily new cases and government policy stringency index) and global financial factors (as proxied by VIX and US's FSI). Specifically, we want to identify factors that play the most significant role in driving FSI ever since the outbreak of COVID-19 in Singapore.

The rest of this chapter is organised as follows. In Section 2, we present the COVID-19 statistics and highlight key policy responses, both in terms of public health and economic aspects, that have been taken by the Singapore government to tackle COVID-19 thus far. In Section 3, we construct the composite FSI based on stresses of banking, equity, and foreign exchange markets, and identify episodes of financial stress based on the index. We then present our VAR model and the impulse responses of Singapore's FSI facing a COVID-19 or a global factor shock in Section 4. And the last section concludes.

2. Policy Responses of Singapore Government

2.1 *Singapore's COVID-19 cases*

Singapore's first COVID-19 case, a 66-year-old man from Wuhan was confirmed on 23 January 2020. On 4 February, first local community case was identified at a Chinese medical hall Yong Thai Hang. Other earliest clusters include Life Church and Missions Singapore cluster identified on 8 February, Grace Assembly of God church and Seletar Aerospace Heights construction site clusters emerged on 12 February, SAFRA Jurong cluster was reported on 5 March, as well as several key clusters found at S11 Dormitory, Westlife Toh Guan, Mustafa Centre, and Sungei

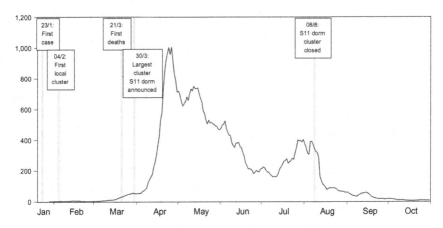

Figure 3:   Daily confirmed COVID-19 cases, rolling 7-day average between 20 January and 31 October 2020.

Source: European CDC COVID-19 situation update worldwide, *Channel NewsAsia* and *The Straits Times*.

Tengah Lodge that were announced between 30 March and 4 April. As shown in Figure 3, the number of COVID-19 cases began to surge since March 2020, of which many infections in later period were concentrated in foreign worker dormitories. In fact, the largest cluster identified was the S11 Dormitory cluster in Punggol that took around 5 months of surveillance and mass-testing before it was finally announced cleared on 8 August. At the time of writing, Singapore's COVID-19 curve seems to plateau since October 2020.

2.2 *Coronavirus containment measures*

Like many other affected places, Singapore saw an exponential rise in infections shortly after its first local community case occurred in February 2020. As a surge in infections could potentially stretch the capacity of the health-care system, Singapore has implemented various preventive measures that aim to restrain people's mobility and interactive social activities. Figure 4 plots the government response stringency index collected from OxCGRT database (Hale *et al.*, 2020). The stringency policy index quantifies

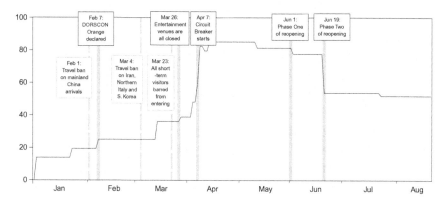

Figure 4: Government response stringency index between 1 January 2020 and 21 August 2020.

Source: Hale *et al.*'s (2020) Oxford COVID-19 Government Response Tracker (OxCGRT, *Channel NewsAsia* and *The Straits Times*).

strictness of disease control policy imposed by the government to combat COVID-19 transmission. Specifically, the dataset provides comprehensive daily information on the rigour of government-imposed containment actions on the following: (1) school closure, (2) workplace closure, (3) cancellation of public events, (4) restrictions on gatherings, (5) closure of public transport, (6) stay at home requirements, (7) restrictions on internal movement, (8) international travel controls, and (9) provision of public information campaigns. In the following paragraph, we mainly highlight travel restrictions and other COVID-19 containment measures that are congruent with the rise in the stringency index in Figure 4.

In terms of cross-border activity, on 23 March, not long after WHO's declaration of the pandemic status of COVID-19, all short-term visitors were barred from entering or transiting in Singapore. Furthermore, all returning travellers were required to go on quarantine at dedicated facilities from 9 April onwards. Domestically, the government elevated Disease Outbreak Response System Condition[2] (DORSCON) alert level to Orange, which is the third rank out of four levels (Green, Yellow, Orange,

---

[2]The colour (Green, Yellow, Orange, and Red) of the DORSCON is defined based on the severity and spread of the disease. For each colour, it shows the impact of the disease on

and Red, respectively) and is the first time since the SARS experience in 2003. Under DORSCON Orange, the nature of the outbreak is defined as severe and easily transmittable but still contained. Moderate disruptions to daily activities due to measures such as quarantine, temperature screening, and visitor restrictions at hospitals are to be expected. In the end of March, all religious gatherings were cancelled, while tuition centres and entertainment venues were closed. As cases continued to rise, Singapore followed in the footsteps of many countries to launch its stay-at-home order known as Circuit Breaker from 7 April to 1 June 2020, during which people were only allowed to leave home for exceptional reasons, such as working for essential services, providing assistance to seniors or disabled persons, buying groceries, and so on. When the Circuit Breaker period ended, the country was re-opened in three phases, namely *Phase One: Safe Reopening* (from 2 to 18 June 2020), *Phase Two: Safe Transition* (from 19 June to 27 December 2020), and *Phase Three: Safe Nation* (from 28 December 2020 to present).

As stated by Janil Puthucheary, the Senior Minister of State for Health on 25 February 2021, Singapore has no intention to exit from *Phase Three* reopening anytime soon and all practices and habits of this phase will remain as "new normal" until the majority of population has been vaccinated and low risk of COVID-19 resurgence is ensured (Lai, 2021). The government has been administering free vaccination for all Singaporean citizens and long-term residents in progressive orders prioritising the elderly and other vulnerable groups as well as healthcare workers in the first tranche. As of 18 April 2021, 1,364,124 have received the first dose and 849,764 people (approximately 14.9% of total population) have completed full vaccination regimen under the nationwide vaccination programme (Ministry of Health, 2021).

2.3 *Key economic policy responses to COVID-19*

During the early pandemic period, the Circuit Breaker enforcement and global supply chain disruption had played havoc on most of the business

---

the community, such as the measures to be taken in daily life, which include temperature screening and border measures, and advice to the public.

Table 1: Quarter-on-quarter seasonally adjusted growth rate of GDP in chained (2015) dollars.

	1Q20	2Q20	3Q20	4Q20	2020
Overall GDP	**−0.6**	**−13.1**	**9.0**	**3.8**	**−5.4**
Goods Producing Industries	7.9	−15.4	11.9	1.8	0.3
Manufacturing	10.5	−7.6	0.7	−1.4	7.3
Construction	−1.5	−65.6	37.5	55.6	−35.9
Services Producing Industries	−3.2	−10.4	5.5	4.1	−6.9
Wholesale & Retail Trade and Transportation & Storage	−1.6	−10.4	2.0	4.1	−9.5
Information & Communications, Finance & Insurance and Professional Services	−2.9	−3.8	3.4	5.1	0.9
Accommodation and Other Services	−7.6	−17.7	12.0	5.7	−12.8

Source: Singapore Department of Statistics.

activities and caused massive layoffs in the local job market. According to the report of the Ministry of Manpower, in August 2020, overall unemployment rate soared to 3.4%, slightly surpassing the 3.3% recorded in September 2009 during the GFC. At the end of 2020, the decline in employment had surpassed the previous largest record seen 20 years ago in AFC, with 166,600 job cuts amid non-residents accounting for most of the employment fall.

Table 1 reports the quarter-on-quarter seasonally adjusted change in real GDP growth for different industries of Singapore. For the whole of 2020, Singapore's economy shrunk by 5.8%. Among all industries, the *Construction* sector and the more tourism-dependent services, such as *Accommodation and Other Services* as well as *Wholesale & Retail Trade and Transportation & Storage* were the hardest-hit industries.

Despite the fact that economic uncertainty continues into 2021, Singapore's economy sees gradual recovery with a projected growth at 4 to 6% by the Ministry of Trade and Industry, thanks to global economic recovery as well as immediate support schemes implemented by the government in response to the COVID-19 crisis.

In this subsection, we will highlight the key fiscal as well as monetary and macro-financial policies rolled out by the government against the COVID-19 as summarised by the International Monetary Fund Policy Tracker (IMF, 2020).

2.3.1 *Fiscal policy*

Several fiscal support packages were announced on 18 February, 6 March, 6 April, 21 April, 26 May, and 17 August 2020, with an amount totalling up to approximately SGD 100 billion. Financial support schemes to households include cash payouts to all Singaporeans and payments to low-income or unemployed individuals. Support to businesses include wage subsidies, rental cost subsidies, enhancement of financing schemes, and additional payments to self-employed and the most affected industries such as aviation, tourism, construction, transportation, arts, and culture. The authorities have also prepared loan capital of SGD 20 billion to help businesses and individuals with cash flow difficulty.

As an extension to FY2020 stimulus package, a narrower budget deficit of SGD 11.01 billion is deployed for COVID-19 Resilience Package under the FY2021 budget. The main focuses of the package are: (1) SGD 4.8 billion healthcare spending, including expenditure for testing, contact tracing, and vaccination, to safeguard public health and support safe reopening; (2) Jobs Support Scheme (SGD 700 million), SGUnited Jobs and Skills Package (SGD 5.4 billion), and COVID-19 Recovery Grant are extended to support workers and businesses where needed; (3) relief funds such as SGD 870 million for aviation sector, SGD 45 million for Arts, Culture, and Sports sectors, and SGD 133 million for COVID-19 Driver Relief Fund, in order to support sectors that are still under stress.

2.3.2 *Monetary and macro-financial policy*[3]

The central bank, Monetary Authority of Singapore (MAS), eased its exchange-rate based monetary policy on 30 March 2020 with a 0% per annum rate of appreciation. Macro-financial policies that targeted mitigating liquidity issue and relaxing regulatory requirement of the financial

---

[3] For more detailed information, please visit the MAS webpage that reports its response to COVID-19, at https://www.mas.gov.sg/regulation/covid-19.

system were also put in place. For instance, on 31 March, the MAS and the financial industry announced a package of measures, including deferring repayment for loans and insurance, to help individuals and small and medium-sized enterprises (SMEs) facing cashflow challenges. A second package put forth on 30 April extended the scope of relief for individuals to a wider range of loan types. On 7 April, the MAS announced adjustments to selected regulatory requirements and supervisory measures, such as lowering banks' capital and liquidity requirements, deferring implementation of regulatory reform, and suspending supervisory measures. On 8 April, the MAS launched a SGD 125 million support package, funded by the Financial Sector Development Fund, to bolster financial services and FinTech capabilities. To ensure USD liquidity in the banking system, on 19 March, a USD 60 billion swap facility was established between the MAS and the US Federal Reserve. On 30 July, the MAS extended the swap facility to the end of March 2021. On 3 September, the MAS announced measures to enhance the banking system's access to SGD and USD liquidity facilities to strengthen banking sector resilience. On 5 October, the MAS and the financial industry extended support for individuals and SMEs that need more time to resume loan repayments. On 12 October, the MAS announced it would provide SGD funding at 0.1% annual interest rate for a 2-year tenor to eligible financial institutions to support their lending to SMEs. On 23 November, the MAS announced that it will provide up to RMB 25 billion (SGD5.1 billion) of funding to banks in order to deepen renminbi liquidity.

In January 2021, the authorities announced that small firms severely impacted by COVID-19 could (1) apply for a Simplified Insolvency Programme for debt restructuring or orderly winding up and (2) enter the Re-Align Framework to renegotiate certain contracts for businesses significantly impacted by COVID-19.

3. Constructing FSI and Identifying Stress Episodes

At the time of writing this chapter, the COVID-19 pandemic is still lingering across the globe, while some countries have seen second/third waves of outbreaks. Therefore, it is important to come up with a measure to closely monitor and quantify the current financial vulnerability given the constantly evolving global pandemic situation. Our objective to build a financial monitoring indicator is closely related to the previous studies of Early Warning System (EWS) that serve the purpose of predicting the onset of financial crises. However, EWS is criticised for treating the crisis as a binary variable (crisis vs. no crisis) and thus failing to measure the intensity of the crisis and even neglecting near miss episodes that did not morph into full-blown crises but still impact the macroeconomy (Borio and Lowe, 2002). To address these drawbacks, FSI — a synthetic variable that is built with market-based indicators of various financial segments — is developed to serve as a continuous measure of financial stress. Well-known FSI indicators include the daily Canadian FSI as developed by Illing and Liu (2006), the weekly Financial Fragility Indicator by Nelson and Perli (2007), and the monthly Kansas City FSI by Hakkio and Keeton (2009) constructed for the US financial system, the financial systemic stress index that incorporates time-varying correlations between different financial market segments for Greece by Louzis and Vouldis (2012) as well as the weekly Composite Indicator of Systemic Stress for Euro area by Hollo *et al.* (2012).

In this chapter, we aim to build the daily FSI for Singapore. Our choice of variables largely follows the FSI construction of the extant literature (see for examples, Melvin and Taylor, 2009; Apostolakis and Papadopoulous, 2014), while also hinging on the availability of daily data of the variables. Our FSI encapsulates six components that cover three key financial sectors:

(1) **Banking sector:** The banking stress is compiled by (a) the banking sector's β, constructed as 12-month rolling covariance of banking stock returns and the overall market returns relative to variance of the overall market returns, (b) the TED spread, spread between 3-month interbank rates and yield on Treasury Bill, and (c) the inverted yield curve measured by the difference between government short-term and long-term Treasury Bill yields.
(2) **Equity market:** The equity market stress comprises both the inverted daily stock returns and the conditional stock market volatility derived from a GARCH $(1,1)^4$ model.

---

[4] Numerous FSI studies have adopted GARCH (1,1) model in deriving time-varying conditional variances of stock and exchange rate returns (Cardarelli *et al.*, 2011; Apostolakis and Papadopulous, 2019), in which its superior predictive performance among a set of

(3) **Foreign exchange market:** The foreign exchange pressure is measured by the time-varying volatility of daily changes of nominal effective exchange rates (NEER) derived from a GARCH (1,1) model.

To aggregate all components and form a single FSI, we use a variance weighted method that is widely adopted in the existing literature (Cardarelli *et al.*, 2009, 2011; Melvin and Taylor, 2009; Apostolakis and Papadopoulous, 2014). All sub-indices are standardised (by subtracting their mean and dividing by their standard deviation) and summed to obtain FSI:

$$FSI = \beta + TED \; spread + Inverted \; yield \; curve + Stock \; returns + Stock \; volatility + NEER \; volatility$$

The series of daily FSI for Singapore between 30 March 2001 and 21 August 2020 is illustrated in Figure 5. The peaks of Singapore's FSI coincided with several crisis episodes, such as 2001 dot-com bubble burst, 2008 GFC, 2011 Black Monday stock market crash, 2015 Chinese stock market turbulence, and the recent COVID-19 crisis. The top panel of Figure 5 shows that the composition of Singapore's FSI varies overtime, in which equity stress is dominant in GFC, whereas the banking sector is the main financial sector affected by the COVID-19 crisis.

We also compare FSI to its trend as derived by Hodrick–Prescott filtering method (with smoothing parameter $\lambda = 6,812$) and define financial stress episodes as periods when FSI exceeds two standard deviations (SD) above its trend. The bottom panel of Figure 5 highlights the stress periods (12 September 2001–26 September 2001, 21 August 2007–2 December 2008, 23 September 2011–10 November 2011, and 9 March 2020–21 April 2020). The latest stress episode has been identified during the COVID-19 period, which is almost a decade away from the previous stress episode identified during the Eurozone crisis in 2011. Referring to the bottom panel of Figure 5, the peaked FSI fell on 23 March 2020 at 13.36, which surpasses slightly the peaked FSI during Eurozone crisis on 26 September 2011 at 13.13 but is below the GFC's peak at 20.58 on 27 October 2008.

---

volatility models has been supported by a number of studies (Hansen and Lunde, 2005; Sharma, 2015).

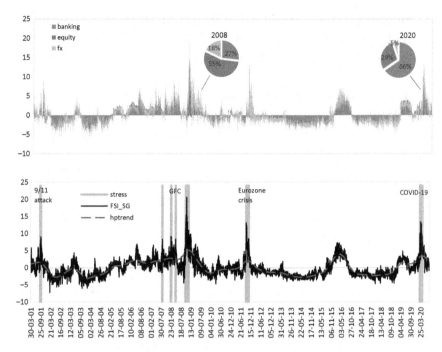

Figure 5: Singapore's FSI for banking, equity and foreign exchange markets during 30 March 2001 and 21 August 2020 (top). Episodes of financial stress defined as FSI exceed two SD above trend (bottom).

4. FSI, COVID-19, and Global Financial Cycle

In the previous section, we provided evidence of stress for Singapore's financial system at the time of COVID-19. In this section, we will further analyse the impact of two main factors, COVID-19 indicators and global financial factors, on Singapore's FSI.

4.1 *Data*

To represent shocks of COVID-19, we focus on two variables: (1) the number of daily confirmed COVID-19 cases (*NEW_CASE*) that captures directly the prevalence of the pandemic, and (2) government response stringency index (*STRINGENCY*), which represents the indirect shock induced by the pandemic due to policy measures in attempts to contain the disease spread. Besides, Singapore as a small open economy is susceptible

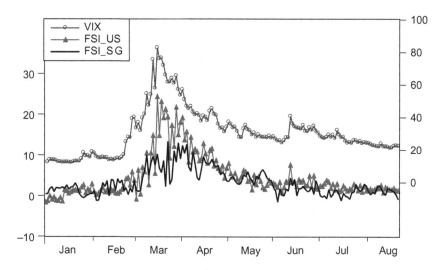

Figure 6: VIX (right-axis); the US's and Singapore's FSI (left-axis), between 1 January 2020 and 21 August 2020.

to the global financial cycle, a notion brought up by Rey (2015) that suggests the increased comovement across the integrated financial system globally that follows the monetary policy stance of the central economy, particularly the US. We will proxy the global factors using Chicago Board Options Exchange's Volatility Index (*VIX*) and FSI of the US (*FSI_US*) constructed using the same method as described in Section 3, given the global prominence status of the US's financial system. The dynamics of Singapore's FSI (*FSI_SG*), *VIX*, and *FSI_US* since January 2020 are shown in Figure 6. A quick look at the figure suggests correlations across the three series in most periods.

4.2 *Empirical method*

A vector autoregression (VAR) method is used to model the interdependencies among the key variables:

$$y_t = c + \sum_{j}^{p} A_j y_{t-j} + u_t$$

where $y = [DNEW\_CASE, DSTRINGENCY, DVIX, DFSI\_US, DFSI\_SG]^T$ and p denotes the maximum number of lagged observations included in the model.[5] Analyses of impulse responses and forecast error variance decomposition have been carried out under the framework of VAR.

4.3 *Empirical results*

We present impulse responses of Singapore's FSI for a 10-day period facing one-SD shocks of all the other variables in Figure 7 and Table 2.[6] The figure suggests that global financial factors, i.e. *VIX* and *FSI_US*, are the significant factors underlying the dynamics of *FSI_SG*, whereas both the *STRINGENCY* and new COVID-19 cases have no significant impact on *FSI_SG*. The immediate responses of *FSI_SG* to *VIX* and *FSI_US* are positive, but the responses afterwards oscillate between positive and negative signs, signalling the volatile market responses towards external shocks. As such, we take the 10-day average of the impulse responses as presented in Table 2, which shows that *FSI_SG* responds positively to the shocks of *VIX* and *FSI_SG* with mean responses of 0.0386 and 0.0303, respectively.

We further perform forecast error variance decomposition in order to quantify the amount of information each variable contributes to *FSI_SG*. Table 3 tabulates the variance decomposition of *FSI_SG* to all other variables for a 10-day period. Taking the average of the 10-day variance decomposition, we find that *VIX* and *FSI_SG* contribute to as high as 8.69% and 19.09% of the forecast error (S.E.) of *FSI_SG*, respectively, corroborating the importance of global factors in driving Singapore's domestic financial stress.

---

[5] Null hypothesis of unit root is not rejected in ADF test for each variable, and all variables enter VAR in their first differences (denoted by *Dvariable*). We choose lag length, $p = 3$, according to Akaike information criterion. Results can be made available upon request.

[6] We impose Cholesky ordering: *DNEW_CASE, DSTRINGENCY, DVIX, DFSI_US, DFSI_SG*, in which the first variable is assumed to be the most exogenous and the last is the least exogenous.

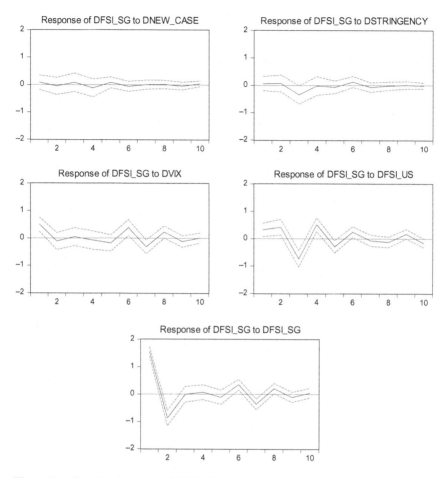

Figure 7: Impulse responses of *DFSI_SG* to Cholesky (d.f. adjusted) one-SD innovations of each variable.

4.4 *Discussion about the empirical findings*

The empirical findings shed light on the main driver of Singapore's financial stress during the earlier phase of COVID-19 pandemic. In particular, our results suggest that the number of COVID-19 cases and the containment measures taken by the government to deal with the COVID-19 outbreak are not the main factors underlying Singapore's financial stress dynamics during this period. Rather, Singapore's financial stress

Table 2:   Impulse responses of *DFSI_SG* to Cholesky (d.f. adjusted) one-SD innovations of each variable.

Period	DNEW_CASE	DSTRINGENCY	DVIX	DFSI_US	DFSI_SG
1	0.0874	0.0588	0.5057	0.3253	1.5591
	(0.1311)	(0.1309)	(0.1279)	(0.1234)	(0.0864)
2	–0.0503	0.0686	–0.1146	0.4182	–0.8757
	(0.1573)	(0.1551)	(0.1556)	(0.1455)	(0.1377)
3	0.0853	–0.3491	0.0528	–0.7322	–0.0060
	(0.1682)	(0.1663)	(0.1651)	(0.1482)	(0.1419)
4	–0.1182	–0.0201	–0.0722	0.5178	0.0706
	(0.1625)	(0.1709)	(0.1690)	(0.1255)	(0.1354)
5	0.0855	–0.0701	–0.1784	–0.2894	–0.1156
	(0.0995)	(0.1146)	(0.1500)	(0.1105)	(0.1297)
6	–0.0560	0.1282	0.3898	0.2463	0.3504
	(0.0909)	(0.1024)	(0.1462)	(0.0973)	(0.0966)
7	0.0078	–0.0737	–0.3152	–0.0678	–0.3608
	(0.0827)	(0.0852)	(0.1260)	(0.1010)	(0.0968)
8	0.0164	–0.0176	0.2315	–0.1230	0.2076
	(0.0772)	(0.0749)	(0.1141)	(0.0966)	(0.0928)
9	–0.0436	0.0046	–0.1196	0.1710	–0.1100
	(0.0702)	(0.0692)	(0.1040)	(0.0864)	(0.0913)
10	0.0412	–0.0146	0.0063	–0.1632	0.0449
	(0.0514)	(0.0522)	(0.0918)	(0.0801)	(0.0874)
Mean	**0.0055**	**–0.0285**	**0.0386**	**0.0303**	**0.0764**

Note: Standard errors in parentheses.

synchronises with that of the US financial stress. This is not surprising given that a large body of international finance literature has documented the global dominance of the US in financial risk transmission, which is especially evident in the events of extreme downside risk (see for examples, Kim *et al.*, 2015; Liu, 2014). Our findings further substantiated the US financial stress spillover to Singapore amid the COVID-19 crisis. This implies that, as a small and highly open regional financial centre, Singapore's financial stability during the pandemic hinges heavily on the

Table 3:   Variance decomposition of *DFSI_SG*.

Period	S.E.	DNEW_CASE	DSTRINGENCY	DVIX	DFSI_US	DFSI_SG
1	1.6744	0.27	0.12	9.12	3.77	86.71
2	1.9405	0.27	0.22	7.14	7.45	84.92
3	2.1056	0.39	2.93	6.13	18.42	72.12
4	2.1740	0.66	2.76	5.86	22.95	67.76
5	2.2062	0.80	2.78	6.34	24.01	66.07
6	2.2853	0.80	2.91	8.82	23.54	63.93
7	2.3371	0.77	2.88	10.25	22.59	63.51
8	2.3610	0.76	2.83	11.01	22.41	63.00
9	2.3732	0.78	2.80	11.15	22.70	62.57
10	2.3796	0.81	2.79	11.09	23.04	62.27
Mean	**2.1837**	**0.63**	**2.30**	**8.69**	**19.09**	**69.29**

external financial shock. Thus, against the backdrop of elevated global economic uncertainty, extra policy efforts have to be devoted to monitoring and sustaining financial system soundness even if domestic COVID-19 cases are under good controls in Singapore.

Further, the analysis in Section 3 shows that financial stress levels vary across three different financial segments, among which the banking sector was under the greatest strain in the latest identified financial stress episode of the emergence of the pandemic. This indicates that the pandemic effect is not homogeneous across financial markets. Worryingly, the banking sector has always been the underpinning of the financial system, facilitating financial intermediation among a diverse group of market participants including SMEs and retail investors who often do not have access to direct financing, and thus plays a vital role for a healthy economy. Also, foreign banks constitute a large proportion of the banking system of Singapore given its role as a major banking hub in Asia.[7] There is a chance that external financial risk may be transmitted to the whole financial system through the banking industry and

---

[7]Referring to MAS Financial Institutions Directory, as of 2021, Singapore has four local banks and 127 foreign banks out of total 131 commercial banks.

derail economic recovery if not properly handled. Hence, banking supervision as well as credit support schemes are essential to guarantee sufficient liquidity and credit to the economy.

5. Conclusion

In this chapter, we provided a detailed analysis about Singapore's financial stability during the pandemic period through constructing daily FSI for Singapore. This study consists of two main parts.

In the first part, we identified financial stress episodes in Singapore by comparing FSI to its trend and confirm that a stress period has indeed occurred during 9 March–21 April 2020. The FSI seems to stabilise towards the end of our sample period but is still higher than the pre-pandemic level. Not to mention, the global economic uncertainty remains significant given the recurring waves of COVID-19 outbreaks in multiple regions around the world. Moreover, the staggering magnitude of the COVID-19 financial stress episode is comparable to the previous GFC and Eurozone crisis, which may insinuate similar predicament ahead of our time.

In the second part, we discovered that Singapore's financial stress is attributed to global financial factors instead of a direct consequence of the domestic COVID-19 outbreak. This means that despite the improving COVID-19 situation domestically, the financial system of Singapore is still highly fragile to changes in external financial conditions.

The policy implications of our study are twofold. Since financial stress of Singapore is mainly driven by the external financial shock, the retraction of stimulus packages and financial support schemes must also factor in global financial factors. The protracted mitigation measures and liquidity facility to support vulnerable individuals and local businesses may be expected, given the world economy continues to face exceptional uncertainty over pace of recovery. International cooperation should be in place to fight against COVID-19 resurgence, facilitate international trade and direct investment flows, and set up international regulatory framework for coordinated financial surveillance across borders. Next, as the financial stress concentrates mainly on the banking sector, which is the principal sector in the financial system, a thorough and timely risk assessment must be made to ensure the well-functioning of the banking system in order to avoid a domino effect to other segments of the financial system. The monetary authority must also keep a close eye on the overall credit condition, specifically after the expiry of COVID-19 loan relief packages going forward.

Acknowledgements

We gratefully acknowledge the funding support from Singapore Ministry of Education AcRF Tier 1 Research Grant (RG132/20) and James Cook University Singapore Internal Research Grant (IRG20210009).

References

Apostolakis, G. and Papadopoulos, A. P. (2014). Financial stress spillovers in advanced economies. *Journal of International Financial Markets, Institutions and Money*, 32: 128–149.

Apostolakis, G. and Papadopoulos, A. P. (2019). Financial stability, monetary stability and growth: A PVAR analysis. *Open Economies Review*, 30(1): 157–178.

BBC News. (April 21, 2020). US oil prices turn negative as demand dries up. *BBC News*. https://www.bbc.com/news/business-52350082.

Borio, C. E. and Lowe, P. W. (2002). Asset prices, financial and monetary stability: Exploring the nexus. BIS Working Paper No. 114.

Cardarelli, R., Elekdag, S., and Lall, S. (2011). Financial stress and economic contractions. *Journal of Financial Stability*, 7(2): 78–97.

Hakkio, C. S., and Keeton, W. R. (2009). Financial stress: What is it, how can it be measured, and why does it matter? *Economic Review*, 94(2): 5–50.

Hale, T., Petherick, A., Phillips, T., and Webster, S. (2020). Variation in government responses to COVID-19. Blavatnik School of Government Working Paper, 31.

Hansen, P. R. and Lunde, A. (2005). A forecast comparison of volatility models: Does anything beat a GARCH (1,1)? *Journal of Applied Econometrics*, 20(7): 873–889.

Hollo, D., Kremer, M., and Lo Duca, M. (2012). CISS - a composite indicator of systemic stress in the financial system. ECB Working Paper No. 1426.

Igan, D., Kirti, D., and Peria, S. M. (2020). The disconnect between financial markets and the real economy. Special Notes Series on COVID-19, IMF Research.

Illing, M., and Liu, Y. (2006). Measuring financial stress in a developed country: An application to Canada. *Journal of Financial Stability*, 2(3): 243–265.

IMF. (2020). Policy responses to COVID-19. https://www.imf.org/en/Topics/imf-and-covid19/Policy-Responses-to-COVID-19.

Jones, M. (September 14, 2020). BIS warns of gap opening between markets and COVID-19 reality. *Reuters*. https://www.reuters.com/article/bis-report-markets/bis-warns-of-gap-opening-between-markets-and-covid-19-reality-idUKL8N2GB2S1.

Khanna, V. (January 2, 2021). Covid-19's impact to still weigh on Singapore's economy in 2021. *The Straits Times*. https://www.straitstimes.com/opinion/virus-impact-to-still-weigh-on-economy-0.

Kim, B. H., Kim, H., and Lee, B. S. (2015). Spillover effects of the US financial crisis on financial markets in emerging Asian countries. *International Review of Economics & Finance*, 39: 192–210.

Lai, L. (February 25, 2021). Singapore not expected to move out of phase 3 any time soon: Janil. *The Straits Times*. https://www.straitstimes.com/singapore/parliament-singapore-not-expected-to-move-out-of-phase-three-any-time-soon.

Liu, L. (2014). Extreme downside risk spillover from the United States and Japan to Asia-Pacific stock markets. *International Review of Financial Analysis*, 33: 39–48.

Louzis, D. P., and Vouldis, A. T. (2012). A methodology for constructing a financial systemic stress index: An application to Greece. *Economic Modelling*, 29(4): 1228–1241.

Mazur, M., Dang, M., and Vega, M. (2020). COVID-19 and the March 2020 stock market crash. Evidence from S&P1500. *Finance Research Letters*, 38: 101690.

Melvin, M., and Taylor, M. P. (2009). The crisis in the foreign exchange market. *Journal of International Money and Finance*, 28(8): 1317–1330.

Ministry of Health. (2021). COVID-19 vaccination. https://www.moh.gov.sg/covid-19/vaccination.

Nelson, W. R., and Perli, R. (2007). Selected indicators of financial stability. *Risk Measurement and Systemic Risk*, 4: 343–372.

Rey, H. (2015). Dilemma not trilemma: The global financial cycle and monetary policy independence (No. w21162). *National Bureau of Economic Research*.

Sharma, P. (2015). Forecasting stock index volatility with GARCH models: International evidence. *Studies in Economics and Finance*, 32(4): 445–463.

About the Authors

Sook-Rei Tan is currently a lecturer of Economics at James Cook University Singapore. She graduated from NTU with a Ph.D. in Economics. Her research interests focus on applied macroeconomics and international finance. Her research works have been accepted and presented at several conferences, such as The American Finance Association (AFA) Ph.D. Student Poster Session, Conference of Computing in Economics and Finance, INFER Workshop on Applied Macroeconomics, and the *Singapore Economic Review* Conference.

Wei-Siang Wang received his Ph.D. in Economics from Michigan State University. His current research interests are Applied Econometrics and Machine Learning. He has published papers in *Journal of Econometrics* and *Journal of Productivity Analysis*. Before joining NTU, he was teaching at Michigan State University and Kettering University. He has taught various courses including Macroeconomics, Data Analytics, Survey Methods and Sampling Techniques, and Econometrics at various levels. He was nominated for Humanities and Social Sciences Excellence in Teaching Award in 2017. In 2019 and 2020, he received the Excellence in Teaching Award from the MSc in Applied Economics programme at NTU.

Wai-Mun Chia obtained her bachelor's degree in Economics from the University of London with a first class honors in 1996. She received the Datuk Paduka Hajjah Saleha Ali Outstanding Award for her exceptional academic performance at the international level in 1997. She was granted the London School of Economics Scholarship to pursue her master's degree at LSE in 1998. She obtained her Ph.D. degree at Nanyang Technological University (NTU) in 2006. She is currently an associate professor at NTU. Before joining NTU, she was an industry analyst at the Federation of Malaysian Manufacturers and a lecturer at HELP University College, Kuala Lumpur. She has published her work in some refereed journals and presented at various international conferences. She also serves as Treasurer Manager to the *Singapore Economic Review* and Co-Director to the Economic Growth Centre.

Chapter 7

Impacts of COVID-19 Pandemic on Thai Fruit: A Case Study of Longan Supply Chain

Roengchai Tansuchat*[,†,**], Tanachai Pankasemsuk[‡,§,¶,††], and Chanita Panmanee[‖,‡‡]

*Center of Excellence in Econometrics, Faculty of Economics,
Chiang Mai University, Chiang Mai, Thailand
†Center for Socio-Economic Impact Assessment
and Economic Possibility Study for Research Project,
Chiang Mai University, Chiang Mai, Thailand
‡Department of Plant and Soil Sciences, Faculty of Agriculture,
Chiang Mai University, Chiang Mai, Thailand
§International College Digital Innovation,
Chiang Mai University, Chiang Mai, Thailand
¶Academic Services and Research, Payap University,
Chiang Mai, Thailand
‖Faculty of Economics, Maejo University, Chiang Mai, Thailand
**roengchaitan@gmail.com
††pankasemsuk@gmail.com
‡‡golffychicha@gmail.com

‖Corresponding author.

169

Abstract

COVID-19 has had tremendous ripple effect upon every sector in the system since its beginning in 2019. Not only the effect of the pandemic itself, but the preventive measures of the government also affected the system, especially the agriculture supply chain widely considered to be the most important part of Thailand. The aims of the research chapter were to investigate and analyse the effects of COVID-19 and government measures towards the fruit supply chain in Thailand, together with reviewing on-season longan as a case study. Consequently, the instrument utilised was the supply chain mapping. The result was collected additionally by in-depth interviews, focus-group interviews, and questionnaires from Thai farmers. As a result, COVID-19 pandemic and preventive measures indicated the entire fruit supply-chain system's impacts on activities and stakeholders from start to finish nationally and internationally. Besides, the labour markets were affected, particularly seasonal foreign harvesting workers. These effects are in accordance with the agricultural overproduction, farm price and export price decreases, and other export volumes. In case of on-season longan, the shortage of fruit harvesting workers from disease preventive measures, including the prohibition of cross-border travel, were highlighted as significant problems. Additionally, the 14-day quarantine measure lessened the number of brokers, traders, and agricultural workers. These problems put pressure on involved people and changed the consumer behaviour. In sum, the noteworthy results lead to the policy recommendations for the new normal of the marketplace, comprising promoting comprehensive learning and training (reskill, upskill, and new skill) courses for agricultural practices and so forth.

Keywords: COVID-19; pandemic; agriculture; supply chain; Thailand; fruit; longan.

1. Introduction

The ongoing situation of the coronavirus disease 2019 (COVID-19) pandemic known as the coronavirus pandemic was first identified and declared in December 2019. Later, the World Health Organization (WHO) declared the outbreak a Public Health Emergency of International Concern in January 2020 and announced it a pandemic in March 2020. The governments in several countries have immediately responded to COVID-19 with a number of different non-pharmaceutical measures to prevent infections and the spread of COVID-19. Most of the preventative measures are curfew declarations or lockdowns in varying degrees (i.e. throughout the country or particular region, province, district, or community), prohibiting mass public gatherings, closing public spaces, restricting public transportation, implementing Working from Home (WFH) arrangements, as well as the border closure together with suspension of commercial international flights. Despite passing the legislation and measures in response to the pandemic, these measures disrupt the global supply chain and logistic services of agriculture and food systems which is the crucial key and needed most in order to access the essential agriculture and food resources as well as other key necessities.

Due to the economic consequences of the ongoing COVID-19 pandemic, economic depression began in numerous nations (Jackson *et al.*, 2020; Kanu, 2020). The COVID-19 recession appears to be severe and has become the worst global economic crisis since the Great Depression of the 1930s. Thus, it is of great significance that COVID-19 inevitably has impacted the global agriculture and food supply chain, which is one of the most important sectors of the economy (IMF, 2020; Ivanov, 2020). COVID-19 resulted in the movement restrictions of agricultural labour supply and transportation, changes in consumer demand and purchasing behaviour for food products, shutdowns of food manufacturers and service providers, shipping disruption and temporary port closures, increased costs from public health measures requirements, and financial pressures in food supply chain (Aday and Aday, 2020). All of these situations lead to the intensive increase in global food insecurity, economic and social impacts, which affect the well-being of households presently and almost every country subsequently.

Among initial measures, many governments are concerned about guaranteeing food availability for domestic consumption, food security, and alleviating problems for agricultural and food manufacturers to survive under many restrictions. Owing to the significance of food for life and income-inelasticity of food demand, trade in agricultural products has

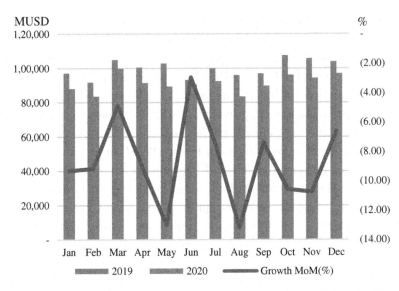

Figure 1: The value and growth of global agriculture export of 2019 and 2020.
Source: Trade Map (2020).

been more resilient than other sectors in the system, such as industry and tourism sectors.

Figure 1 presents the value and growth rate of total global agriculture export of 2019 and 2020. In 2020, the total value of global agricultural export (HS 01-21) decreased to USD 1,095.8 million compared with USD 1,200.4 million from 2019, or equivalent to a diminishing of –8.72%. The export value growth rates have shown negative signs since the beginning of the COVID-19 pandemic. In January 2020, the agriculture export value shrank from USD 97.1 million to USD 88 million or decreased 9.32% compared with the same month in 2019. On account of the ongoing COVID-19 pandemic, the inability to control the pandemic in some regions with long-lasting economic impacts affects the consumer confidence index. The line represents the global agriculture export value growth rate in comparison with the same period between 2019 and 2020. The result shows that all have negative values, especially in August, which has the highest negative growth rate at –13.17%.

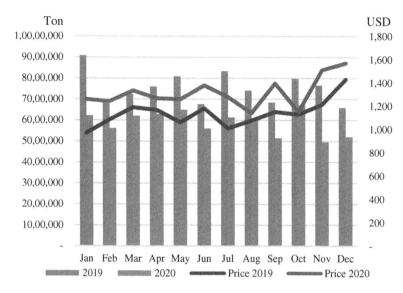

Figure 2: The volume and price of global edible fruit export of 2019 and 2020.
Source: Trade Map (2020).

The total volumes and average prices of global edible fruit export are displayed in Figure 2. The overall global edible fruit export volume in 2020 was less than in 2019, while its average price increased. The highest percentage average price change in the same period between 2019 and 2020 was 29.8% in January followed by 26.55% and 24.5% in July and November, respectively. The main causes are simultaneous disruptions in supply, demand, supply chain, and logistics infrastructure due to the COVID-19 pandemic. In addition, edible fruits normally have a greater price and income elasticity than staple food that provides more energy and calories than fruits, such as grains, rice, wheat, corn, and cassava (Andreyeva *et al.*, 2010; Femenia, 2019).

It is noted that the decrease in agricultural export has arisen from several causes. All of them relate to the many activities and stakeholders in the agricultural supply chain. To illustrate, labour sickness and short-age, and social distancing measures in some countries significantly reduced agricultural labour supply leading to the loss of agricultural pro-duction and food security (World Bank, 2020). They accordingly forbid food export in order to ensure sufficient food for domestic consumption (Aday and Aday, 2020). For example, the governments of Vietnam and Cambodia were considerably concerned about food security in their countries, therefore they placed an export ban on their rice. In addition, cross-border shipping delays, interruptions in logistics, and restrictions on exports from various measures in each country cause a decline in export volumes. The increase in export cost resulted in higher export prices correspondingly (Evenett *et al.*, 2020). Most hotels, restaurants, catering, and cafes were closed as a result of the government measures in provision for demand reductions of fruits and vegetables. Although food demand, especially of fresh fruits and vegetables, has lessened; food-security concerns to food importing countries, in terms of the lower production volumes and restrictions on exports, pushed the global food price up by 18% on average (Espitia *et al.*, 2020).

Moving to the case of Thailand, the first case of COVID-19 was confirmed on 13 January 2020. The Prime Minister declared a state of emergency, effective on 26 March 2020, and a curfew went into effect on 3 April 2020. All commercial international flights were suspended from 4 April 2020; consequently, lockdown measures were implemented in varying degrees throughout the country. Measures as mentioned have had a direct impact on plenty of economic activities, including production of goods and services, household consumption, private businesses and commerce, along with transportation and logistics.

Thai tropical fruits are considered an important economic crop in Thailand, generating billions of US dollars each year (more than USD 3.6 billion in 2019) and popularly consumed both domestically and internationally. It is noteworthy to mention that Thai tropical fruits are economically important and have high export value, specially longans, durians, mangosteens, mangoes, rambutans, etc. Figure 3 shows the monthly value and growth of Thailand edible fruit export. In the first 2 months of 2020, it was pointed that the export values decreased, and the export value growth rates were negative. However, between March to May, which is the prior and high season for tropical fruits of Thailand, the export value increased from THB 327 million in March to THB 785 million in May. The export value growth rates of March and May compared to the same period between 2019 and 2020 were 13.68% and 143.82%, respectively.

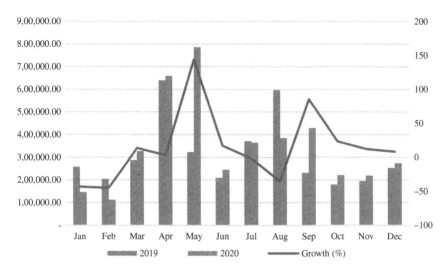

Figure 3: Value and growth of Thai edible fruit export.

Source: Trade Map (2020).

To shed light on this issue, this chapter firstly aims to document and analyse what the impacts of COVID-19 are on Thai fruits, and in what way the government can alleviate the fruit growers and stakeholders. According to this study, most Thai fruits were adversely affected by the COVID measures, excluding durians. It should be noted that the major problems in Thai fruit supply chain are labour shortages, lower farm-gate prices, increased domestic and international transport restrictions, including sanitary requirements, rising freight costs, and lower consumer purchasing power (Attavanich, 2020; Suriyankietkaew *et al.*, 2020).

Besides, longan is a tropical fruit that is classified as the main economic fruit and product champion of Thailand that can be produced for domestic and international consumption, with the second largest export value after durian, holding China as the main export market. While durian export values increased compared with the previous year, longan export values dropped significantly. Therefore, the research question is what the economic and social impacts of COVID-19 are on in-season longan supply chain in Thailand.

In short, the specific objectives are: (1) to systematically review and empirically investigate the effects of COVID-19 and the government alleviation strategies regarding it on the fruit sectors in Thailand considering different aspects, (2) to study the impacts of COVID-19 pandemic on in-season longan supply chain in Thailand, and (3) to provide the possible balance recovery policies in order to alleviate the impact of COVID-19 on stakeholders in Thai fruit supply chain. This chapter is organised as follows. Section 1 gives a brief overview of the rationale of the chapter and objectives. Section 2 is literature about the impact of previous pandemics and the COVID-19 pandemic on agricultural sector and supply chain, emphasising on fruits. In Section 3, the research methodology and data collection are presented. Section 4 shows the empirical results. Finally, the conclusion and policy recommendations are stated in Section 5.

2. Literature Review

In the last 30 years prior to the COVID-19 pandemic, there have been global outbreaks affecting people, the agricultural sector, and food supply chain, such as H5N1, H7N9, H1N1, SARS, MERS, and Ebola. The first group is a group of influenza A viruses (H5N1, H7N9, and H1N1) which directly affect the meat production used as human food source, and meat supply chain. The avian influenza virus (H5N1 and H7N9), also known as avian flu or bird flu, is a concern due to the global spread of H5N1 that constitutes a pandemic threat. It can be transmitted between different birds and poultry, and to humans. The H5N1 and H7N9 outbreaks have had a negative impact on the poultry meat industry and supply chain, and poultry trade in many countries, particularly major export countries such as China, USA, and Thailand (Taha, 2007; Nicita, 2008; Mohan *et al.*, 2009; Kumar and Chandra, 2010; Kumar, 2012; Khokhar *et al.*, 2015). Shifting consumer food choices have decreased poultry consumption, resulting in lower domestic poultry prices (Taha, 2007; Beach, 2008). H5N1 was first confirmed in poultry and humans in Thailand in January 2004 (Tiensin *et al.*, 2005). Between 2004–2006, the H5N1 caused 25 human cases and 17 deaths in Thailand. Thailand had a 75% drop in poultry exports in the first quarter of 2004 (Blayney *et al.*, 2006; Taha, 2007).

In 2009, H1N1 influenza pandemic, also known as swine flu pandemic, was found in Mexico, and later was confirmed as human cases of infection spread throughout Mexico, in parts of the United States, and in several countries worldwide. It can be transmitted between swine, and to humans. H1N1 also affected the pig industry, pork supply chain, and exports (Rassy and Smith, 2013). At the initial stage, it immediately caused a downturn in domestic and international pork markets. Domestic pork demand and prices dropped sharply because of food safety concerns of consumers. Several pork-importing countries such as China, Indonesia, and Azerbaijan, banned and restricted pork imports from certain countries. H1N1 pandemic effect also spilt over to other agricultural markets in the supply chain, such as feed grain and other livestock markets.

The second group is a group of coronaviruses which are respiratory infectious diseases such as severe acute respiratory syndrome coronavirus (SARS-CoV or SARS-CoV-1) in 2003, Middle East respiratory syndrome-related coronavirus (MERS-CoV) in 2009, and coronavirus disease 2019 (COVID-19 or SARS-CoV-2). In many countries, the situation worsens as the disease progresses. Therefore, many measures such as lockdowns, social distancing, movement restrictions, public health measures, and social and economic measures were implemented by governments worldwide in response to the pandemic. These measures indirectly affected agriculture and food supply chain through restricted tourism, transportation, and labour movement in the agricultural sector. In case of the MERS outbreak in the Republic of Korea, measures indirectly affected the agriculture and food supply chain through tourism, and travel-related service sectors, including food and beverages, and transportation (Joo *et al.*, 2019). SARS also has a significant impact on domestic consumption, tourism, and related industries, as is the spread of SARS in China and other countries. For instance, it intervenes in the household food demand and consequently causes the drastic decline in the number of hotel guests (Siu and Wong, 2004; Qiu *et al.*, 2018).

In case of Ebola virus disease, De La Fuente (2020) studied the impact of the West African Ebola epidemic on agricultural production and rural welfare, and found that the 2014–2015 Ebola epidemic had devastated both humans and economies. The agricultural sector of three countries, namely Sierra Leone, Guinea, and Liberia, has been severely affected by the Ebola pandemic (Qureshi, 2016). The higher Ebola prevalence disrupted the mobilisation of labour for cultivation and harvest, and many farms were abandoned. This resulted in a decrease in rice cultivation areas and rice yields that may in turn have led to food price increases. Household welfare, as measured by per capita expenditures, was much lower in Ebola-endemic areas, especially those areas that were negatively impacted by a shortage of agricultural workers.

In case of COVID-19, there are considerable research papers reviewing and anticipating the impacts of COVID-19 on the agriculture sector. It impacts agriculture in two key areas: demand and supply for food (Siche, 2020). In accordance with Pan *et al.* (2020), studying the influence of COVID-19 on agricultural economy and emergency relief measures in China, plenty of impacts on many aspects were highlighted such as production, product supply, income and employment, and product sales model and trade. In addition, COVID-19 pandemic control measures have delayed and interrupted transport and logistics services. The border closures and further procedures, together with investigations, create congestion and delays affecting the transport of perishable products (OECD, 2020).

The declaration of export restrictions and more sanitary requirements in several countries restricted the global agri-food trade and market access. The COVID-19 outbreak has had a broader impact, bringing about a continued decline in agricultural products (Espitia *et al.*, 2020; Miller, 2020; Pulubuhu *et al.*, 2020). To illustrate, food products seem to be expensive due to transport restrictions and the steadily declining volumes of agricultural products (Pulubuhu *et al.*, 2020). Additionally, the COVID-19 epidemic could affect the availability of important intermediate inputs for farmers. Low inputs and/or high prices, such as pesticides, could negatively affect crop yields in 2020 and 2021, especially in developing countries (Schmidhuber *et al.*, 2020).

The number of labour in the agricultural sector tends to decline in terms of availability, number of labourers, and labour productivity (Gong, 2020; World Bank, 2020) due to labour sickness and shortage, 14-day quarantine measures, and restrictions on the movement of workers across the country and specific areas. Government guidance of urging residents not to leave home has incommoded plenty of farmers from doing their activities, leading to lower incomes (Pulubuhu, 2020). Hence, restrictions on the movement of people across borders have contributed to labour shortages in agriculture in many countries, particularly during peak seasonal labour demand or labour-intensive production (OECD, 2020).

In case of Thailand, Attavanich (2020) has evaluated and reported the impacts of COVID-19 on food systems, food security and nutrition, and livelihoods. From in-depth interviews, focus group and survey data from 1,449 farm households and 1,345 general households across the country showed that farm households likely received higher negative impact than general households. The COVID-19 preventive and containment measures of Thai government caused migrant labour shortage of fruit harvesting, food supply chain disruption, contraction in domestic consumption, the delay of exports or inability to export to international market from Thai-border trade checkpoints closing and raising of transportation, logistic, and shipping cost, which lead to an oversupply problem. The fresh fruit farmers were the most affected compared to other stakeholders in the fruit supply chain system. The report revealed that the highest income per capita reduction among Thai tropical fruits is longan farm households.

Concerning perspectives of ASEAN community, many countries in ASEAN depending on agriculture also responded immediately to COVID-19 pandemic. Suriyankietkaew *et al.* (2020) reported that each ASEAN country has different measures to deal with this pandemic. Many key sectors such as agriculture, supply chain and logistic, and tourism have been affected by lockdown and other measures. The lockdown damaged not only the incomes, employment, and social welfare but also food security and sustainability of the country. Although ASEAN response was slow and lacked consistency in the early stage, ASEAN later proposed the Declaration of the Special ASEAN Summit on Coronavirus Disease 2019 which has some measures related to recuperate the agricultural sector, to maintain supply chain connectivity, and to take collective actions and coordinate policies in alleviating the economic and social impact, safeguarding the people's well-being and preserving social economic stability in the face of the pandemic.

3. Research Methodology and Data Collection

This study will be conducted to gather relevant literature, documents, and information about impact of COVID-19 crisis on Thai fruit sector in macro views, and primary data from multi-lateral stakeholders in the Thai fruit supply chain. Data will be derived from various data collection methods, including (1) primary data from in-depth interviews and focus group interviews from multiple stakeholders and questionnaires, (2) secondary data from recent reports and related statistics from government agencies (The Office of Agricultural Economic, National Statistical Office, Ministry of Agriculture and Cooperatives, and Ministry of Commerce), and private agencies (CEIC database, Trade Map database) plus research reports from academic institutions, and international organisations.

Primary data are used in order to gain insightful perspectives and better understanding about the situations and contexts. This research proceeded with in-depth interview with key opinion leaders and influential stakeholders with various parties of fruit and longan supply chains in seven provinces, comprising Chiang Mai, Lamphun, Loei, Samut Sakhon, Chanthaburi, Sa Kaeo, and Songkhla. The stakeholders are fruit growers, local collectors, contract merchants, cooperatives, middle men (Lhong), wholesalers, retailers, and exporters totalling 58 observations. In terms of longan, this study provides focus group interviews with several stakeholders in the longan supply chain in Chiang Mai and Lamphun province (40 participants) in order to observe their opinions on the issues and impacts of the coronavirus situation on in-season longan supply chain. It is remarkable that Chiang Mai and Lamphun provinces have the most in-season longan cultivation in Thailand and represent the in-season longan supply chain in the northern part of Thailand.

In addition, 200 questionnaires were collected from longan growers in Chiang Mai and Lamphun provinces by random sampling method, where the major in-season longan plantations are, in order to investigate the impacts of COVID-19 pandemic on in-season longan farmers. Inexplicably, it is crucial to note that only in Chiang Mai and Lamphun provinces the productive area of longan is 92,531 hectares, accounting for almost 50% of the total areas (Office of Agricultural Economics, 2020a). In the following stage of the process, the questionnaires were divided into three parts as follows: the general information of respondents, longan growers' production, and the impacts of COVID-19 on post-harvesting and sales. For the secondary data, relevant documentations were reviewed, then appropriate data were used for systematic mapping, further data validation, and content analysis.

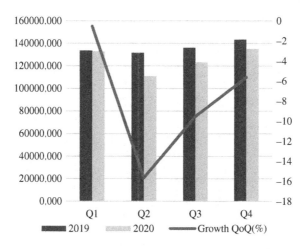

Figure 4: Nominal GDP and growth rate.

Source: CEIC Database (2020).

4. Results

4.1 *Overview of macro-level analysis*

The economic impact of COVID-19 on Thailand's economy has been devastating because of Thailand's openness to trade, food export, and tourism. As demonstrated onwards, Figure 4 presents the quarterly nominal gross domestic product (GDP) and GDP growth rate of Thailand. In the first quarter, the outbreak had trivial impact on the nominal GDP with a decrease in growth rate –0.55%, while in the second quarter of 2020, it dramatically decreased from USD 131.6 to USD 111 million or shrank by –15.65% compared with the same quarter in 2019, which is the sharpest decline in the Southeast Asia region. However, after Thailand controlled the spread of COVID-19 and implemented a gradual easing of the restrictions, the value of nominal GDP in the third and fourth quarters increased to USD 123 million and USD 135 million, respectively. However, this was the fourth consecutive quarter of contraction in the GDP, but the smallest decline since the Q1, as an improvement in both global demand and domestic activity. Considering the whole of 2020, the economy shrank by 7.78%, the sharpest drop since the 1998 Asian financial crisis.

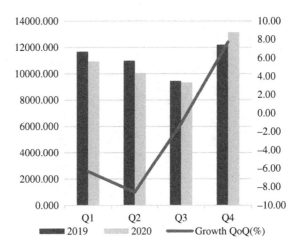

Figure 5:   Agriculture, forestry, and fishing nominal GDP and growth rate.
Source: CEIC Database (2020).

Figure 5 presents the GDP of Agriculture, Forestry, and Fishing (AFFGDP) of Thailand. In the first quarter, AFFGDP decreased from USD 11.7 million to USD 10.9 million, accounting for –6.33% compared with the same quarter in 2019. In the second quarter, the AFFGDP still declined from USD 10.9 million of 2019 to USD 10.0 million or –8.58%. However, the AFFGDP has recovered in the third quarter, restoring to USD 9.34 million, close to the value of AFFGDP in 2019 or an increase of 1.13%. Surprisingly, the AFFGDP in the fourth quarter increased at 7.72% to USD 13.13 million. According to the trade statistics from the Ministry of Commerce (2020), in 2020, the agricultural products with the highest export value are the preparations of meat with export valued USD 6.55 billion, followed by edible fruit and cereals, respectively. Remarkably, even during the COVID-19 pandemic, the edible fruit and cereals were higher than 2019 with an export value of USD 4.16 billion, an increase by 10.86%.

4.2 *Thai fruits*

The COVID-19 outbreak has had a strong impact both economically and socially on the stockholders of the different activities along the Thai fruit

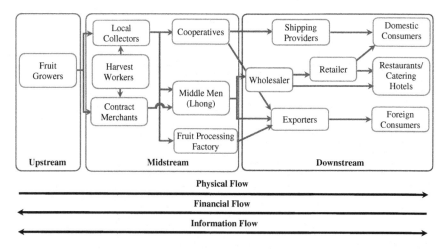

Figure 6:   General Thai fruit supply chain.

supply chain. Figure 6 explains the stakeholders in the Thai fruit supply chain. In the upstream, the person who plays the critical role is the fruit grower or farmer who plants the fruit trees commercially. At the middle stream, there are many players undertaking different activities, namely, collectors, fruit harvest workers, contract merchants (who would buy in advance), middle men (Lhong), exporters and traders, agriculture cooperatives, wholesalers and retailers, domestic shipping providers, and supermarkets. The players downstream are consumers, restaurants, catering units, hotels, and foreign imports.

4.2.1 *Fruit growers or farmers*

Although many kinds of Thai tropical fruits and harvesting season began in March together with pandemic controllability of China, the epidemic without borders outside China has become more serious. China has continued to tighten measures to curb foreign travel in and out, and to encourage all airlines to reduce passenger flights to China. In the meanwhile, the government of Thailand announced a nationwide curfew starting on 3 April 2020, all borders had to be closed, and all normal commercial international flights in Thailand were suspended. This condition affected the arrival of fruit buyers, brokers, and traders from abroad, especially China

Table 1:   On-season fruit price index 2019–2020.

Month	Durian			Rambutan			Mangosteen		
	2019	**2020**	**% Change**	**2019**	**2020**	**% Change**	**2019**	**2020**	**% Change**
May	539.79	439.51	−18.58	190.48	115.28	−39.48	259.22	138.69	−46.50
June	578.81	463.78	−19.87	218.79	172.42	−21.19	240.05	115.97	−51.69

Source: Office of Agricultural Economics (2020b).

and Vietnam who come to Thailand to evaluate both the quantity and quality of the product each year, and to negotiate and enter into trade contracts. In addition, the pandemic has changed international trade patterns and behaviours as more and more people took to digital media such as Line or WeChat. As a consequence, the restrictions resulted in fewer contracts for fruit purchases and contracts of lesser size and value. It is empirically demonstrated that the total demand for on-season fresh fruit and the farm-gate fruit prices had been reduced as shown in Table 1, the on-season (i.e. May and June) fruit price index of durians, rambutans, and mangosteens.

4.2.2 *Harvest workers*

Farmers and local workers indicated that they are not affected by the COVID-19 epidemic and curfew measures as they are able to maintain social distancing while harvesting, and their working time is during daytime. However, the affected groups are foreign workers and ethnic workers, particularly in the fruit harvesting season in which they have to work laboriously to meet harvest scheduling. The lockdown measures, setting up of the border control, prevented foreign workers (from Cambodia and Myanmar) from crossing the border at harvest time. From in-depth interviews with fruit farmers in Chiang Mai and Chanthaburi provinces, it was found that the effects of COVID-19 caused migrants to return to their home countries and they could not cross the border back to work in Thailand due to labour mobility prohibition across the border. Moreover, a key problem in relation to the hill tribe workers is that they cannot leave their hometown or village for job seeking during the fruit harvest season. This problem has raised the scarcity of labour supply in the short harvesting season. It has become a limitation for contract merchants, local collectors, and lhong, leading to wage increases.

4.2.3 *Wholesaler and retailer*

A variety of measures which the government applied in the early stages of the COVID-19 pandemic, such as the curfew pass and work from home arrangement, had a drawback on domestic fruit consumption, transportation, and logistics. After applying government work from home guidance, fruit sales in both the fresh market (wholesale and retail markets) and the modern trade market (supermarkets) fell. A number of businesses have temporarily ceased their operations, causing local workers to lose their jobs and move back to their hometowns corresponding to declining demand and sales of fruits. In addition, the recent COVID-19 crisis has led consumers to change their purchasing behaviour, substituting traditional markets for online shopping and delivery platforms such as Grab, Food Panda, and Line Man. Furthermore, the suspension of cross-provincial and international travel also has a tremendous impact on hotels, restaurants, and catering; significantly related to the declining demand for fruits from wholesalers and retailers when these businesses were temporarily shut down.

4.2.4 *Fruit processing business*

The COVID-19 outbreak has heightened the need for processed fruit (canned fruit or dried fruit) to continually maintain food security at the household level. The effects are multidimensional. For example, the sluggish global economy resulting from COVID-19 decreased the orders of processed pineapples or canned pineapples in Thailand from foreign markets, related to the reduction of production capacity. Moreover, the manufacturing labour shortage, which occurred with labour mobility restriction measures, leads to the delay in purchasing raw materials for farmers. Consequently, the fresh pineapple factory price was lessened.

4.2.5 *Transportation and logistics*

The government's stringent measures in the early stages of the COVID-19 pandemic, such as a strict night-time curfew, severely affected the transportation and logistics systems needed to transport fruits from orchards to fresh wholesale markets, local fresh markets, and foreign countries. The acute problem of fruit exporters by land transport is the 14-day quarantine requirement for workers and truck drivers if they cannot return to Thailand within 5 hours, and some international border checkpoints required they remain for a period of 3 days and nights. The issue in relation to these situations arises from a shortage of containers. As a matter of fact, at some border checkpoints, the government officer requires COVID-19 health certificate for drivers and workers to cross international borders. In particular, at the Vietnam checkpoint on route R12 (connecting Thailand, Laos, Vietnam, and China), the officer randomly examines the medical certificate of the driver transporting durians without prior notice. The transport companies and exporters were unable to provide documents in a timely manner; therefore, fruit container vehicles could not cross the Cha Lo border, Vietnamese checkpoint. Similarly, the sea freight had to encounter insufficient containers for the products. In case of air freight, lower number of flights and higher air freight rates dominated the higher export and overseas retail prices.

4.3 *Longan case study*

Longan is a tropical fruit that is classified as the main economic fruit and product champion of Thailand that can be produced for domestic consumption and export, with the second largest export value after durian, holding China as the main export market. While durian export values increased compared with the previous year, longan export values dropped significantly. Figure 7 displays the value and month-over-month growth rate of fresh longan export. In 2020, the total longan export value of Thailand declined to USD 256 billion compared with USD 407 billion of 2019 or equivalent to –37%. The longan export value growth rate is negative every month except December, when a log of off-season longans is exported to China before Chinese New Year's Eve. The longan production in Thailand has been categorised into two types, namely in-season and off-season. Likewise, their supply chains from farms to consumers have been affected by COVID-19 shocks. Therefore, the research question is what are the economic and social impacts of COVID-19 on in-season longan supply chain in Thailand.

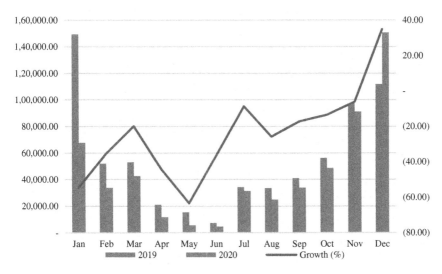

Figure 7: Value and growth of fresh longan export.

Source: Trade Map (2020).

Most of the in-season longan cultivation areas are in Northern Thailand, especially Chiang Mai and Lamphun provinces. In 2019, Thailand had 192,268.48 hectares of longan plantation area, rising by 1.46% from 2018. The longan output in 2019 was 1.01 million tons, declining from 2018 by 3.53%. As mentioned earlier, there are two types of longan production in Thailand: in-season longan and off-season longan. In-season longan refers to the longan production in natural conditions; the flowering commences in late December to late February, while the harvest time is from late June to late August.

Based on Tansuchat *et al.* (2016) and Panmanee *et al.* (2018), Figure 8 represents the on-season longan supply chain mapping. There are many stakeholders in the longan supply chain classified by activities as follows: (1) upstream: longan growers or farmers, (2) midstream: harvest workers, collectors, contract merchants, middlemen (Lhong), agriculture coopera-tives, and longan processing factors, and (3) downstream: wholesalers and retailers, domestic shipping providers, and exporters. Each stakeholder has different roles, functions, and priorities.

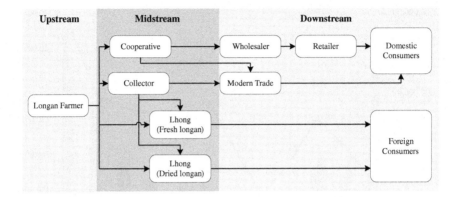

Figure 8:   On-season longan supply chain mapping.

To clarify, the upstream starts with farmers growing longan as vigorously as possible by pruning together with providing water and farm management to protect longans from weeds, pests, and diseases. The coronavirus outbreak (COVID-19) and implementation of various government measures coincided with the on-season longan harvesting periods (June–August). Measurements were taken using 200 questionnaires collected from longan farmers in both Chiang Mai and Lamphun provinces. Of the study samples, the respondents are male (66.5%) and female (33.5%). The average age of respondents is 59 years old, and most of them are in the range 51–60 years old (33%). Most respondents (67%) have longan cultivation as their principal occupation. They have more than 15 years of experience in on-season longan farming. The average cultivation area is 3.97 rai or 0.64 hectares.

In response to the harvesting and selling of products, it was found that 56.28% of them have the capability to sell their products, comprising 39.7% of farmers fending for themselves and the rest of them undertaking the contract-merchant process. The majority of respondents (70.89%) harvest fresh longan by themselves, while the minority (29.11%) employ harvest workers. Complying with the COVID-19 pandemic situation and lockdown measure leading to the scarcity problem of the seasonal foreign workers, 95.65% of harvest workers are local workers. When the subjects were asked about the product sales under harvesting and sorting worker scarcity issue, the result indicated that they sold in the loosened longan

Table 2: Number of farmers affected by COVID-19 (province).

	Lamphun		Chiang Mai	
Province	**Frequency**	**Percentage**	**Frequency**	**Percentage**
Affected by COVID	89.00	89.00	99.00	99.00
Not affected by COVID	11.00	11.00	1.00	1.00
Total observation	100.00	100.00	100.00	100.00

Table 3: Effects of COVID-19.

	Lamphun		Chiang Mai	
Effects	**Number**	**Percentage**	**Number**	**Percentage**
Longan cheaper	85.00	95.51	98.00	98.99
No merchants	16.00	17.98	5.00	5.05
Hard to sell longan	6.00	6.74	6.00	6.06
Other	5.00	5.62	7.00	7.07

Note: Respondents can choose more than one effect.

(detached from their inflorescences) 52.69%, longan in basket 37.63%, and bunched longan 9.68%. This is because the bunched longan and longan in basket required more skilled and meticulous labour to handle than loosened longan.

According to Table 2, 188 respondents or 94% reported that they experienced COVID-19 effect. The respondents agreeing on the decrease in longan price were 80.26% (Table 3). This corresponds to lower farm-gate prices of grade A fresh longan, compared with rates in the same month of 2019, as shown in Figure 9. In addition, 9.21% of respondents faced the problem of none of the collectors and merchants being able to buy fresh longan. Therefore, farmers decided to switch their selling pattern from longan in basket or bunched longan to a loosened longan sale. Normally, the Office of Commercial Affairs Lamphun (2020) reported that the farm-gate price of longan in basket is about 30–32B/kg. and bunched longan is about 26–28B/kg, which are higher than loosened longan (19–20B/kg). Consequently, farmers are more likely to suffer from deficiency compared to selling on-season longan.

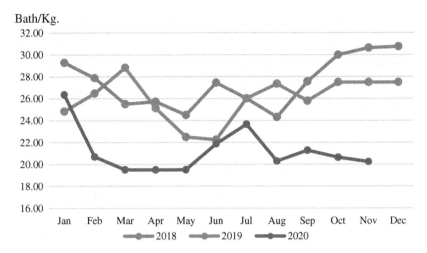

Figure 9:   The price of grade-A longan in bunch form between 2018–2020.

Source: Office of Agricultural Economics (2020b).

In the harvesting process, longan picking is the activity requiring skilled labourers, so a large number of skilled labourers are needed for collectors, contract merchants, or farmers. In Northern Thailand, most of them are foreign workers from Myanmar and hill tribe workers. Measures to prevent the spread of COVID-19 include controlling the labour mobility across the border, thus obstructing them to do the harvesting jobs. Furthermore, during the harvesting season, from July to August, or the rainy season, longan should not be picked as the additional risk of breakdown after harvest. In sum, labour shortage raised problems of late harvesting, resulting in crop damage and lowering farmers' income, leading to additional financial burden and household debt.

The problems of cross-provincial travel and the shortage of harvest workers affected the collector/contract merchant, causing the decline of workers and financial liquidity problems. Adversely affected domestic retailers and wholesalers as a result of curfew restrictions are unable to open because of the public concerns bringing about the change of consumer buying behaviour. Hence, some operators comply with selling fresh longan online by means of website or Facebook, and delivering them through domestic shipping providers, such as Thailand Post and Kerry in lieu of traditional marketing. Apparently, the online market is fairly popular among consumers as it helps in avoidance of gatherings, which reduces the risk of contracting the virus.

The processed longan with the most economic value is dried longan (dried longan with shell, and gold dried longan without shell), and the major in-demand import country is China with 68.88%. From interviewing with dried-longan peeling workers, it was found that the situation of the COVID-19 pandemic resulted in low product demand. It is confirmed by the report of the agriculture office of the Royal Thai Consulate-General, Shanghai, that the COVID-19 pandemic and drastic measures to suppress the pandemic have reduced demand for dried longan, resulting in a large amount of dried longan remaining in Chinese stock. In addition, the dried longan for domestic consumption can be produced and supplied from three provinces, namely Guangdong, Fujian, and Guangxi, resulting in a decrease in demand for imported dried longan from Thailand. Moreover, the uncertainty of the pandemic situation heightened Chinese consumers' awareness of their spending being more focused on essential products for life purchase; in consequence, markedly declining demand for dried longan. Another problem that arose was concerned with the issue of trade agreements with the importers. In general, the importers or brokers originally commuted to Thailand to cope with the situation on fresh and dried longan, including negotiating the price, quality, and quantity of the dried longan. Despite the 14-day quarantine for all arrivals, trade negotiations of foreign traders, brokers, and importers were impracticable. Cross-border negotiations were altered into trading by means of online media, such as WeChat, Line, and Email. Unfortunately, exporters have to confront excessive pricing with excessively complicated procedures, such as creating animated videos to serve the purpose of marketing campaign and providing consumer product safety documentation for the decision concerning requirements. The export quantity of dried longan in the previous 9 months of 2020 thus decreased to 112.4 tons or equivalent to −1.8%.

Based on the impact of COVID-19 from the respondents, the Thai government has eased the measures to alleviate the affected longan farmers satisfactorily correlating with and further adopting these following measures. In the first place, the government generates the financial remedy measures for longan plantations compensating THB 2,000 per rai with the conditions of not more than 25 rai in order to comprehensively compensate other farmers. Second, launching the Online to Offline (O2O) model project under the concept of modern commercial agriculture model aims to accelerate the distribution of fresh on-season longan in the northern region by approximately 30% of the total longan production. The O2O model project operates under the collaboration of private e-commerce companies and Thailand Post. Third, the Department of Cooperative Promotion would buy longan from members of the cooperative at a leading market price and distribute them for sale across provinces and across regions. Fourth, establishment of "Longan Institute" in the form of Agritech and Innovation Centre (AIC) and Centre of Excellence (COE) would conduct research and development aiming to reduce costs, focus on processing, add value to longan, and reduce dependence on exports as a sustainable solution.

4.4 *Discussion*

The results of the study confirmed that the COVID-19 pandemic and government measures had adversely impacted the agricultural and food supply chain system, which comprises many activities included in a "farm to fork" such as farming, harvesting, process management, packaging, transportation, distribution and marketing, and demand management, in at least three ways. Firstly, it is the demand channel. The COVID-19 pandemic destroys consumer confidence and creates uncertainty conditions in the country's economy. Therefore, people will stay connected to their homes and work from home to reduce the chance of contracting the disease. The consumption expenditure then declined, and shopping behaviour changed to online platforms. The reduction in consumption expenditure affects gross demand. For instance, international tourism is banned, affecting the tourism industry and tourism-related industries such as food and beverages industry, aviation industry, hotel and accommodation industry, and retail industry. Secondly, supply channels are changed. To demonstrate, gross demand reduction directly affects real sector production, employment, a considerable drop in sales, and business operations. Ceasing business and reducing employment has a direct impact on the income and living condition of household members. Lastly, the concern of supply chain channels is growing. The nation-wide lockdowns and safety measures from COVID-19 created the agriculture supply chain risks due to harvest labour shortages for fruit growers, agriculture supply chain disruption, shortage and fluctuation in the supply markets, inadequacy of the logistics providers, restrictions on interprovincial and interstate transportation, and rising of logistics cost.

In case of longan, which is a tropical tree species that produces edible fruit, the COVID-19 pandemic destroyed many activities and stockholders. Nevertheless, the analysis did not confirm any significant differences between the overall fruit export. The result pointed to the strategy that farmers altered their products in terms of the loosened longan instead of bunched longan and longan in basket. It also created much risk in supply chain such as supply-side risks due to harvest labour shortages for fruit growers, fresh longan over supply, and reduced farm-gate price; demand-side risk due to unanticipated consumer demand, reduced purchasing power of domestic consumers, changes in food safety requirements, logistics; and transportation risk due to underperformance of the logistics providers because of nation-wide lockdowns and safety measures.

5. Conclusion

This chapter has documented and analysed the impacts of COVID-19 pandemic on Thai fruit sectors along with studying a special case in longan with its dominance. The findings of this study indicate that the variety of COVID-19 measures have adversely ripple effects on the stakeholders of Thai fruit supply chain. The lockdown and containment measures dwindle the fruit trading volume, on-season fruit export prices, farm-gate prices, leading to the increase in skilled harvest labour shortage, transportation and logistics cost, and higher food safety measures and requirements. The upshot of the current farmers' income and future production planning is under consideration. This possibility also obliges every stakeholder involved in the fruit supply chain sectors. In the case of longan, coronavirus and preventive measures point to the considerable impact towards the idea of business operations and exports of longan. This research also underlined the economic impact in terms of the lower demand for fresh on-season longan, bringing about the lessened prices, lower farmer's income, and reduced financial liquidity of longan-related businesses, especially farmers and merchants. Moreover, it is crucial to note that the problems of supply-chain disruptions consist of logistics delays and jams, customs clearance delays, logistics and transportation costs, and changes in product distribution channels.

The results of the study can lead to policy recommendations. First, it would be necessary for the government to provide financial capacity with low interest rates for the next season's production. Second, promoting learning and training (reskilling, upskilling, and new skilling) courses about careful advance planning, fruit supply chain management, food safety, and traceability system are crucial for farmers and stakeholders with emphasis on digital skills; for instance, promoting Climate-Smart Agriculture (CSA) and Good Agricultural Practices (GAP); building high-value food industries such as in processing, packaging and retailing; and enhancing Food Value Chain (FVC) approach to food safety, security, and quality by promoting Public and Private Partnership (PPP) based on FVC and CSA. Third, food safety will become a mega trend in the future. Entrepreneurs in the agriculture and food supply chain should pay more attention and the government should accelerate the search for ways to promote safe food production, such as raising awareness of the importance of safe food for consumers. If consumers are willing to pay more, it will increase incentives for farmers to produce safer agricultural products. Fourth, the public and private sectors should try to optimise the customer's understanding about the correspondence between COVID-19 and fruit and vegetable products to reduce consumption anxieties. Fifth, although the restrictions of cross-border labour should be applied under the pandemic situation, liberalisation with the regulation of internal labour migration, especially fruit picking workers across provinces, should be taken into consideration. Lastly, the government should promote convenient export and import of agricultural and food products, and enhance regional and international cooperation to alleviate trade restrictions on agricultural and food products from measures to prevent the spread of COVID-19.

Acknowledgement

This research is a part of the study performed within the framework of research title "Food Loss Assessment of Longan Products for Identifying the Food Loss Reduction Measures along the Whole Value Chain and Reporting SDG 12.3.1" which was made possible by a grant from the Agricultural Research Development Agency (Public Organisation) under Ministry of Agriculture and Cooperatives.

References

Aday, S., and Aday, M. S. (2020). Impact of COVID-19 on the food supply chain. *Food Quality and Safety*, 4(4): 167–180.

Andreyeva, T., Long, M. W., and Brownell, K. D. (2010). The impact of food prices on consumption: A systematic review of research on the price elasticity of demand for food. *American Journal of Public Health*, 100(2): 216–222.

Attavanich, W. (2020). *COVID-19 Country Assessment of Impacts and Response Options on Food Systems, Food Security and Nutrition, and Livelihoods.* FAO Regional Office for Asia and the Pacific (FAORAP).

Beach, R. H., Kuchler, F., Leibtag, E., and Zhen, C. (2008). *The Effects of Avian Influenza News on Consumer Purchasing Behavior: A Case Study of Italian Consumers' Retail Purchases.* United States Department of Agriculture. doi: 10.22004/ ag.econ.56477.

Blayney, D. P., Dyck, J. H., and Harvey, D. J. (2006). Economic effects of animal diseases linked to trade dependency. *Economic Research Service*, 4: 23–29. No. 1490-2016-127902, August 2008.

CEIC. (2020). CEIC Database. https://info.ceicdata.com/en-products-global-database.

De La Fuente, A., Jacoby, H. G., and Lawin, K. G. (2020). Impact of the West African Ebola epidemic on agricultural production and rural welfare: Evidence from Liberia. *Journal of African Economies*, 29(5): 454–474.

Espitia, A., Rocha, N., and Ruta, M. (2020). Covid-19 and food protectionism: The impact of the pandemic and export restrictions on world food markets. World Bank Group. http://documents.worldbank.org/curated/en/417171589912076742/ Covid-19-and-Food-Protectionism-The-Impact-of-the-Pandemic-and-Export-Restrictions-on-World-Food-Markets.

Evenett, S., Fiorini, M., Fritz, J., Hoekman, B., Lukaszuk, P., Rocha, N., Ruta, M., Santi, F., and Shingal, A. (2020). Trade policy responses to the COVID-19 pandemic crisis. VOX, CEPR Policy Portal. https://voxeu.org/article/ trade-policy-responses-covid-19-pandemic-new-dataset.

Femenia, F. (2019). A meta-analysis of the price and income elasticities of food demand. *German Journal of Agricultural Economics (Online)*, 68: 77–98.

Gong, B., Zhang, S., Yuan, L., and Chen, K. Z. (2020). A balance act: Minimizing economic loss while controlling novel coronavirus pneumonia. *Journal of Chinese Governance*, 5(2): 249–268. doi: 10.1080/23812346.2020.1741940.

IMF. (6 April 2020). Policy responses to Covid-19. International Monetary Fund. https://www.imf.org/en/Topics/imf-and-covid19/Policy-Responses-to-COVID-19#I.

Ivanov, D. (2020). Predicting the impacts of epidemic outbreaks on global supply chains: A simulation-based analysis on the coronavirus outbreak (COVID-19/SARS-CoV-2) case. *Transportation Research Part E: Logistics and Transportation Review*, 136: 101922.

Jackson, J. K., Weiss, M. A., Schwarzenberg, A. B., Nelson, B. M., Sutter, K. M., and Sutherland, M. D. (2020). Global economic effects of COVID-19. Congressional Research Service. https://fas.org/sgp/crs/row/R46270.pdf.

Joo, H., Maskery, B. A., Berro, A. D., Rotz, L. D., Lee, Y. K., and Brown, C. M. (2019). Economic impact of the 2015 MERS outbreak on the Republic of Korea's tourism-related industries. *Health Security*, 17(2): 100–108.

Kanu, I. A. (2020). COVID-19 and the economy: An African perspective. *Journal of African Studies and Sustainable Development*, 3(2): 29–36.

Khokhar, S. G., Min, Q., and Su, C. (2015). Bird flu (H7N9) outbreak and its implications on the supply chain of poultry meat in China. *Journal of Applied Poultry Research*, 24(2): 215–221.

Kumar, S., and Chandra, C. (2010). Supply chain disruption by avian flu pandemic for US companies: A case study. *Transportation Journal*, 49(4): 61–73.

Kumar, S. (2012). Planning for avian flu disruptions on global operations: A DMAIC case study. *International Journal of Health Care Quality Assurance*, 25(3): 197–215.

Miller, S. R., Malone, T., and Schaefer, A. K. (2020). Economic impact of COVID-19 on Michigan agricultural production sectors. (Publication No. 1098-2020-812). Doctoral dissertation, Michigan State University. AgEcon Search.

Ministry of Commerce. (2020). http://tradereport.moc.go.th/TradeThai.aspx.

Mohan, U., Viswanadham, N., and Trikha, P. (2009). Impact of Avian Influenza in the Indian poultry industry: A supply chain risk perspective. *International Journal of Logistics Systems and Management*, 5(1–2): 89–105.

Nicita, A. (2008). *Avian Influenza and the Poultry Trade*. The World Bank. doi: 10.1596/1813-9450-4551.

OECD. (2020). OECD scheme for the application of international standards for fruit and vegetables. Preliminary report: Evaluation of the impact of the coronavirus (COVID-19) on fruit and vegetables trade. OECD: Organisation for Economic Co-operation and Development. https://www.oecd.org/agriculture/fruit-vegetables/oecd-covid-19-impact-on-fruit-and-vegetables-trade.pdf.

Office of Agricultural Economics. (2020a). Longan production area and productive area in 2019. Ministry of Agriculture and Cooperatives. http://www.oae.go.th/assets/portals/1/fileups/prcaidata/files/longan%2062%20dit.pdf.

Office of Agricultural Economics. (2020b). Agricultural price index. Ministry of Agriculture and Cooperatives. http://www.oae.go.th/assets/portals/1/fileups/aeocdata/files/Table1_en_agriPriceIndex_11_63.XLS.

Office of Agricultural Economics. (2020c). 3rd quarter 2020 and outlook for 2020. Ministry of Agriculture and Cooperatives. http://www.oae.go.th/assets/portals/1/fileups/bappdata/files/Outlook%20Q3_2563%20final.pdf.

Office of Commercial Affairs Lamphun. (2020). https://region3.prd.go.th/region3_ci/topic/news/12621.

Pan, D., Yang, J., Zhou, G., and Kong, F. (2020). The influence of COVID-19 on agricultural economy and emergency mitigation measures in China: A text mining analysis. *PLoS ONE*, 15(10): 1–20. doi: 10.1371/journal.pone.0241167.

Panmanee, C., Tansuchat, R., and Arkornsakul, P. (2018). Green efficiency analysis of longan supply chains: A two-stage DEA approach. *Chiang Mai University Journal of Economics (CMJE)*, 22(2): 1–9.

Pulubuhu, D. A. T., Unde, A. A., Sumartias, S., Sudarmo, S., and Seniwati, S. (2020). The economic impact of COVID-19 outbreak on the agriculture sector. *International Journal of Agriculture System*, 8(1): 57–63.

Qiu, W., Chu, C., Mao, A., and Wu, J. (2018). The impacts on health, society, and economy of SARS and H7N9 outbreaks in China: A case comparison study. *Journal of Environmental and Public Health*, 2018: 1–7. doi: 10.1155/2018/2710185.

Qureshi, A. I. (2016). Economic and political impact of Ebola virus disease. *Ebola Virus Disease*, 177–191. doi: 10.1016/B978-0-12-804230-4.00013-3.

Rassy, D., and Smith, R. D. (2013). The economic impact of H1N1 on Mexico's tourist and pork sectors. *Health Economics*, 22(7): 824–834.

Schmidhuber, J., Pound, J., and Qiao, B. (2020). COVID-19: Channels of transmission to food and agriculture. Food and Agriculture Organization of the United Nations. http://www.fao.org/policy-support/tools-and-publications/resources-details/en/c/1269557/.

Siche, R. (2020). What is the impact of COVID-19 disease on agriculture? *Scientia Agropecuaria*, 11(1): 3–6.

Siu, A., and Wong, Y. R. (2004). Economic impact of SARS: The case of Hong Kong. *Asian Economic Papers*, 3(1): 62–83.

Suriyankietkaew, S., Nimsai, S., Bunnag, C., Tonsuchart, R., Petisan, P., Kaewsompong, N., Buppasiri, T., Ngampramuan, S., and Chumnasiew, P. (2020). *Research on Sustainable Development and Covid-19 Pandemic in ASEAN*. ASEAN Center for Sustainable Development Studies and Dialogues.

Taha, F. A. (2007). How highly pathogenic avian influenza (H5N1) has affected world poultry-meat trade. United States Department of Agriculture. doi: 10.22004/ag.econ.7360.

Tansuchat, R., Piboonrungroj, P., and Nimsai, S. (2016). Exploring opportunities and threats in logistics and supply chain management of Thai fruits to India. *International Journal of Supply Chain Management*, 5(2): 150–157.

Tiensin, T., Chaitaweesub, P., Songserm, T., Chaisingh, A., Hoonsuwan, W., Buranathai, C., ... and Stegeman, A. (2005). Highly pathogenic avian influenza H5N1, Thailand, 2004. *Emerging Infectious Diseases*, 11(11): 1664–1672.

Trade Map. (2020). Imports and Exports data. https://www.trademap.org/Index. aspx.

World Bank. (2020). World Bank East Asia and Pacific economic update, April 2020: East Asia and Pacific in the time of COVID-19. The World Bank. http://hdl.handle.net/10986/33477.

About the Authors

Roengchai Tansuchat is currently an associate professor of Faculty of Economics, and Director of Centre of Excellence in Econometrics at Chiang Mai University, Chiang Mai, Thailand. His research interests include econometrics, data analytics, risk modelling, energy finance, commodity finance, international commodity trade, agricultural economics and supply chain, quantum econometrics and finance. His research outcomes have been published widely including in *Energy Economics, Thai Journal of Mathematics, Tourism Economics, Mathematics and Computers in Simulation, North American Journal of Economics and Finance, International Journal of Supply Chain Management, Soft Computing, Applicable Algebra in Engineering, Communications and Computing, International Journal of Theoretical Physics, Discrete Mathematics*, and Springer Verlag book series. He has received the Golden Elephant Award 2019 for Outstanding Researcher in Social and Human Science from Chiang Mai University and National Research Council Award (Research

Award) 2016 from the National Research Council of Thailand (NRTC). He is a member of Centre for Socio-Economic Impact Assessment and Economic Possibility Study for Research Project, Faculty of Economics, Chiang Mai University.

Tanachai Pankasemsuk is currently a lecturer in Department of Plant and Soil Sciences, Faculty of Agriculture, and assistant dean in International College Digital Innovation, Chiang Mai University, Chiang Mai, Thailand. His research interests include phytomone, plant physiology, post-harvest technology, food safety, plasma technology, and nanotechnology in agriculture. His research outcomes have been published widely, including in *HortScience, The Journal of the American Society for Horticultural Science, International Journal of Food Engineering,* and *Journal of Wood Science.* He was a member of the Chiang Mai Think Tank Team, a consulting team of Chiang Mai city; a leader of agricultural nanotechnology and plasma technology research teams; Director of Post-harvest Technology of Chiang Mai University.

Chanita Panmanee is an assistant professor of the Faculty of Economics in Maejo University, Chiang Mai, Thailand. She completed her bachelor's and master's degree in economics and obtained doctoral degree in agricultural systems from Chiang Mai University. Her research interests associate with community-based economics, circular economy, agricultural marketing, and supply chain and logistics, especially agricultural and agri-business supply chain and logistics. Her recent research engagement includes food loss assessment of longan products for identifying the food loss reduction measures along the whole value chain and enhancement of konjac in Mae Hong Son province to acquire Thai geographical indication mark. She is also involved in consultancy and training activities in strengthening and competitiveness enhancement for many community enterprises and farmer groups.

Chapter 8

COVID-19 in Vietnam: Perception of Urban Workers and Compliance with the National Social Distancing Policies

Thanh-Long Giang[*,†,¶], Tham Hong-Thi Pham[*],
Thi-Thu Do[‡], and Manh-Phong Phi[§]

*National Economics University, Hanoi, Vietnam
†Menzies Institute of Medical Research,
University of Tasmania, Hobart, Australia
‡Banking Academy, Hanoi, Vietnam
§University of Mining and Geology, Hanoi, Vietnam
¶longgt@neu.edu.vn

Abstract

Using an online survey with about 650 persons living in urban areas in Vietnam and working in different job positions, this chapter aimed to explore how they perceived various measures in containing COVID-19 and how they complied with and evaluated different government policies in controlling the pandemic. In particular, we disaggregated data of

¶Corresponding author.

the urban workers into gender (male vs. female), job positions (wage-earners vs. other), social insurance participation (mandatory, voluntary, and non-participating), and self-rated health (good vs. bad). We found that the respondents highly appreciated the government with the provided information of COVID-19 and the implemented policies to contain the pandemic. People showed quite good compliance with the national social distancing policies since they went out of their homes mostly for essential work, while very rarely for other reasons or non-essential work. We could see various differences in perceptions and compliance levels of the respondents in terms of age, gender, residential area, and health status. Based on those findings along with the existing studies, we recommended that appropriate measures stabilising social and economic activities within the country should be continuously implemented so as to maintain or alternate jobs for people working in severely affected economic sectors. Also, providing accessible and affordable healthcare measures to all people, especially for poor and informal workers who are particularly risky to infectious diseases, should also be given great consideration. Sufficient goods and services for people to meet their basic needs during social distancing should be continuously maintained.

Keywords: COVID-19; compliance; pandemic; perception; Vietnam.

1. Introduction

According to the WHO COVID-19 Dashboard, on 1 December 2020, there were 62.66 million infected cases and 1.46 million deaths. From the first COVID-19 case, it took 90 days for the global total to reach 1 million cases. The number of days to reach every following 10th million reduced over time: from 86 days for increasing from 1 million to 10 million cases to only 17 days for increasing from 50 million to 60 million cases. The COVID-19 pandemic has created a human and economic crisis like no other since the Second World War (ILO *et al.*, 2020). It has hit more than 200 countries and regions with different levels of spreading and consequences. COVID-19 has pushed several households into poverty with great losses in labour income and remittances (Sumner *et al.*, 2020). ILO *et al.* (2020) showed that the long-term impact of COVID-19 might affect the implementation of the Sustainable Development Goals (SDGs) and targets, among which poverty alleviation, food security, decent work, health outcomes, and gender equality are of great concern.

To prevent COVID-19 outbreak and spreading-out, many countries introduced social distancing or lockdown measures with strict home isolation and restricted travelling. As argued by some reports (see, for instance, Jones *et al.*, 2020; Aljazeera, 2020a), such measures could be adopted quite well in high-income countries, but they might create heavy difficulties for low- and middle-income countries. In addition, 1,568 social protection measures were implemented in 209 countries in the world, 339 measures of which were implemented in 40 countries in Asia and the Pacific region, to provide special allowance/grant for income/jobs protection, unemployment benefit, housing/basic services, healthcare support, food and nutrition, pensions, children and families, sickness, access to education, maternity/parental support, and employment injury (ILO, 2020).

As a low middle-income country with a long border with China where the COVID-19 pandemic was exposed, Vietnam recorded the first COVID-19 infected case on 23 January 2020. As of 1 December 2020, there were 1,358 infected cases and 35 deaths. Since the reveal of the first case on 23 January 2020, Vietnam has implemented various strong measures to avoid the spread of COVID-19 to its about 97 million citizens. To date, Vietnam implemented the first national social distancing and some local lockdowns in late March and mid-April to contain the first wave of COVID-19, and the second local lockdowns in some provinces and cities in mid-July to contain the second wave of COVID-19. In the first 3-week social distancing period, for the first time in many people's lifetime, they were asked to "stay at home for the sake of your own and your community's welfare", and restricted travelling and transportation were implemented. The same as in many other countries in the Asia and the Pacific region, such measures severely influenced economic activities throughout the country, which has been presented with job losses and economic slow-down (World Bank, 2020). GSO (2020a) showed that the first two quarters in 2020 had much lower growth rates for the whole economy and the main economic sectors than at the same time in 2018 and 2019. GSO (2020b) showed that about 32 million people aged 15 and over have been negatively affected by COVID-19 pandemic with job loss, job rotation, reduced working hours, and thus income loss or reduction. About 69%

workers in services sector, 66% workers in industrial and construction sector, and 27% workers in agriculture, forestry, and fishery sectors were seriously affected. To deal with those problems, the government of Vietnam (GOV) issued the Resolution 42/NQ-CP to approve a support measure worth VND 62 trillion (or about USD 2.66 billion) to support people affected by the COVID-19 pandemic for 3 months (from April to June). Moreover, various measures to support firms and organisations were also implemented, such as corporate tax exemption and delayed contribution.

To date, Vietnam has been embraced by the World Health Organization (WHO) and other international organisations for its successful containment of COVID-19. As discussed by La *et al.* (2020) and Huynh (2020), Vietnam considered the COVID-19 pandemic as a serious public health issue at the beginning and thus it took a variety of measures to use "the golden time" to contain the spread of COVID-19. For example, La *et al.* (2020) argued that official news and continuous dissemination of COVID-19 infected cases provided by the GOV and its ministries delivered important health policy messages to people in order to change their healthcare behaviours such as hand washing and limiting direct contacts. Moreover, Huynh (2020) added that, instead of forcing the citizens with the compulsory regulations, the GOV well disseminated nudging-behaviour policies, which could increase the "virality" of the information.

To understand reactions of people, particularly urban persons, to the social distancing policies to contain the COVID-19 in Vietnam, we conducted an online survey with nearly 700 people right after the first national social distancing in late April 2020. The survey was conducted with the ethical approval of the Institute of Social and Medical Studies (ISMS) under Decision No.2/HDDD-ISMS dated 4 March 2020. This research explored perception of and compliance with social distancing measures by those persons.

This chapter has been organised as follows. Section 2 provides a literature review on perception and compliance of social distancing policies in various countries in the previous epidemic or pandemic events. Section 3 discusses data and analytical methods. The key findings along with discussions have been provided in the fourth section. The last section provides some concluding remarks with policy implications.

2. Literature Review

2.1 *Conceptual framework*

Perception is defined as the process of receiving, selecting, organising, interpreting, checking, and reacting to sensory stimuli or data (Pareek *et al.*, 1981). Perception is a conscious, or phenomenal, experience of seeing, hearing, or touching, etc. Perceptual experience provides the final output of perceptual processing (Styles, 2005).

Aswathappa (2009) analysed three main groups of factors affecting perception, including characteristics of the perceiver, the perceived, and the situation. Characteristics of the perceiver (such as needs, attitudes, values, and experiences) impact the process of perception. Characteristics of the perceived (such as appearance and behaviour) also influence how they are being perceived. Perceivers tend to notice physical appearance characteristics that contrast with the norm, that are intense, or that are new or unusual. Physical attractiveness often catches the attention quickly. In addition, characteristics of the situation show that the physical, social, and organisational settings of the situation also influence the process of perception. For example, a conversation with the boss held in the reception area of a dance club will be perceived differently than the conversation held in the office with the door closed.

Compliance can be defined as "conscious obedience to or incorporation of values, norms or institutional requirements" (Oliver, 1991, cited in Burdon and Sorour, 2020). In behavioural economics, there are two main approaches related to compliance, *decision theory and game theory*. In decision theories, Becker and Stigler (1977) assumed that the choice of people is decided based on the target of maximising their utility and minimising their cost. Accordingly, higher levels of fines for infractions in relation to fighting crime or higher subsidy levels in environmental policies make for more compliance. Besides, in game theory decisions of people depend on a fixed set of constraints. People adjust their behaviour according to other people's choices. In general, according to the decision theory or game theory, the compliance depends on the maximising of individual utility but does not cover other motivations.

Besides, theoretical studies of compliance are also based on the *psychological and sociological theories*. Compliance with rules or regulations relates to both internal characteristics of each individual and external effects of environment. These factors are explored using two theories, i.e. cognitive theory (Bandura, 1999) and social learning theory (Bandura, 1973). According to cognitive theory, the key variables influencing compliance are the individual's personal morality and level of moral development. The social learning theory concentrates on the effects of the environment. Therefore, the determinants of compliance are peers' opinions and the extent of social influence that an individual encounters.

2.2 *Factors affecting perception and compliance in containing a pandemic*

The lockdown and social distancing policies have positive effects on containing the pandemic. However, there are differences in the effectiveness of social distancing policies to control the spread of the COVID-19 implemented by the high-income and low- and middle-income countries (Maire, 2020). This is caused by many demographic and employment characteristics of citizens in each country such as age, gender, education level, living area (urban or rural), health status of respondents and their trust in government's policies and responses, job positions, and income levels. These factors can have positive, negative, or non-linear effects on compliance with and perception of the pandemic-containing policies in different countries.

Based on these theoretical frameworks, many empirical studies have been carried out about determinants of perception and compliance in pandemic-containing policies, including three main groups of factors: demographic, employment characteristics, and the attitude of people towards government regulation. Demographic and employment characteristics are not only the perceiver characteristics affecting people's perception, but are also internal factors influencing their compliance. In addition, the trust in government regulation is a perceiver factor affecting the perception first, then it impacts on compliance with the policies.

Firstly, compliance depends on demographic characteristics of respondents, including age, gender, education level, health status.

Age has a positive effect on compliance and perception of people in most territories such as Italy, Hong Kong, Singapore, Taiwan, in many different epidemics including SARS and COVID-19 pandemic (Barari *et al.*, 2020; Blendon *et al.*, 2006). In particular, Blendon *et al.* (2006) used data from a survey of residents of Hong Kong, Taiwan, Singapore, and the United States to explore attitudes towards and compliance with the use of preventive measures, including wearing a mask, having temperature taken, and quarantine that could protect the health of the community and prevent the spread of an infectious disease in a public health emergency. The findings showed that there was also large support for the mentioned measures and compliance with them in the four territories. Nonetheless, the respondents in the U.S. had less experience with them: 88% and 44% of respondents favoured the measure of having temperature taken in Singapore and in the U.S., respectively. For the quarantine measures of people suspected of having been exposed to an infectious disease, there was still strong support in Taiwan, Hong Kong, and Singapore after citizens were told that a person could be arrested if he or she did not comply, with 54%, 68%, and 70% in favour of the measures in Hong Kong, Singapore, and Taiwan, respectively. However, only 42% of the public supported these measures in the United States.

The impacts of age on compliance also might be non-linear. Using data from the Avian Influenza pandemic in the U.S., both studies by Blake *et al.* (2010) and Bass *et al.* (2010) showed that older people (those aged 60 and older) were more likely than younger people to say that they would have stayed at home if the government had asked. This was explained as being possible as a lot of older people had no work outside their homes, so they were willing to stay at home to comply with the policies. In contrast, younger people, especially the youth, had to go for work to their companies, and they were scared of losing their jobs. In addition, older people had much more health problems, and thus they were more cautious with their health than younger people in responding to the serious spread of the virus.

In regard to gender differences in complying with the anti-virus policies, most of the existing studies (see, for instance, Blendon *et al.*, 2006; Bass *et al.*, 2010; Blake *et al.*, 2010; Barari *et al.*, 2020) showed that women were much more likely to comply than men in every solution for controlling spread of the viruses in various pandemics. In particular, Bass *et al.* (2010), applying an ANOVA analysis to explore gender differences in complying with quarantines, concluded that women were much more likely than men to comply with all types of quarantines. Such results could be explained by employment characteristics and health protective behaviours of women: there were some groups of women who worked at home as family workers, and they believed that staying at home was a solution to avoid diseases from the pandemic. Barari *et al.* (2020) also showed that about 77% female respondents had anxiety or shock from the COVID-19 pandemic, while that was the case for about 71% of the male respondents.

Education level has negative correlation with compliance and perception of people in containing pandemic. This was demonstrated in many studies in different pandemics including SARS, influenza pandemic in Hong Kong, Singapore, Taiwan, the U.S. (see Blendon *et al.*, 2006; Bass *et al.*, 2010; Blake *et al.*, 2010). For example, Bass *et al.* (2010) analysed the compliance of people in the Avian Flu pandemic in the U.S. The results showed that generally people with a higher educational level were more likely to be compliant to quarantine orders than those with a lower educational level. Exceptionally, however, those without a high school diploma were more willing to comply with the social distancing to contain the pandemic than those with university level education, and this could be explained as people with lower education level usually having lower income and social capital, and thus being more worried about the government's punishment.

It is very interesting that people with excellent and good health statuses are much more likely to comply with and highly evaluate the solutions of the government in controlling the spread of virus in pandemics than those with poor health (Blake *et al.*, 2010; Barari *et al.*, 2020; Rothstein and Talbott, 2007). Barari *et al.* (2019), for example, investigated a nationally representative survey about public health crisis caused by SARS-COV-2 virus to evaluate the government's public health efforts and the compliance of citizens in Italy. The authors concluded that people having poor health were less likely to stay at home because they had to go to hospitals and pharmacies in order to take care of their health problems. Rothstein and Talbott (2007) assumed that legal, personal, or economic risks made undocumented immigrants and individuals with a substance use disorder unwilling to comply with the quarantine. In order to ensure compliance with quarantine, they suggested that arrest, deportation, or similar adverse consequences must be applied. Barari *et al.* (2020) employed one of the first nationally representative surveys on the unprecedented COVID-19 crisis in Italy for evaluating the Italian government's public health policies and Italian citizens' responses. They found that all respondents understood how to protect themselves and others from the SARS-COV-2 virus, but young people usually had a lower compliance rate. The authors, however, also found that there were severely negative impacts of the quarantine on the population's mental health, and they recommended that public health procedures be made more desirable by virtual social interactions, and online social reading activities.

Secondly, compliance is also associated with employment characteristics of respondents, particularly job position and income. Rothstein and Talbott (2007) and Blake *et al.* (2010) showed that there were differences in complying to contain a pandemic between groups of workers in terms of job position (such as wage earners vs. self-employed). For example, by reviewing the international experiences with SARS from Taiwan, Singapore, Hong Kong, and the U.S. in 2003, Rothstein and Talbott (2007) suggested some recommendations to achieve more voluntary quarantine compliance, including providing job security and income replacement during the pandemic. After that, based on data from the 2006 Harvard School of Public Health Pandemic Influenza Survey and multivariable logistic regression, Blake *et al.* (2010) found employment characteristics that were associated with compliance with recommendations in the event of a pandemic influenza outbreak. Those respondents who were unable to work from home, suffered from lack of pay due to being absent from work, or were self-employed would be less likely to comply with social distancing recommendations

By using a sample of 1,204 adult Pennsylvania residents to interview people's attitudes, awareness of avian influenza, measure for containing the pandemic of governments, and their compliance, Bass *et al.* (2010) also concluded that people who had no work were more likely to stay at home because they did not fear losing their job.

Income has positive or non-linear effects on compliance of labour (Blake *et al.*, 2010; Bass *et al.*, 2010). Particularly, Blake *et al.* (2010) showed that people in low- and middle-income groups were less likely to comply with policies for containing the pandemic than upper-income groups. If the strong social distancing policies were applied for 3 months, people at every income level, especially low-income, would face greater financial problems. However, Bass *et al.* (2010) also studied compliance during the Avian Flu pandemic of the U.S. with different results. The authors explained that lower income labour were either not working at all or did not think about choices different from the social distancing policies that the government required them to make such as the quarantine policy. In contrast, people in the highest income group were the least likely to comply with these policies because they may also fear reprisal less.

Finally, factors reflecting the trust in government regulation have positive effects on high evaluation and compliance of citizens (Bish and Michie, 2010; DiGiovanni *et al.*, 2004; Barari *et al.*, 2019). Bish and Michie (2010) employed data from 26 papers to review the key demographic and attitudinal factors of three types of protective behaviours during an influenza pandemic, including prevention, avoidance, and management of illness behaviours. They concluded that perceived susceptibility, perceived severity, belief in the effectiveness of the recommended behaviours to protect against the disease, levels of state anxiety, trust in authorities were factors linked to behaviours. Similarly, based on data from interviews, telephone polling, and focus groups, DiGiovanni *et al.* (2004) investigated obstacles to compliance with quarantine during the 2003 SARS pandemic in Toronto. They found that psychological stress and communications to the public were among the important factors influencing compliance with the quarantine.

3. Data and Analytical Methods

3.1 *Data*

In collaboration with a research team at the Institute of Social and Medical Studies (ISMS) in Hanoi, Vietnam, we conducted a web-based survey immediately after the GOV relaxed its social distancing measures during the 3 weeks of 1–21 April 2020. The survey was approved by IRB in Biomedical Research at ISMS under Decision No.2/HDDD-ISMS dated 4

March 2020. We have provided in the Appendix the English translation of the part of the survey questionnaire that we analysed as follows.

The survey consisted of four sections with 46 questions, which collected data on individual characteristics (such as age, sex, job, education, and health status), and their evaluations about the effectiveness of the government's policies against COVID-19. We focus in this chapter on the data related to their perception of and compliance with the social distancing policies.

We employed the snowball sampling method and invited individuals in our network to participate in the survey. We contacted these individuals through popular social media platforms in Vietnam such as Facebook and Zalo. We received 677 respondents to our survey in total. After checking the data, however, we removed 24 respondents due to their incomplete answers to the survey questionnaire. Consequently, the final sample for analysis included 653 respondents. Due to the way of collecting data via social media platforms, we acknowledge that the survey could not fully cover rural residents and informal workers. Also, the survey was not nationally representative, and it was biased towards urban residents, who had higher education levels and mostly worked in the formal sector.

Table 1 provides the descriptive statistics. The age of the individuals in our sample averaged 39 and ranged from 18 to 68. The majority of them were female (71%), Kinh (98%), married (80%), lived in urban areas (90%), and followed no religion (78%). In terms of educational achievement, 34% of individuals had a college degree, while 62% had a graduate degree (i.e. master's degree or higher levels). Around 64% of all individuals had a permanent job contract, and 14% have a short-term job contract (i.e. one that is less than 3 years). Only 8% of the survey respondents were self-employed.

3.2 *Analytical methods*

For each of the questions on the perception of and compliance with the social distancing policies, we disaggregated data into different individual characteristics of the respondents (such as age groups, gender, and health status). Explanations for the results were based on the policies

Table 1:   Individual characteristics of the surveyed persons.

Surveyed Workers' Situation	%
Have a job	86
Self-employed	8
Have a permanent job contract	64
Have a short-term job contract	14
Good health	68
Age	38.6
Female	71
Kinh	98
Have a college education	34
Have a graduate education (master's or higher)	62
Married	80
Follow no religion	78
Urban	90

Source: Own calculations from the Survey Data.

implemented in Vietnam as well as compared with those found in other studies as discussed in the literature review.

4. Key Findings

4.1 *Perception of the respondents on the COVID-19 pandemic*

Figure 1 provides the results for self-assessment on efficiency of measures to contain COVID-19 by the respondents of the survey. The maximum score for assessment was 10, and the minimum score was 0. As can be seen, social distancing was considered the most effective way while curfew was seen as the least effective way to contain COVID-19, with respective scores being 9.24 and 8.53.

Figure 2 provides the results for self-assessment on efficiency of measures to contain COVID-19 by gender of the respondents. In general, female respondents had higher assessment scores than the male

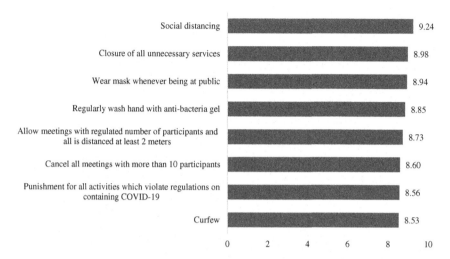

Figure 1: Average score for self-assessment on efficiency of measures to contain COVID-19.

Source: Own calculations from the survey data.

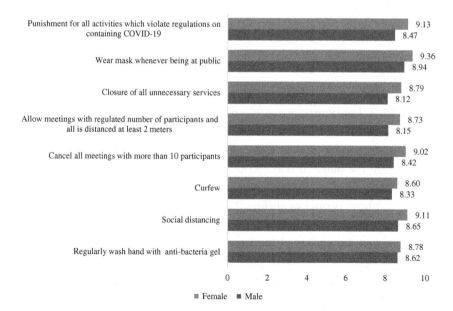

Figure 2: Average score for self-assessment on efficiency of measures to contain COVID-19, by gender.

Source: Own calculations from the survey data.

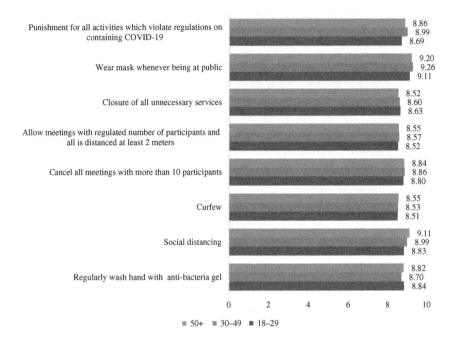

Figure 3:   Average score for self-assessment on efficiency of measures to contain COVID-19, by age group.

Source: Own calculations from the survey data.

respondents. For both genders, the most effective way to contain COVID-19 would be "wear mask whenever being at public". However, they had different assessment for the least effective way: for females, it was "curfew", while for males it was "Allow meetings with regulated number of participants and all is at a distance of at least 2 meters".

To see how people of different age groups assessed effectiveness of measures to contain COVID-19, Figure 3 presents our survey results. The respondents were classified by three age groups: youth (18–29), middle-age (30–49), and near-elderly and older persons (aged 50 and over). Their average scores were not much different within a certain measure, but different across the measures. In general, "wear mask whenever being at public" was considered the most effective way for containing COVID-19 by people in all three age groups. For other measures, the oldest group

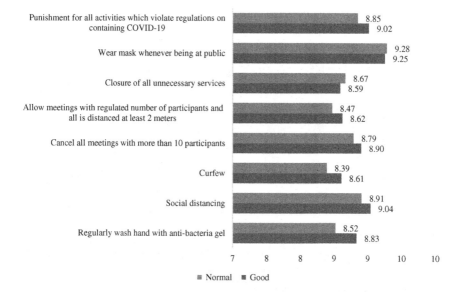

Figure 4: Average score for self-assessment on efficiency of measures to contain COVID-19, by health status of respondent.

Source: Own calculations from the survey data.

(those aged 50 and over) believed that "social distancing" would be the most effective way (scored 9.11), while it was "Punishment for all activities which violate regulations on containing COVID-19" for the middle-age group (scored 8.99), and "Regularly wash hand with anti-bacteria gel" for the youth (aged 18–29).

By health status of the respondents, the results presented in Figure 4 generally indicate that there were significant differences in assessing measures between those with normal and good health.[1] Both those with normal health and good health had the highest rate for "Wear mask whenever being at public" (with a score of 9.28 and 9.25, respectively). The least effective way to control COVID-19 was "Curfew" for those with

---

[1] In the survey, there were only three persons who responded with "bad health status", so we did not analyse this sample.

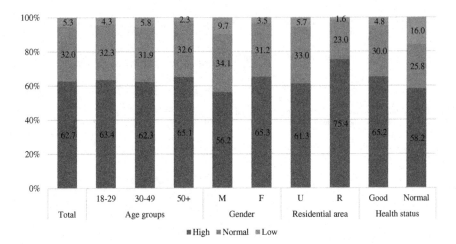

Figure 5: How much do you believe in the government's measures to contain the pandemic?

Source: Own calculations from the survey data.

normal health (scored 8.39) and "Closure of all unnecessary services" for those with good health (scored 8.59).

In order to assess how much the respondents believed in the government's measures to contain the COIVID-19 pandemic, Figure 5 shows the survey results by age groups, gender, residential area, and health status. In general, about 63% of the respondents strongly believed in the government's measures; about 33% had normal belief in these measures, and only about 5% of them had low belief.

There were significant differences among the respondents in terms of age, gender, residential area, and health status. In particular, the oldest groups had higher rates of "high" and "normal" beliefs than those for youth and middle-age groups. Female respondents had significantly higher rate of "high belief" than male respondents (65.3% vs. 56.2%). This was also the same for rural and urban respondents (75.4% vs. 61.3%).

In terms of health status, for "high belief", the rate for those with normal health was 58.2%, while that for those with good health was 65.2%. In contrast, among those who had low belief in the government's

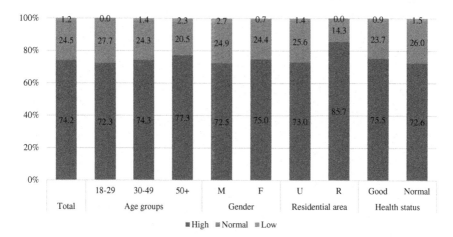

Figure 6: How much do you believe in the information about the pandemic provided by mass media?

Source: Own calculations from the survey data.

measures, the rate for those with normal health was much higher than that for those with good health (16% vs. 4.8%).

"Infodemic" is always going along with any epidemic or pandemic, and thus it is important to know whether citizens believe in the information provided by various mass media sources. Figure 6 provides the survey results for the respondents in terms of age, gender, residential area, and health status.

In general, about 99% of the respondents believed in the information provided by mass media sources, of which 74% had strong belief while about 25% had normal (average) belief. The same as the results in Figure 5, there were significant differences among the respondents in terms of age, gender, residential area, and health status. In specific, the oldest group, women, rural people, and those with good and normal health had higher rates of belief in information about the pandemic provided by mass media sources than did their younger, men, urban, and bad health counterparts.

Going further with assessments of the respondents on how the government has responded to contain the COVID-19 pandemic, Figure 7 shows

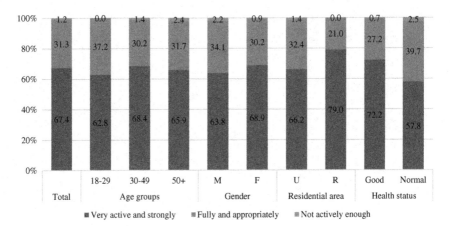

Figure 7:   How do you think the government has reacted to the pandemic?
Source: Own calculations from the survey data.

quite similar results as those in Figure 6. About 99% of the respondents thought that the government had reacted to the pandemic strongly, timely, and appropriately, while only 1% did not think so. There were significant differences in assessment rates among the respondents in terms of gender (women had higher rate of positive thoughts than did men), residential area (rural respondents had higher rate of positive thoughts than did urban counterparts), and health status (those with normal health had lower rate than did those with good health).

4.2 *Compliance of the respondents to the policies for containing COVID-19 pandemic*

To see how the respondents complied with the social distancing policies, we explored their frequency of going out of their houses, as well as the main reasons for going out.

Figure 8 presents the survey results for the respondents in terms of age, gender, residential area, and health status. Overall, about 49% of the respondents went out of their houses 1–2 times per week, followed by

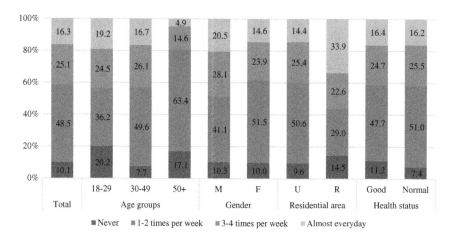

Figure 8:   Frequency for going out of the house during the social distancing period.
Source: Own calculations from the survey data.

25.1% who went out 3–4 times per week, and about 16.3% who went out of their houses every day.

These frequencies were different among the respondents in terms of age group (the youth had the highest rate for going out every day (19.2%), followed by the middle-age (16.7%), which were much higher than that for the oldest group (4.9%). The youngest and the oldest groups had higher rates to "never go out" than the middle-age group (20.2% and 17.1% vs. 7.7%) and this could be explained by the fact that the former groups included students and retirees, so they stayed at home for studying online or relaxing, while the latter group included those who were working so they might still go out for working and other reasons.

In terms of gender, there were not significant differences between two groups for "never go out" (10.3% for men and 10% for women). However, men had a significantly higher rate for "go out everyday" than the women (20.5% vs. 14.6%), and this could be attributed to differences in working status and housework responsibilities.

The distributions of frequencies to going out for urban and rural respondents were quite diverse. Rural people had higher rates for "never

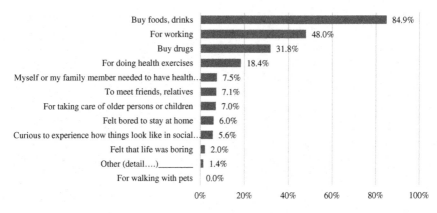

Figure 9:   Purposes for going out of the houses during the social distancing period.
Source: Own calculations from the survey data.

go out" and "go out everyday", but had much lower rates for "1–2 times per week" than urban people.

In terms of health status of the respondents, there were no significant differences between those with normal health and those with good health, except for the "going out 1–2 times per week" (51% for the former and 47.1% for the latter).

Figure 9 provides various reasons for the respondents to go out of their houses during the social distancing period. The main reason was "to buy foods and drinks" (84.9%), followed by "to work" (48%), "buy drugs" (31.8%), and "for doing exercises" (18.4%), while other reasons were less than 8%. To present the data in more details, Figure 10 describes the results for the reasons to go out by age groups, while Figure 11 shows those by gender.

Overall, Figure 10 shows that "buy foods and drinks" was the main reason for the respondents in all age groups, in which the middle-aged persons — who were mostly working and responsible for taking care of their families — had the highest rate for this reason. The oldest group had the lowest rate for "working", but had much higher rates (and the highest rates) for "taking care of older persons and/or children" and "for doing health exercises" than did the respondents in other two age groups.

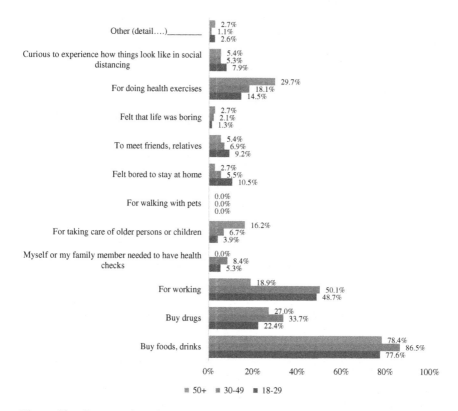

Figure 10: Purposes for going out of the houses during the social distancing period, by age group.

Source: Own calculations from the survey data.

There were significant differences between women and men in their reasons to go out of their houses during the social distancing period, as presented in Figure 11. Both had "buy foods and drinks" as the main reason to go out, but women had a higher rate for this reason than did men (88.2% vs. 76.6%) and this could be easily understood by gender differences in housework, including "buy foods and drinks", in Vietnam. For all other reasons, men had higher rates than women (for instance, 50.9% vs. 46.8% for "working"; 28.7% vs. 14.1% for "doing health exercises").

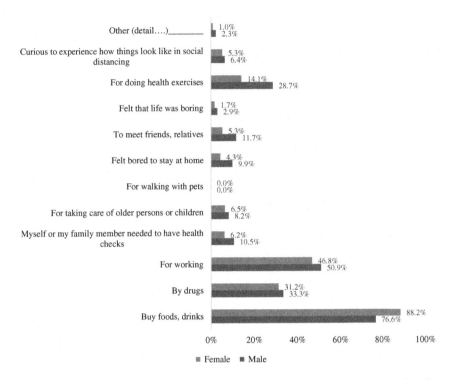

Figure 11: Purposes for going out of the houses during the social distancing period, by gender.

Source: Own calculations from the survey data.

Figure 12 shows how those with normal health and those with good health had different reasons for going out of their houses during the social distancing period. It is interesting to see that these two groups were not much different for the most popular reason, i.e. "buy foods and drinks", but they were significantly different in other reasons, such as in "buy drugs" (for which those with normal health had a higher rate than those with good health: 34.9% vs. 30.4%), in "working" (for which those with normal health had a much lower rate than those with good health: 42.3% vs. 50.9%), and in "for doing health exercises" (for which those with normal health had a much lower rate than those with good health: 15.9% vs. 19.7%).

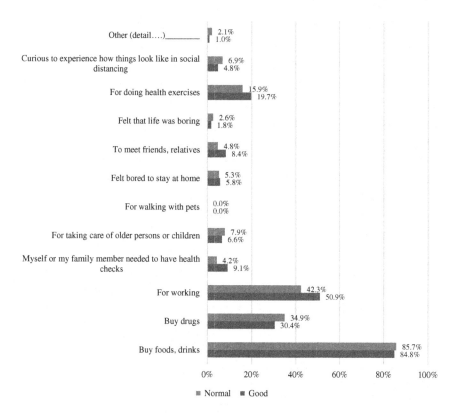

Figure 12: Purposes for going out of the houses during the social distancing period, by health status.

Source: Own calculations from the survey data.

5. Further Discussions and Concluding Remarks

We conducted a web-based survey in Vietnam — among the first in the early time of the COVID-19 pandemic — to understand individuals' assessments of their perception of and compliance with the national social distancing policies in April 2020. We found that the respondents highly appreciated the government with the provided information of COVID-19 and the implemented policies to contain the pandemic. These findings could be supported by those found in previous studies (such as Giang,

2020; UNDP & ISMS, 2020) and this research itself that the government provided information and support in a timely manner to people in need right after the first week of social distancing, particularly the Resolution 42 dated 10 April 2020 that provided cash transfers to poor and vulnerable households as well as informal sector workers. Also, we found that people showed quite good compliance with the national social distancing policies since they went out of their homes mostly for essential work only such as "buy foods and drinks", "working", "buy drugs", and "for doing health exercises", with very low rates for other reasons which could be considered as non-essential work such as "meeting friends, relatives", "feeling that life was bored", and "curious to experience how things look like in social distancing".

The assessment rates, however, were different between the respondents in terms of age groups, gender, residential area, and health status. Due to possible work, study, and familial duties, younger people, men, and urban people had lower rates of perception of measures to contain COVID-19 but higher rates for going out of their homes than their counterparts. To some extent, this trend might reflect causal relation, and as such more policy actions should be focused on these groups of people so as to avoid possible infections.

Along with other studies on the impact of COVID-19 on the Vietnamese people and households (such as Giang *et al.*, 2021; UNDP & ISMS, 2020), we would like to propose the following policy recommendations.

- Appropriate measures in containing COVID-19 to stabilise social and economic activities within the country should be continuously implemented. Among various economic solutions, maintaining or alternating jobs for people working in more affected economic sectors (such as tourism and hospitality) should be prioritised. Experiences from various countries showed that lockdowns or social distancing are not the same for all people, which has been tough for those with poor living conditions to follow.
- Health condition is clearly an important factor influencing people's perception of and compliance with social distancing policies, and thus providing accessible and affordable healthcare measures to all

people should be given greater consideration, especially the poor and informal workers who are particularly at risk from the infectious diseases — not only because of their job per se, but also due to their poor living conditions (such as lack of sufficient housing and sanitation conditions, low access to clean water, etc.).

• Along with social and health protection measures, well-organised logistics providing sufficient goods and services for people to meet their basic needs during social distancing should be continuously maintained. This would help people stay at home without being concerned about shortage of — for instance — food and vegetables, which in turn helps prevent frequent contacts among people.

As mentioned above, we acknowledged that our survey sample was biased towards those who had higher education levels, lived in urban areas, and had formal jobs. The current sample thus provided quite promising results on perception of COVID-19 and compliance with the national social distancing policies. This also means that those who were more vulnerable (such as people with lower educational levels or those who worked without a labour contract) might be even more affected by the COVID-19 pandemic, but they were not included in our study. More specifically, informal sector workers — who usually have no labour contract and have unstable jobs without social protection benefits — should be considered in the next study. Under any measures to contain COVID-19 (such as social distancing or lockdown), these workers may be likely to suffer more income losses, and thus their compliance with policies might be different to those in our studied sample.

References

Aljazeera. (2020a). Chaos and hunger amid India coronavirus lockdown. Retrieved on 1 May 2020 from https://www.aljazeera.com/news/2020/03/chaos-hunger-india-coronavirus-lockdown-200327094522268.html.

Aljazeera. (2020b). "Future is scary": Poor hit hardest by India coronavirus lockdown. Retrieved on 1 May 2020 from https://www.aljazeera.com/news/2020/04/scary-poor-hit-hardest-india-coronavirus-lockdown-200409105651819.html.

Aswathappa, K., and Reddy, G. S. (2009). *Organisational Behaviour*, Vol. 20, Mumbai: Himalaya Publishing House.

Bandura, A. (1973). *Aggression: A Social Learning Analysis*, Englewood Cliffs, NJ: Prentice- Hall.

Bandura, A. (1999). A social cognitive theory of personality. In: L. Pervin and O. John (Eds.), *Handbook of Personality*, 2nd ed., New York: Guilford Publications, pp. 154–196. (Reprinted in Cervone, D. and Shoda, Y. (Eds.) *The Coherence of Personality*, New York: Guilford Press).

Barari, S., Caria, S., Davola, A., Falco, P., Fetzer, T., Fiorin, S., … and Slepoi, F. R. (2020). Evaluating COVID-19 public health messaging in Italy: Self-reported compliance and growing mental health concerns. doi: 10.1101/2020.03.27.20042820.

Bass, S. B., Ruzek, S. B., Ward, L., Gordon, T. F., Hanlon, A., Hausman, A. J., and Hagen, M. (2010). If you ask them, will they come? Predictors of quarantine compliance during a hypothetical avian influenza pandemic: Results from a statewide survey. *Disaster Medicine and Public Health Preparedness*, 4(2): 135–144.

Becker, G. J. and Stigler G. S. (1977). De Gustibus Non Est Disputandum. *The American Economic Review*, 67(2): 76–90.

Bish, A., and Michie, S. (2010). Demographic and attitudinal determinants of protective behaviours during a pandemic: A review. *British Journal of Health Psychology*, 15(4): 797–824.

Blake, K. D., Blendon, R. J., and Viswanath, K. (2010). Employment and compliance with pandemic influenza mitigation recommendations. *Emerging Infectious Diseases*, 16(2): 212–218.

Blendon, R. J., DesRoches, C. M., Cetron, M. S., Benson, J. M., Meinhardt, T., and Pollard, W. (2006). Attitudes toward the use of quarantine in a public health emergency in four countries: The experiences of Hong Kong, Singapore, Taiwan, and the United States are instructive in assessing national responses to disease threats. *Health Affairs*, 25(Suppl1): W15–W25.

Burdon, W. M., and Sorour, M. K. (2020). Institutional theory and evolution of 'a legitimate'compliance culture: The case of the UK financial service sector. *Journal of Business Ethics*, 162(1): 47–80.

DiGiovanni, C., Conley, J., Chiu, D., and Zaborski, J. (2004). Factors influencing compliance with quarantine in Toronto during the 2003 SARS outbreak. *Biosecurity and Bioterrorism: Biodefense Strategy, Practice, and Science*, 2(4): 265–272.

Giang, T. L. (2020). Successful social distancing to contain COVID-19: How well were the Vietnamese households prepared? Unpublished manuscript.

GSO (General Statistics Office, Viet Nam). (2020a). Socio-economic situation in the first three quarters in 2020 (in Vietnamese). Retrieved on 20 October 2020 from https://www.gso.gov.vn/du-lieu-va-so-lieu-thong-ke/2020/09/thong-cao-bao-chi-tinh-hinh-kinh-te-xa-hoi-quy-iii-va-9-thang-nam-2020.

GSO. (2020b). Report on the impact of the COVID-19 pandemic on employment and work in Vietnam in the third quarter of 2020. Retrieved on 20 October 2020 from https://www.gso.gov.vn/du-lieu-va-so-lieu-thong-ke/2020/10/bao-cao-tac-dong-cua-dich-covid-19-den-tinh-hinh-lao-dong-viec-lam-tai-viet-nam-quy-iii-2020.

Huynh, L. D. T. (2020). The COVID-19 containment in Vietnam: What are we doing? *Journal of Global Health*, 10(1): 1–3. doi: 10.7189/jogh.10.010338.

ILO, ESCAP, UNICEF and other. (2020). *Social Protection Responses to COVID-19 in Asia and the Pacific: The Story so Far and Future Considerations*. Bangkok: ILO.

Jones, S., Egger, E. M., and Santos, R. (2020). Is Mozambique prepared for a lockdown during the COVID-19 pandemic? Retrieved on 1 May 2020 from https://www.wider.unu.edu/publication/mozambique-prepared-lockdown-during-covid-19-pandemic

La, V. P., Pham, T. H., Ho, M. T., Hoang, N. M., Linh, N. P. K., Trang, V. T., *et al.* (2020). Policy response, social media, and science journalism for the sustainability of the public health system amid COVID-19 outbreak: The Vietnam lessons. *Sustainability,* 12: 2931. doi: 10.3390/su12072931.

Maire, J. (2020). Impact of COVID-19 lockdowns on individual mobility and the importance of socioeconomic factors. Peterson Institute for International Economics, Policy brief. Retrieved on 1 February 2021 from www.google.com/covid19/mobility.

Pareek, U., Rao, T. V., and Pestonjee, D. M. (1981). *Behavioural Processes in Organizations*. New Delhi: Oxford & IBH Publishing Co.

Rothstein, M. A., and Talbott, M. K. (2007). Encouraging compliance with quarantine: A proposal to provide job security and income replacement. *American Journal of Public Health*, 97(Supplement_1): S49–S56.

Sakib, S. M. N. (2020). Bangladesh: Poor struggle to survive amid COVID-19. Retrieved on 1 May 2020 from https://www.aa.com.tr/en/asia-pacific/bangladesh-poor-struggle-to-survive-amid-covid-19/1819868.

Styles, E. A. (2005). *Attention, Perception and Memory: An Integrated Introduction.* London: Psychology Press.

Sumner, A., Hoy, C., and Ortiz-Juarez, E. (2020). Estimates of the impact of COVID-19 on global poverty. Helsinki. doi: 10.35188/UNU-WIDER/2020/800-9.

UNDP (United Nations Development Programme) and ISMS (Institute of Social and Medical Studies). (2020). Impacts of COVID-19 on livelihood and access to healthcare services of ethnic minority households living nearby the border with China.

World Bank. (2020). *Taking Stock July 2020: What will be the New Normal for Vietnam — The Economic Impact of COVID-19.* Washington D.C: World Bank.

Appendix — Questions for the Survey

(Extracted from the full survey with four sections and 46 questions)

I	PERSONAL INFORMATION	
1	Year of Birth	
2	Sex	
	Male	1
	Female	2
3	Ethnicity	
	Kinh	1
	Other (detail)_____	99
4	Permanent living place (more than 6 months in the past 12 months)	
	Urban	1
	Rural	2
5	Highest educational level	
	Never schooling	1
	Incomplete primary school	2
	Complete primary school	3
	Complete secondary school	4
	Complete upper-secondary school	5
	College/University	6
	Postgraduate (Master, Ph.D.)	7
	Other (detail)_____	99
6	Marital status	
	Currently married	1
	Never married	2
	Separated	3
	Divorced	4
	Widow	5
7	In the past 14 days, were you working?	
	Yes	1
	No	2

8	In the past 14 days, how did you feel about your health?		
		Good	1
		Normal	2
		Not good	3

II   ASSESSMENTS ON ACTIVITIES TO CONTAIN COVID-19

1   Have you ever heard about any policies of the Government related to COVID-19?

Yes   1

No   2

2   How confident are you about Government's policies in containing COVID-19?

High   1

Normal   2

Low   3

3   How do you assess information related to the pandemic which was provided by the official media agencies?

Reliable   1

Normal (half reliable, half unreliable)   2

Fully unreliable   3

Do not know   98

4   How do you assess Government's reactions to contain COVID-19?

Active, strong   1

Appropriate, sufficient   2

Inappropriate, insufficient   3

Do not know   98

III   ON REGULATION AND COMPLIANCE OF SOCIAL DISTANCING

1   How often did you get out of your house during social distancing period?

Never   1

1–2 times per week   2

3–4 times per week   3

Almost everyday   4

III ON REGULATION AND COMPLIANCE OF SOCIAL DISTANCING

2   Why did you go out of your house? (**multiple choices**)

Buy foods, drinks	1
By drugs	2
For working	3
Myself or my family member needed to have health checks	4
For taking care of older persons or children	5
For walking with pets	6
Felt bored to stay at home	7
To meet friends, relatives	8
Felt that life was boring	9
For doing health exercises	10
Curious to experience how things look like in social distancing	11
Other (detail....)_____	99

3   How do you assess the following activities in containing COVID-19? (**grading from 1 to 10, in which 1 is fully inefficient and 10 is fully efficient**)

Regularly wash hand with anti-bacteria gel

Social distancing

Curfew

Cancel all meetings with more than 10 participants

Allow meetings with regulated number of participants and all is distanced at least 2 meters

Closure of all unnecessary services

Wear mask whenever being at public

Punishment for all activities which violate regulations on containing COVID-19

About the Authors

Thanh-Long Giang is currently an associate professor in Economics at the National Economics University, and a senior researcher at Institute of Social and Medical Studies (ISMS) — both are in Hanoi, Vietnam. His research interests include ageing, social protection, and health protection. His research outcomes have been published widely, including in *Asian Economic Journal*; *Asia Pacific Migration Journal*; *Asia Pacific Economic Literature*; *Development and Change*; *International Social Science Journal*; and *Social Science and Medicine*. He was a member of the drafting team for Vietnam's Social Protection Strategy (2011–2020); a key member of taskforce and research group for reforming social assistance system in Vietnam (2017–2021), under Ministry of Labour, War Invalids, and Social Affairs, Vietnam. Prof. Long has provided various consultancy services for ADB, GIZ, ILO, World Bank, World Health Organization, among others.

Tham Hong-Thi Pham is a senior lecturer at the Faculty of Mathematical Economics in National Economics University. She obtained her master's degree in actuarial sciences from Institute of Actuarial and Financial Sciences at Lyon 1 University (France), and her Ph.D. degree in mathematical economics at the National Economics University (Vietnam). Her main research areas include applied mathematical models in finance, economics, and insurance. Her research outcomes have been published in *Journal of Social Insurance*, *Journal of Economics and Development*, and *Social Science and Medicine*. She is also involved in consultancy and training activities in actuarial work of insurance for many insurance corporations and the Health Finance and Governance (HFG) project of USAID.

Thi-Thu Do is a lecturer at the Banking Academy of Vietnam. She has taught microeconomics, public economics, and environmental economics. Her research interests include topics related to social security and sustainability development such as social insurance, ageing population, poverty reduction, and corporate social responsibility. Ms. Thu has published in many prestigious Vietnamese academic journals. She completed a Ph.D. programme in economics at National Economics University.

Manh-Phong Phi is a senior lecturer at the Faculty of Political Studies in University of Mining and Geology, Hanoi. He completed his master's degree and doctoral degree in political economy from Vietnam National University, Hanoi. His research interests lie in social protection issues, especially poverty, social health insurance, health care, long-term care for older people group, from the analysis to the evaluation of social protection policy. His recent research engagement includes poverty of older people, social health insurance for older people, and productive activities of older people. He has also been involved in consultancy for World Bank in Vietnam.

Chapter 9

Successful Social Distancing to Contain COVID-19: Mapping the Readiness of the Vietnamese Households

Thanh-Long Giang*

*Faculty of Economics, National Economics University (NEU),
207 Giai Phong Street, Hai Ba Trung District,
Hanoi 11616, Vietnam
Menzies Institute of Medical Research,
University of Tasmania, 17 Liverpool Street, Hobart,
Tasmania 7000, Australia
longgt@neu.edu.vn

Abstract

This chapter — among the few in the world — examined how well the households were prepared to contain COVID-19 in Vietnam under the first national social distancing in late April 2020 by mapping their related indicators presenting living conditions. It used the provincial data from Vietnam's Population and Housing Census 2019. Following Jones *et al.*

---

*Corresponding author.

(2020)'s approach, it constructed various readiness indicators for households in 63 provinces/cities in Vietnam in order to see how they were ready for the social distancing period. The results showed that Vietnam's social distancing in late April 2020 was successful because it was applicable and implementable along with readiness of all households with sufficient resources. At the provincial level, however, there were differences in readiness levels, in which some provinces were consistently lower than the other. As such, supplementing social assistance policies during the social distancing period was timely and appropriate. This chapter concluded that, given its position as a middle-income country with limited resources and a population of nearly 97 million, Vietnam has been among the few countries in the world to successfully contain COVID-19 in a short time. Early interventions and timely social assistance measures combined with households' readiness strongly determined Vietnam's success.

Keywords: COVID-19; social distancing; readiness; policy; Vietnam.

1. Background

As of 15 January 2021, the World Health Organization (WHO)'s COVID-19 Dashboard reported 93.96 million infected cases and 2.03 million deaths. Also, COVID-19 has hit more than 200 countries and regions with different levels of spreading and consequences. To prevent COVID-19 outbreak and spreading-out, many countries introduced social distancing or lockdown measures with strict home isolation and restricted travelling. As argued by some reports (see, for instance, Jones *et al.*, 2020; Aljazeera, 2020a, 2020b), such measures could be adopted quite well in high-income countries, but they might create heavy difficulties for low- and middle-income countries.

As a low middle-income country with a long border shared with China where the COVID-19 pandemic was exposed, Vietnam recorded the first COVID-19 infected case on 23 January 2020. As of 15 January 2021, there were 1,530 infected cases with 35 deaths and 1,406 recovered. Of these infected cases, the number of imported cases accounted for less than 20%, and most of the domestically infected cases were due to cross-infection among those staying in isolated places for patients or in provinces/cities with high concentration of industrial zones and tourism. To cope with the spreading-out of the COVID-19 to its about 97 million

Table 1: Timeline of COVID-19 outbreak in Vietnam and policy responses until mid-May 2020.

No.	Time	Events/Policy Responses
1	23 January 2020	The first COVID-19 infected case was found
2	24 January 2020	Civil Aviation Administration of Vietnam (CAAV) cancelled all flights from Wuhan (Hubei, China)
3	1 February 2020	All schools were forced to close
4	13 February 2020	Launched health mobile apps
5	14 February 2020	Limitation of outside activities
6	3 March 2020	Stopped migration of Italian citizens
7	10 March 2020	Compulsory health declaration via health mobile apps
8	18 March 2020	Stopped issuance of visas to all foreigners
9	22 March 2020	Stopped all immigration to Vietnam
10	1 April–22 April 2020	Social distancing nationwide. Lockdown of some specific locations
11	23 April–4 May 2020	Relaxed social distancing with limited re-opening of economic activities
12	Since 5 May 2020	Relaxed social distancing with re-opening of all activities, with careful warnings to all citizens
13	18 May 2020	33 consecutive days without new infections within communities

Source: Own compilations, using Huynh (2020) and various government mass media sources.

people, the government of Vietnam (GOV) conducted timely and strong measures immediately from the beginning, including social distancing for a 3-week period — from 1 to 22 April 2020. Table 1 shows various policy actions taken up till mid-May 2020.

Vietnam has been embraced by the WHO and other international organisations for its successful containment of COVID-19. As discussed by La *et al.* (2020), Huynh (2020), and Gan (2020), Vietnam considered the COVID-19 pandemic a serious public health issue from the beginning and thus it took a variety of measures to use "the golden time" to contain the spread of COVID-19. For example, La *et al.* (2020) argued that official news and continuous dissemination of COVID-19 infected cases provided by the GOV and its line ministries delivered important health policy messages to people in order to change their healthcare behaviours such as hand washing and limiting direct contacts. Moreover, Huynh (2020) added that, instead of forcing the citizens with the compulsory regulations, the GOV well disseminated nudging-behaviour policies, which could increase the "virality" of the information. During 1–21 April 2020, the GOV announced and applied a 3-week social distancing period, in which people were asked to "stay at home for the sake of your own and the community's welfare", and restricted travelling and transportation were implemented. As reported by various mass media sources, social distancing was implemented quite well. At the beginning, there was a great concern about implementing social distancing in Vietnam since evidence from other middle-income countries showed that lower-income people found it difficult to follow restrictions and live under lockdown, such as India (Aljazeera, 2020a, 2020b), Bangladesh (Sakib, 2020), and the Philippines (Aspinwall, 2020). In these countries, among a number of reasons, poor living conditions and loss or substantial reduction of income sources made people become violators of social distancing or lockdown policies.

An important question was whether anti-COVID-19 propaganda on mass media and social distancing were sufficient measures for ensuring Vietnam's success in containing COVID-19. This chapter argues that, along with timely information dissemination and social assistance policies, households' readiness was a necessary condition for the success of the social distancing policies in Vietnam.

2. Data and Methods

2.1 *Data*

This research used the final data from the Vietnam's Population and Housing Census (PHC) 2019, which was conducted by the General Statistics Office of Vietnam (GSO). This was the fifth Census in Vietnam since 1979. The PHC 2019 applied a two-stage clustered sampling approach, and the final sample accounted for 9% of the households nationwide. Data were representative at national level, at regional level (for six ecological regions in Vietnam), at area level (urban vs. rural), and at provincial level (for 63 provinces/cities throughout Vietnam).

The Census provided rich information at individual level (such as age, sex, educational level, marital status, and employment status) and household level (such as housing conditions, electricity use, and sanitation).

2.2 *Methods*

To evaluate readiness of provinces/cities in Vietnam, this chapter applied the readiness or suitability index proposed by Jones *et al.* (2020), which was based on five indicators: (i) access to electricity in the household; (ii) access to clean drinking water in the household; (iii) access to adequate sanitation in the household; (iv) having a phone in the household; and (v) the household head being employed (in work). In addition, Jones *et al.* (2020) simply defined a household as "fully ready" if all five indicators were met, and as "partially ready" if at least three out of five indicators were met.

These indicators are extremely important to keep the most basic human needs covered. However, in order to provide a more comprehensive set of indicators which could reflect how a household was ready to be "blocked" due to social distancing, this chapter followed the Maslow's Hierarchy of Needs theory, which argued that human needs were hierarchically arranged, and they superseded the ones that were satisfied. Needs included physiological needs, safety needs, social needs, esteem needs, and self-actualisation needs (Singh, 2020). Physiological needs — which include water, sanitation, and other routine essentials — are the lowest and fundamental for the survival of individuals, and thus these needs should be met under social distancing periods.

For the data from the PHC 2019 in Vietnam, and for possible comparisons with other middle-income countries with similar data from population and housing censuses, this chapter modified the aforementioned indicators proposed by Jones *et al.* (2020) taking into consideration physiological needs, as follows.

(1) *Access to electricity in the households* was measured by the percentage of households in a province/city which used electricity from the national grid system;

(2) *Access to clean water in the households* was measured by the percentage of households in a province/city which used tapped or canned/bottled water for cooking;

(3) *Access to adequate sanitation in the households* was measured by the percentage of households in a province/city which had flush toilet(s) inside their homes;

(4) *Having at least a phone in the households* was measured by the percentage of households in a province/city which had either a fixed/table phone or a mobile phone at home; and

(5) *Population being employed (in work)* was measured by the percentage of population aged 15 and over in a province/city that are employed.

(6) *Living in permanent and semi-permanent* houses was measured by the percentage of households in a province/city having houses which were constructed with bricks, concrete and other durable materials.

For each indicator, this chapter used Maps Chart in Excel 2016 version to draw the map of 63 provinces/cities in Vietnam with their respective percentages for the six indicators.

This research considered that a province/city was "fully ready" if all six indicators were rated at least 75%, and "partially ready" if at least three out of the six indicators were 75% and higher. The rate "75%" was randomly chosen, based on an intuition that at least 75% population being covered by basic social services were acceptable for a low middle-income country. It is worth noting that a sensitivity test could be conducted to see how the levels of readiness would be changed.

3. Results

Figure 1 presents the percentages of households using electricity from the national grid system for all 63 provinces/cities in Vietnam in 2019. As reported by GSO (2020) for PHC 2019, the national average was 99.4%, with urban areas at 100% and rural areas at 99%. Compared to many other countries at low-middle income level as defined by World Bank (2020), such rates were quite high for Vietnam, and this resulted from extension of national electricity grid system in the mid-1990s. Among 63 provinces, however, some in the Northern Mountains and Central Highlands had significantly lower rates of using electricity from the national grid system than did other provinces/cities (such as Cao Bang in the Northern

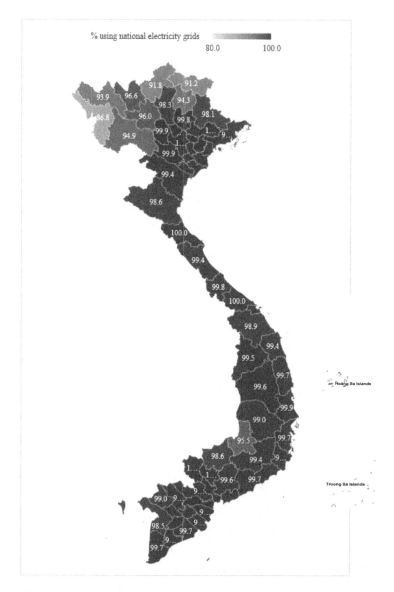

Figure 1: Percentage of households that used electricity from the national grids by province, 2019.

Note: The boundaries, colours, denominations, and other information shown on this map do not imply any judgement on the part of the author concerning the legal status of any territory or the endorsement or acceptance of such boundaries.

Source: Own illustration, using Population and Housing Census 2019 data.

Mountains with 86.8%, and Dak Nong in the Central Highlands with 95.5%).

Figure 2 presents the percentages of households in 63 provinces/cities using tapped or canned/bottled water — both of which were considered as cleaned water — for cooking. According to GSO (2020), in 2019, 54.5% of the people nationwide used such water sources, of which the rates for urban and rural areas were 86.3% and 37.4%, respectively. Figure 2 also shows significant disparities between regions and provinces in this indicator. As expected, the poorer the provinces were, the lower their rates of households using cleaned water for cooking. In particular, households located in provinces with higher rural rates had lower rates of households having cleaned water for cooking. Also, the Northern Mountains, the Central Highlands, and the Southwest regions had significantly lower rates of households having cleaned water for cooking than did other regions.

Figure 3 delineates the map showing the percentages of households in 63 provinces/cities which had flush toilet(s) inside their houses. The rates for the whole of Vietnam, urban areas, and rural areas were 65.9%, 89.8%, and 52.8%, respectively (GSO, 2020). The same as other above indicators, provinces in the Northern Mountains and the Central Highlands had significantly lower rates of households having flush toilet(s) inside their houses than did those in other regions. In particular, provinces with higher urbanisation rates had significantly higher rates of households having flush toilet(s) inside their houses than those with lower urbanisation rates. These differences resulted from differences in per-capita income and socio-economic development levels (MPI and World Bank, 2015).

For the communication during social distancing, fixed/table phones or mobile phones were important because people could get calls for personal contacts as well as text messages for information on COVID-19 from Ministry of Health or Ministry of Information and Communication. Figure 4 shows the percentages of households in 63 provinces/cities in Vietnam having at least a fixed/table phone or mobile phone at their houses. It was extremely impressive that, in 2019, the rates were 91.7%, 94.5%, and 90.1% for the whole country, urban areas, and rural areas, respectively. There were differences between provinces, particularly those

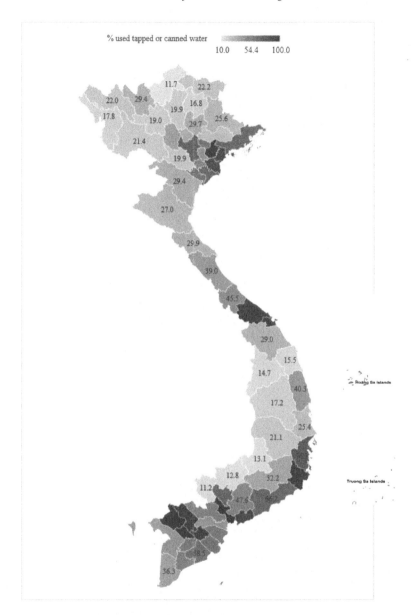

Figure 2:   Percentage of households that had tapped or canned water for daily use, 2019.

Note: The boundaries, colours, denominations, and other information shown on this map do not imply any judgement on the part of the author concerning the legal status of any territory or the endorsement or acceptance of such boundaries.

Source: Own illustration, using Population and Housing Census 2019 data.

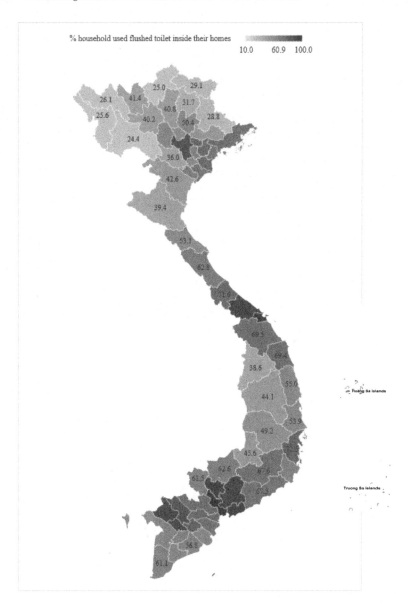

Figure 3:   Percentage of households that used flush toilets inside their houses, 2019.

Note: The boundaries, colours, denominations, and other information shown on this map do not imply any judgement on the part of the author concerning the legal status of any territory or the endorsement or acceptance of such boundaries.

Source: Own illustration, using Population and Housing Census 2019 data.

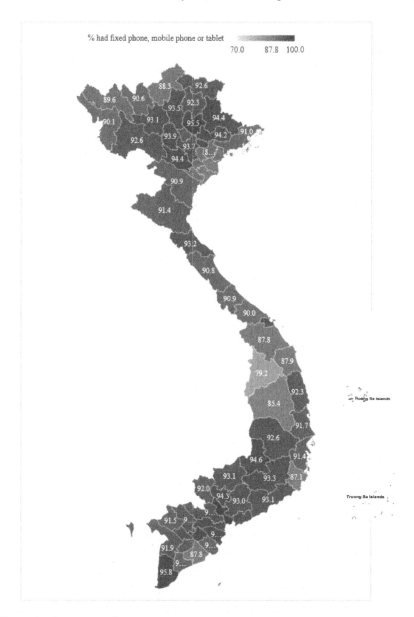

% had fixed phone, mobile phone or tablet

70.0   87.8   100.0

Figure 4: Percentage of households that had phone (fixed or mobile) in their houses, 2019.

Note: The boundaries, colours, denominations, and other information shown on this map do not imply any judgement on the part of the author concerning the legal status of any territory or the endorsement or acceptance of such boundaries.

Source: Own illustration, using Population and Housing Census 2019 data.

located in the Northern Mountains and the Central Highlands had lower rates than the national average.

In the period of social distancing, income — in addition to other above indicators — was extremely crucial for households and their members to stay at home. For this, being employed was a good proxy for income. Figure 5 shows the percentages of households having members aged 15 and over (or adults) who were working. As presented, all 63 provinces/cities had very high rates of working people with the lowest at 96.1% and the highest at 99.3%.

It was worth noting, however, that being employed in different jobs could provide different income levels, and thus financial sufficiency during social distancing. Figure 6 shows significant differences between provinces in terms of having people aged 15 and over who had simple jobs (i.e. jobs with the least skill requirements and low income) who could face income insecurity during social distancing due to the closure/shutdown of businesses. As shown, poorer provinces/cities had significantly higher rates of adult people with simple jobs than did their richer counterparts.

Experiences from India (Aljazeera, 2020a, 2020b), Bangladesh (Sakib, 2020), and Sudan (Assal, 2020) and many other places such as big cities like New Delhi and Metro Manila (Madarcos, 2020), have shown that it would be critically difficult to implement social distancing without sufficient spaces at both private houses (owned by household heads) and public houses (owned by government and rented to households). In particular, for those who must follow home quarantine for a period of 14 days or even 28 days, house structures would be extremely important. For this, permanent and semi-permanent houses could provide safe shelters for all family members. Figure 7 indicates the percentages of households in all provinces in Vietnam which had these types of houses. The rates for the whole of Vietnam, urban areas, and rural areas were respectively 91.3%, 98.2%, and 90.3% (GSO, 2020). The same as other indicators, as shown in Figure 7, provinces/cities in the Northern Mountains, the Central Highlands, and the Southwest had lower rates of households having permanent and semi-permanent houses than did their counterparts in other regions.

To evaluate readiness or suitability of each province to social distancing in COVID-19, as presented in the Methods section, this chapter used

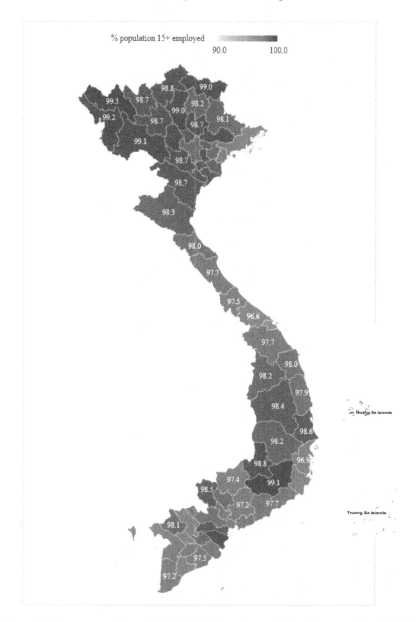

Figure 5: Percentage of households that had people aged 15 and over employed, 2019.

Note: The boundaries, colours, denominations, and other information shown on this map do not imply any judgement on the part of the author concerning the legal status of any territory or the endorsement or acceptance of such boundaries.

Source: Own illustration, using Population and Housing Census 2019 data.

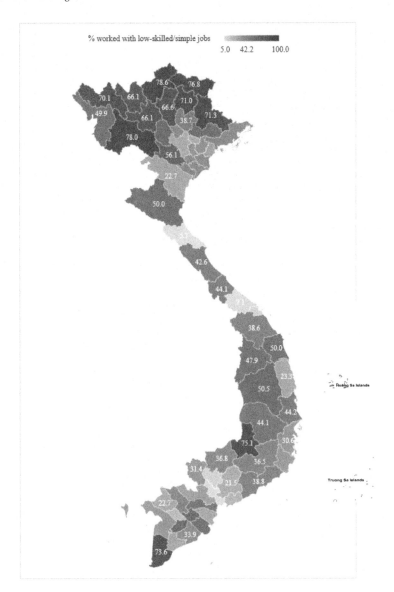

Figure 6.   Percentage of households that had people aged 15 and over employed with simple jobs, 2019.

Note: The boundaries, colours, denominations, and other information shown on this map do not imply any judgement on the part of the author concerning the legal status of any territory or the endorsement or acceptance of such boundaries.

Source: Own illustration, using Population and Housing Census 2019 data.

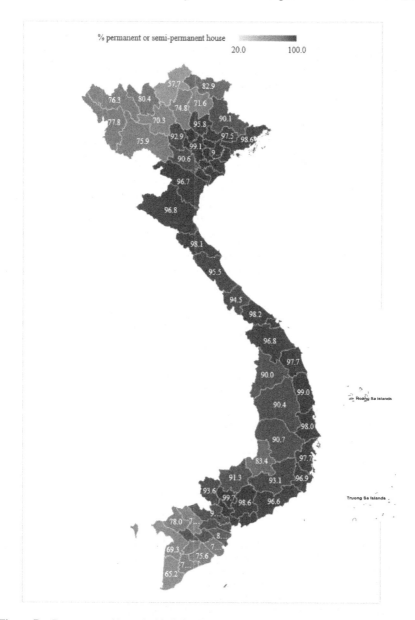

Figure 7.   Percentage of households living in permanent and semi-permanent houses, 2019.

Note: The boundaries, colours, denominations, and other information shown on this map do not imply any judgement on the part of the author concerning the legal status of any territory or the endorsement or acceptance of such boundaries.

Source: Own illustration, using Population and Housing Census 2019 data.

75% as the standardised threshold for any of the six indicators. For any indicator being at least 75%, we scored 1; otherwise, we scored 0. A province/city was "fully ready" if its total score was 6, and "partially ready" if its total score was from 3 to 5. Table 2 presents the results for estimation.

As no provinces had the total score being equal to 0, all provinces in Vietnam could be considered as "generally ready" for social distancing. Exploring the results in further detail, however, Table 2 indicates that only seven out of 63 provinces/cities could be considered as "fully ready", while the remaining 56 out of 63 provinces/cities could be considered as "partially ready". Among the "partially ready" provinces/cities, nine of them met five out of six indicators; 41 of them met four out of six indicators. The remaining, the "partially ready" provinces/cities, met three out of six indicators, and they were either located in the Northern Mountains

Table 2: Readiness score for social distancing in COVID-19 by province/city.

Province/City	% Using National Electricity Network	% Used Tapped or Canned Water	% Household Used Flushed Toilet Inside Their Homes	% Had Fixed Phone, Mobile Phone or Tablet	% Population 15+ Employed	% Permanent or Semi-Permanent House	Total Score
An Giang	1	1	1	1	1	1	6
Ba Ria — Vung Tau	1	1	1	1	1	1	6
Can Tho	1	0	0	1	1	1	4
Đa Nang	1	0	0	1	1	0	3
Đong Thap	1	0	0	1	1	1	4
Thua Thien-Hue	1	0	0	1	1	1	4
Ho Chi Minh City	1	0	0	1	1	1	4
Binh Duong	1	0	0	1	1	1	4
Đong Nai	1	0	1	1	1	1	5
Ha Noi	1	0	0	1	1	1	4

Table 2: *(Continued)*

Province/City	% Using National Electricity Network	% Used Tapped or Canned Water	% Household Used Flushed Toilet Inside Their Homes	% Had Fixed Phone, Mobile Phone or Tablet	% Population 15+ Employed	% Permanent or Semi-Permanent House	Total Score
Hai Duong	1	0	0	1	1	1	4
Hai Phong	1	0	0	1	1	0	3
Khanh Hoa	1	1	1	1	1	1	6
Ninh Thuan	1	0	0	1	1	1	4
Thai Binh	1	1	1	1	1	1	6
Vinh Long	1	0	0	1	1	1	4
Bac Giang	1	0	0	1	1	1	4
Bac Kan	1	0	0	1	1	1	4
Bac Lieu	1	0	1	1	1	1	5
Bac Ninh	1	1	1	1	1	1	6
Ben Tre	1	0	0	1	1	1	4
Binh Đinh	1	0	0	1	1	0	3
Binh Phuoc	1	0	0	1	1	1	4
Binh Thuan	1	0	1	1	1	1	5
Ca Mau	1	0	0	1	1	1	4
Cao Bang	1	1	0	1	1	1	5
Đak Lak	1	1	0	1	1	1	5
Đak Nong	1	0	0	1	1	1	4
Đien Bien	1	0	0	1	1	1	4
Gia Lai	1	0	0	1	1	1	4
Ha Giang	1	1	0	1	1	1	5
Ha Nam	1	0	0	1	1	0	3
Ha Tinh	1	0	0	1	1	1	4
Hau Giang	1	0	0	1	1	1	4
Hoa Binh	1	0	0	1	1	1	4
Hung Yen	1	0	0	1	1	1	4

(Continued)

Table 2:   (*Continued*)

Province/City	% Using National Electricity Network	% Used Tapped or Canned Water	% Household Used Flushed Toilet Inside Their Homes	% Had Fixed Phone, Mobile Phone or Tablet	% Population 15+ Employed	% Permanent or Semi-Permanent House	Total Score
Kien Giang	1	0	0	1	1	1	4
Kon Tum	1	0	0	1	1	1	4
Lai Chau	1	0	0	1	1	1	4
Lam Đong	1	0	0	1	1	1	4
Lang Son	1	0	0	1	1	1	4
Lao Cai	1	1	0	1	1	1	5
Long An	1	0	0	1	1	1	4
Nam Đinh	1	0	0	1	1	1	4
Nghe An	1	0	0	1	1	1	4
Ninh Binh	1	0	0	1	1	1	4
Phu Tho	1	0	0	1	1	1	4
Phu Yen	1	0	0	1	1	1	4
Quang Binh	1	0	0	1	1	1	4
Quang Nam	1	0	0	1	1	1	4
Quang Ngai	1	0	0	1	1	1	4
Quang Ninh	1	0	0	1	1	1	4
Quang Tri	1	1	0	1	1	1	5
Soc Trang	1	0	0	1	1	1	4
Son La	1	0	0	1	1	1	4
Tay Ninh	1	1	1	1	1	1	6
Thai Nguyen	1	0	0	1	1	1	4
Thanh Hoa	1	1	1	1	1	1	6
Tien Giang	1	0	0	1	1	1	4
Tra Vinh	1	0	0	1	1	0	3
Tuyen Quang	1	1	0	1	1	1	5
Vinh Phuc	1	0	0	1	1	1	4
Yen Bai	1	0	0	1	1	0	3

Source: Own calculations.

Table 3:   Beneficiaries of the Resolution 42.

Group	Beneficiaries
1	The employee working under the labour contract regime must agree to postpone the performance of the labour contract, take a leave without pay for 1 month or more due to businesses struggling due to the COVID-19 pandemic, no revenue, or no financial resources to pay the salary is supported with VND 1.8 million person/month. The period of support is based on the actual time of postponement of the labour contract, unpaid leave, monthly according to the actual situation of the epidemic, starting from 1 April 2020 and not exceeding 3 months
2	An employer who is in financial difficulties and has paid at least 50% of the termination salary for the employee under Clause 3, Article 98 of the Labour Code in the period from April to June 2020 is entitled to loans without collaterals up to 50% of regional minimum salary for each employee based on actual pay period but not more than 3 months with 0% interest rate, maximum loan term of 12 months at the Bank Social policy to pay the remainder of the salary and direct disbursement monthly to the unemployed.
3	Individual business households that have a tax return of less than VND 100 million/year temporarily suspended business from 1 April 2020 are supported with VND 1,000,000/household/month depending on the actual situation, but not more than 3 months.
4	— The employee has a labour contract or employment contract terminated but is ineligible for unemployment benefits; — The employee who has not signed the labour contract and has lost his job gets support of VND 1,000,000/person/month depending on the actual situation of the epidemic but not exceeding 3 months at most. Application period is from April to June 2020.
5	People with meritorious services to the revolution, who are enjoying monthly preferential allowances, are entitled to an additional VND 500,000/person/month. The application period is 3 months, from April to June 2020 and is paid once.
6	Social protection beneficiaries who are receiving monthly social allowances are supported with an additional VND 500,000/person/month. The application period is 3 months, from April to June 2020 and is paid once.
7	Poor and near-poor households according to the national poverty line on the list until 31 December 2019 are supported with VND 250,000/person/month. The application period is 3 months, from April to June 2020 and is paid once.

Source: Own compilation from the Resolution 42/2020 dated 9 April 2020.

and the Central Highlands, or poorer than other provinces/cities in the same region.

4. Discussions

The results of this research indicated that all provinces in Vietnam were generally ready for social distancing policies to confront the COVID-19 which was exposed for the first time in late January 2020. Among six indicators showing readiness or suitability index for social distancing, all provinces could meet at least half of them. At the same time, however, there were significant differences between provinces/cities in their readiness for social distancing; in particular, some provinces in poorer regions (such as the Northern Mountains and the Central Highlands) had consistently lower readiness levels than those located in richer regions.

More importantly, in the poorer provinces/cities, the rates of adult people working with simple jobs were substantially higher than those in the richer provinces/cities, and this was a big concern for social distancing policies which required people to stay at home and thus reduced their income opportunities to survive. Such a concern, however, was partially removed because the GOV officially announced Resolution 42 dated 9 April 2020 (a week after the social distancing period started), the social assistance support packages valued at VND 62,000 billion to provide cash transfer to such vulnerable people as those living in poor and near-poor households, working as self-employed workers, and those losing their jobs due to business closures (see Table 3 for a detailed description of R42 beneficiaries).

In general, it could be concluded that the social distancing period in Vietnam was quite successful, and a part of the reason for this success was the readiness of households throughout the country. There have been some important lessons and experiences from Vietnam's work in combating COVID-19, as follows.

— Governments at all levels — from central to communal — have worked out immediately "infodemic" related to COVID-19 at the early stages, so as to remove fake news or information which could result in chaotic actions by people, especially those who were living in the places with outbreaks. Throughout the time, communications activities have been a key tool in responding to the pandemic. The majority of citizens believed in immediate actions of the governments in responding to the COVID-19;

— Used existing systems and resources — not only for health, but also for information, communication, and social protection — from both central and local governments as well as citizens in order to prevent COVID-19 from spreading out at the early stages (La *et al.*, 2020). More importantly, experiences with similar epidemics (such as SARS in 2013) helped the governments in introducing timely precautionary measures so as to provide citizens with a sense of psychological control in prevention (Le *et al.*, 2020);

— Applied e-health system for the large cities and then nationwide in order to track COVID-19 infected cases (from F0 to F4) and applied immediate quarantines or isolation for the outbreak communities.

— Used and updated data to make decisions timely, in which Ministry of Health has played the focal point institution (UNDP & ISMS, 2020).

— Mobilised resources and made strong linkages with emergency response arrangements. For instance, providing sufficient food and other daily necessities as well as regular health checkups to people living in quarantined communities. Local authorities were responsible for identifying poor and vulnerable people (such as the disabled or those with serious diseases) in order to provide cash and other in-kind support (UNDP & ISMS, 2020).

— Paid close attention to the locations with high population density (such as those as large urban areas like Ha Noi and Ho Chi Minh city; those with many industrial zones where hundreds and thousands of people move in and out for working and living; and those as attractive tourism places), so as to avoid local contagion.

5. Conclusions

As a low middle-income country with limited resources and a population of about 97 million, Vietnam has used various measures in a timely manner (such as restricted travelling and transportation, social distancing along with social assistance policies ensuring income for various vulnerable groups) in order to contain COVID-19. As discussed, Vietnam was successful in implementing a national social distancing in late April 2020, partially because households were ready for such a policy measure. Vietnam's current success also provided a number of implications to other middle-income countries in formulating and implementing policies in COVID-19-like pandemics.

Although this research could provide some interesting evidence on how the Vietnamese households were ready in implementing social distancing in COVID-19, it would have been more comprehensive if data could provide further details. First, if we could have data on social distancing compliance rates in all 63 provinces/cities, we could have been able to explore factors associated with those rates, so as to provide more concrete policy implications for local governments. Second, as the PHC 2019 data did not have any information about household-level income, we were not able to simulate how social assistance policies would help reduce impoverishment of local people and thus reduce rates of social distancing non-compliance. These shortages of information and data could be later compensated for with household-level surveys in order to provide better insights for social distancing policies.

References

Aljazeera. (2020a). Chaos and hunger amid India coronavirus lockdown. Retrieved on 1 May 2020 from https://www.aljazeera.com/news/2020/03/chaos-hunger-india-coronavirus-lockdown-200327094522268.html.

Aljazeera. (2020b). "Future is scary": Poor hit hardest by India coronavirus lockdown. Retrieved on 1 May 2020 from https://www.aljazeera.com/news/2020/04/scary-poor-hit-hardest-india-coronavirus-lockdown-200409105651819.html.

Assal, M. (2020). COVID-19 and the challenges of social distancing in Khartoum. Retrieved on 18 May 2020 from https://www.cmi.no/news/2441-covid-19-and-the-challenges-of-social-distancing-in-khartoum.

Aspinwall, N. (2020). The Philippines' Coronavirus lockdown is becoming a crackdown. Retrieved on 1 May 2020 from https://thediplomat.com/2020/04/the-philippines-coronavirus-lockdown-is-becoming-a-crackdown.

Gan, N. (2020). How Vietnam managed to keep its coronavirus death toll at zero. Retrieved on 12 June 2020 from https://amp-cnn-com.cdn.ampproject.

org/c/s/amp.cnn.com/cnn/2020/05/29/asia/coronavirus-vietnam-intl-hnk/
index.html.

General Statistics Office of Vietnam (GSO). (2020). *Vietnam's Population and Housing Census: Key findings* (in Vietnamese). Hanoi: GSO.

Huynh, L. D. T. (2020). The COVID-19 containment in Vietnam: What are we doing? *Journal of Global Health*, 10(1): 1–3. doi: 10.7189/jogh.10.010338.

Jones, S., Egger, E. M., and Santos, R. (2020). Is Mozambique prepared for a lockdown during the COVID-19 pandemic? Retrieved on 1 May 2020 from https://www.wider.unu.edu/publication/mozambique-prepared-lockdown-during-covid-19-pandemic.

La, V. P., Pham, T. H., Ho, M. T., Hoang, N. M., Linh, N. P. K., Trang, V. T., *et al.* (2020). Policy response, social media, and science journalism for the sustainability of the public health system amid COVID-19 outbreak: The Vietnam lessons. *Sustainability*, 12: 2931. doi: 10.3390/su12072931.

Le, T. T. X., Dang, A. K., Toweh, J., Nguyen, N. Q., Le, T. H., Do, T. T. T., Phan, T. B. H., Nguyen, T. T., Pham, T. Q., Ta, T. K. N., Nguyen, T. Q., Nguyen, A. N., Duong, V. Q., Hoang, T. M., Pham, Q. H., Vu, G. L., Tran, X. B., Latkin, C. A., Ho, C. S. H., and Ho, R. C. M. (2020). Evaluating the psychological impacts related to COVID-19 of Vietnamese people under the first nationwide partial lockdown in Vietnam. *Frontiers in Psychiatry*, 11: 824. doi: 10.3389/fpsyt.2020.00824.

Madarcos, E. (2020). In world's megacities, understanding housing is key to fighting COVID-19. Retrieved on 18 May 2020 from https://www.devex.com/news/opinion-in-world-s-megacities-understanding-housing-is-key-to-fighting-covid-19-97027.

Ministry of Planning and Investment (MPI, Vietnam) and World Bank. (2015). *Vietnam 2035: Toward Prosperity, Creativity, Equity, and Democracy.* Hanoi: MPI & World Bank.

Sakib, S. M. N. (2020). Bangladesh: Poor struggle to survive amid COVID-19. Retrieved on 1 May 2020 from https://www.aa.com.tr/en/asia-pacific/bangladesh-poor-struggle-to-survive-amid-covid-19/1819868.

Singh, P. (2020). Abraham Maslow's 'Hierarchy of Needs' becomes even more relevant in the era of COVID-19. Retrieved on 17 May 2020 from https://www.psychreg.org/hierarchy-of-needs-covid-19.

United Nations Development Program (UNDP) Vietnam and Institute of Social and Medical Studies (ISMS). (2020). *Public Health Impact Assessment of the COVID-19 Pandemic on Vulnerable Groups Living Near the Border of Vietnam and China*. Hanoi: UNDP.

World Bank. (2020). World development indicators 2019. Retrieved on 1 May 2020 from http://datatopics.worldbank.org/world-development-indicators.

About the Author

Thanh-Long Giang is currently an associate professor in Economics at the National Economics University, and a Senior Researcher at Institute of Social and Medical Studies (ISMS) — both are in Hanoi, Vietnam. His research interests include ageing, social protection, and health protection. His research outcomes have been published widely, including in *Asian Economic Journal*; *Asia Pacific Migration Journal*; *Asia Pacific Economic Literature*; *Development and Change*; *International Social Science Journal*; and *Social Science and Medicine*. He was a member of the drafting team for Vietnam's Social Protection Strategy (2011–2020); a key member of taskforce and research group for reforming social assistance system in Vietnam (2017–2021), under Ministry of Labour, War Invalids, and Social Affairs, Vietnam. Prof. Long has provided various consultancy services for ADB, GIZ, ILO, World Bank, World Health Organization, among others.

Index

Printed in the United States
by Baker & Taylor Publisher Services